Cinema in a Democratic South Africa

NEW DIRECTIONS IN NATIONAL CINEMAS

Jacqueline Reich, editor

Cinema in a Democratic South Africa

The Race for Representation

Lucia Saks

INDIANA UNIVERSITY PRESS

Bloomington & Indianapolis

This book is a publication of

Indiana University Press
601 North Morton Street
Bloomington, Indiana 47404-3797 USA

www.iupress.indiana.edu

Telephone orders   800-842-6796
Fax orders   812-855-7931
Orders by e-mail   iuporder@indiana.edu

Library of Congress Cataloging-in-Publication Data

Saks, Lucia.
    Cinema in a democratic South Africa : the race for representation / Lucia Saks.
        p. cm. — (New directions in national cinemas)
    Includes bibliographical references and index.
    ISBN 978-0-253-35457-0 (cloth : alk. paper) — ISBN 978-0-253-22186-5 (pbk. :
alk. paper) 1. Motion pictures—Social aspects—South Africa. 2. Motion pictures—
Political aspects—South Africa. 3. Race in motion pictures. I. Title.
    PN1993.5.S6S35 2010
    791.430968—dc22

                                                                        2009051560

1 2 3 4 5 15 14 13 12 11 10

IN MEMORY OF MY FATHER, BOBBY SAKS (1917–2003)

Contents

Acknowledgments

First, I must thank Jane Behnken, my editor at Indiana University Press, and Jacqueline Reich, the editor of the series in which this book is published, for their belief and unflagging interest in my project. They never let me down throughout the long process of bringing the manuscript to publication.

The University of Michigan is a cold and dark place for eight months of the year. Two luminaries, Kelly Askew, director of the Africa Studies Center, and Kevin Gaines, chair of the Center for Afro- and African-American Studies, brought light to the endless gloom. The funding they provided made it possible for me to travel to South Africa so that I could research the changes that had taken place in the media since leaving the University of KwaZulu-Natal in 2002. I thank them most sincerely. I owe a great deal to my former dean, Michael Chapman, for his material support and friendship during the years I worked at the University of KwaZulu-Natal. I must also thank my two readers, Sean Jacobs and anonymous, for their excellent comments and suggestions and for their praise of the manuscript, which buoyed me up considerably.

The concept of a mentor was foreign to me before I came to the United States, but it found embodiment in the person of Marsha Kinder, my advisor and great friend. Her work on Spanish national cinema has proven exemplary for my own, her friendship has sustained me, and her input throughout the incipient articulation of this project have proven invaluable. She continues to be a powerful and positive presence in my life.

Finally, I owe a huge debt of gratitude to my husband, Daniel Herwitz, who focused his brilliant, energetic, and incisive mind on the project and helped me to improve it in innumerable ways.

Cinema in a Democratic South Africa

Introduction

He is running towards us. Into our exile. Into the return of exiles. Running
towards the negotiated settlement. Towards the Democratic elections. He
is running, sore, into the new South Africa. Into our rainbow nation, in
desperation, one shoe on, one shoe off. Into our midst. Running.

Jeremy Cronin

Decolonization, which sets out to change the order of the world, is, obviously
a program of complete disorder.

Frantz Fanon

Since the 1994 elections that swept the African National Congress (ANC)
into power with Nelson Mandela at its head as the nation's first democratically elected president, South Africa has been, in the words of South African philosopher, activist, and poet Jeremy Cronin, "running towards us,"
away from a terrible past and into an uncertain future. En route, the country has embarked on a program of "complete disorder"—one that involves a
rethinking of itself as a nation. This task has not been a gradual one carried
out in small incremental steps, as is the nature of most political action in
the developed world. It has been instantaneous, immediate, in some cases
desperate, and in all cases disturbing. One need only look to the furor un-
leashed by the final report of the Truth and Reconciliation Commission
(TRC) on human rights abuses under apartheid, which implicated both
the ANC and the apartheid regime, to see the depth of local fragmentation.[1] The program has resulted in a complete restructuring of laws, institutions, economic regulations, and electoral and social policies designed
to transform South Africa into a progressive democracy and to integrate the
country into a world economy from which it had been partially excluded. It
has been a process intended to eradicate the horrors of apartheid and bring

1

about, as Frantz Fanon puts it, "the replacing of a certain species of men by another species of men."[2]

But it is not enough for such a profound transformation to take place only at the institutional level. It also requires an act of immense imagination to bring it into existence and to maintain it, often in the face of insuperable diversity. As Benedict Anderson's study of the rise of the nation in the eighteenth century reveals, people develop a sense of national "belongingness" and identity based on something far softer and more subjective than institutions and laws. His seminal definition of the nation as an "imagined political community" has been particularly useful in shifting the terms of the discussion away from the idea of "official" ideology and toward the subjective, the narrative, and the role of the medium (in Anderson's case, the role of print literature) and its dissemination in producing and maintaining new forms of identity and community.[3]

In addition to negotiations over national institutions and laws, a nation is set on the sediment of a further set of articulations that bind people together (often provisionally) and place them in a shared time and space called the national habitus. This process is very much at issue in South Africa, where there is a pent-up desire for what Stuart Hall has called "the struggle of the margins to come into representation."[4] From the dregs of a nation that has imagined itself only in the brutal terms of apartheid and against a backdrop of terrible violence, grinding poverty, escalating crime, utopian dreams, and threatened apocalypse, new forms of consciousness have emerged, many of them from sites previously marginalized or voiceless. Anderson stresses the violence involved in the national experiment, given how old and recalcitrant forms of belonging, group identity, and of course, entrenched hatreds must give way to new forms of national understanding and (it is hoped) tolerance.

The histories of national formation have been fraught with discord, often leading to the most terrible strife. There is a race to establish new terms of representation that will lead the way to harmony, however temporal, transient, and idealized. This is the race to representation, a national story. It is a race to disgorge the old styles of thinking and showing, illustrating and believing, and to supplant them with new images and ideas; a race to get people to reassign values to others and to their place in the new dispensation, indeed to bring that dispensation about by leading the way in the manner of the Pied Piper. It is also a race to stabilize and forestall chaos and a race to plan the future in the wake of the unpredictable contingencies of immense social transition. From these changes comes the first meaning of the title of this book, *Cinema in a Democratic South Africa: The Race for Representation.*

Beyond that specific meaning, however, there is another very different one that conjures up South Africa's past and obtrudes into its present. In South Africa, any mention of race cannot help but evoke the ugly form of racial consciousness based on quasi-scientific constructs garnered from eugenics and biology that supported apartheid.[5] The history of the twentieth century is a tragic testament to the collapse of scientific objectivity into a scientific racism used to justify the colonial projects of the nineteenth century, the genocides of the twentieth, and South Africa's apartheid system. In the post-World War II years, the use of race as an acceptable paradigm went underground in mainstream Western discourse, except in South Africa. Just at the moment when the Western countries were officially jettisoning the race paradigm along with their colonial empires, South Africa was enacting its fundamental ideas into law with terrible consequences for the majority of the population.

Some of these consequences were shown in the 1990s on public television's weekly broadcasts of the TRC's investigations. Others are present in the spatial formations of contemporary southern African cities—Maputo, Harare, Windhoek, Johannesburg, Pretoria, Cape Town, Durban, and Port Elizabeth—with their segregated residential areas, racial buffer zones, and shack settlements spread around and in the major metropolitan areas. The aftereffects have also emerged in epidemiological studies on the spread of HIV/AIDS throughout southern Africa, which show that the virus feeds off the system of migrant labor that has been in place since the inception of South Africa and the homeland policy of the apartheid era. "If you wanted to spread a sexually transmitted disease, you would take thousands of young men away from their families, isolate them in single-sex hotels, and give them easy access to alcohol and commercial sex," says Mark Lurie, a researcher on the effects of migrant labor on HIV/AIDS.[6] Thus the second meaning of the word "race" in this book's title.

Cinema in a Democratic South Africa is about cinema in post-apartheid South Africa, a period that officially dates from 1994 to the present. It is about the race to expand beyond a cinema marked by race. It is about the dream of creating a unified nation out of fragments and the role of the cinema in realizing that dream.[7] Although this is very difficult for cinema to achieve, as Marsha Kinder has noted in her work on post-Franco cinema, "the film medium has always been an important vehicle for constructing images of a unified identity out of regional and ethnic diversity."[8] This desire is a utopian instinct in film. But it is also a kindred instinct of the state at moments of political transition, as it seeks to turn culture into a hand-maiden of change, a foot soldier in its combat missions. And so the race is also about the race of the state and of parastatal organizations to define, di-gest, sketch out, project, imagine, and legislate film into being, to guide and to shape it. This takes place in South Africa through film bills, fund-ing schemes, exhibition circuits, audiences, training schemes, markets, and festivals, and through representations in the cinema of land, sexuality, race, nation, memory, identity, and illness (to mention but a few of the major themes that have lately found cinematic expression). All is produced in the new South Africa with special energy and rapidity because film is not a ro-bust national enterprise, but rather an incipient entity, waiting to be nudged into existence.

It is not that films were not made prior to the repeal of apartheid laws in 1991. Like the rest of the world, South Africa was on the global cinematic map and the apparatus arrived in the country less than a year after its ap-pearance in Europe and the United States. French, American, and Brit-ish films were shown throughout the land on mobile or traveling bioscopes throughout the next decade, and in 1909, the first permanent theater was built in Durban, a port city on the country's east coast. But local produc-tion has always been haphazard, uneven, and fragmented, despite efforts in the early 1900s to produce "South African" films and later, under apartheid, state-subsidized ones that ignored the realities of apartheid and the struggle of the black majority. As Keyan Tomaselli puts it, "until the 1980s, nearly all commentators and filmmakers allied themselves with the white hegemony, which itself acts as a conduit for international monopoly capital."[9] The in-troduction and dissemination of cinema in South Africa therefore have to be understood as part of globalization and the cultural practices that have formed the modern world, which, to quote John Tomlinson, are character-ized by a "rapidly developing and ever-densening network of interconnec-tions and interdependencies."[10]

Interdependency, however, does not mean there is equality on both sides. The story of South African cinema is one of dependency, failure, ab-jection, and dead ends. It is a story that the state is struggling to change, but the battle is not an easy one given the constitution of the global market-place. As Ian Angell puts it, there are winners and losers in the Informa-tion Age, just as there are winning and losing corporations in the global economy.[11] Angell paints a bleak scenario of fragmentation and attenuation as the nation-state struggles to don the designer suit of the entrepreneur and display itself in the global shopping mall, hoping to attract the global dollar. The needs of the global economy are transferred and internalized as the needs of the nation. An efficient infrastructure; a secure, stable working environment with minimal internal regulations; a workforce that has the skills and knowledge needed by global companies—these are the features that attract peripatetic global companies and their money to the nation. The successful nations will be the ones that have developed themselves into a desired brand. The losers, those who seek to maintain an autonomous stance, or a populist one, will be excluded from the magic circle of money and mobility, and they will decline.

There have been three key moments in twentieth-century South African history: first, in 1901, eight years after the Anglo-Boer war when the Cape Colony, Natal, the Transvaal, and the Orange Free State joined to form the Union of South Africa, a self-governing territory, leading to a liberal/segregationist state; second, in 1948, when the apartheid state was "voted" into existence (with a significant amount of voter manipulation by the National Party); and third, in 1991, when apartheid was replaced by the power-sharing government of Nelson Mandela and F. W. de Klerk, leading to the interim constitution and the first truly democratic elections in 1994, the final constitution two years later, and the other events of democratic transition which were so proudly displayed in the world press during the 1990s (at least until HIV/AIDS became a national emergency and government disgrace).

All of this seems tailor-made for a national cinema study, which is almost what this book is, almost but not quite. Here are the provisos: First, a national cinema is a concordance of infrastructure on the one hand and representations on the other. Those who have written the most insightful and richly textured studies of national cinemas outside of the United States (which generally goes unmarked as being national) have had cinemas to write about in which significant amounts of state infrastructure were devoted to the cinema, which in turn produced a set of narrative forms and stylistic strategies reflecting and articulating the nation under a particular description. This was not the case historically in South Africa, and in spite of the endless spate of state pronouncements and the fact of a South African National Film Board, it is not the case today—not sufficiently, anyway. Second, given that South Africa's democracy has emerged in an age that has been described as post-national, global, transnational, hybrid, fluid, porous, multicultural, diverse, and decentered (specifically in the 1990s), it would also be too simple to say that the aspiration within filmmaking has been national, as opposed to becoming globally normalized, a southern wing of Hollywood, a continental "Africanist" enterprise, or more directly, an expression of the will toward liberty in filmmaking, individualist or formulaic, after such a long period of state censorship and repression. Even the state, in spite of its wishes to produce culture for "a new nation," has been more ambivalent than one might have expected given its neoliberal turn and desire to make South African culture worthy of global investment and attention.

The state speaks in many voices, one of which is that of an ex-Communist cell wanting to direct cultural reform toward a radical South African democracy, and another of which is the voice of a player on the global stage wanting investment in culture (as well as in other areas) by the world. South Africa has come late to the scene of democratically evolving countries, perhaps too late for it to exist very much as an "independent" entity, wishing to take control of its future. To write the history of South African state economic practice during the 1990s would be to write the history of the World Bank and of Chinese global domination of industry. To write the history of South African cinema, one must take an equally global or transnational scope.

And there is another point. The South African nation is a celebration of diversity after a century of brutal and racist control. The urge toward national unity in spirit and equality under the law and the desire for equity in the job market for all South Africans and equality of opportunity for the young are offset by a recognition that this is a nation of many languages and peoples, and that a hundred flowers must bloom if the nation is not to crush the spirit of many. Yet national cinema stories tend to focus on nations at the moment when a univocal culture is being formulated and/or foisted on citizens, when the French notion of *citoyen/citoyenne* (those who participate in the political life of the community and enjoy its positive freedoms) is at the foreground. Any national cinema story of South Africa in the 1990s and beyond must be about a nation developing a national spirit at a postmodern moment when diversity is understood to be what the nation requires.

This is not to deny the importance of the idea of nationalism; it is to place nationalism at the center of the story but in a way that understands both the unique context of South African history and also the larger historical moment of global modernity in which nationalism is present. If one still wants to call this book a national cinema story, so be it, but with all the provisos intact.

This book is also not the study of a national *movement* like *Cinema Novo* in Brazil, nor is it a historical survey, nor an auteur study—the other traditional modes used by scholars in writing about African cinemas. It is a book about cinema, and the state pronouncements around it, at a moment of democratic transition, which is a race to rewrite race. Cultural theorists Achille Mbembe and Sarah Nuttall speak of "the failure of contemporary scholarship to describe Africa's complexity."[12] Africa, they state, should be read "in the same terms as we read everywhere else" in order to escape from the conventional categories that have stymied African representation."[13] Taking their injunction seriously, *Cinema in a Democratic South Africa* does not read South African cinema as Third Cinema, third-world cinema, post-third worldist, minoritarian, postcolonial, or African cinema. A central argument of this book is that despite the nationalist rhetoric emanating from state and market players, the situation facing South African cinema is highly contradictory. The race to build a cinema is going in many directions. There are moves to create a national cinema, or as the government's White Paper on Film puts it, "an indigenous film industry which reflects the nation's own culture in its cinema and television."[14] There is a desire to harness cinema in the service of a continent-wide rebirth, an "African Renaissance" that harks back to the pan-Africanist stance advocated by Aimé Césaire and Léopold Senghor in *Présence Africaine*, but at the same time update it as a new, vital, positive African modernity. From another point of view, cinema is a way to create jobs at home, generate economic spin-offs in local economies, earn foreign revenue by touting locations and production expertise, generate revenue from co-productions and sales abroad, and encourage tourism. Such incompatible aims are not unusual in the utopian quest for a national cinema.[15] The task at hand, then, is to critically tease out the specific forms of growth that have emerged in this systemic whirlwind.

One quick example of this double articulation of cinema as industry and cinema as art can be seen in two post-apartheid cinematic institutions: the National Film and Video Foundation and the Industrial Development Corporation's media and motion picture division. Both are state owned and operate in the name of the nation, but they serve two very different constituencies. The Foundation holds to a central ideology that models transformation in postcolonial, nationalist terms and interprets filmmakers as deserving of state patronage because they are cultural workers participating in the construction of South African cinema/media. Its view of cinema is prescriptive, idealistic, artisanal, and auteurist. The Corporation concentrates on productions that will attract international players, and considers a project feasible if it can be shot in South Africa *and* find an international market, a goal it calls "globalizing from both ends."[16]

Finally, this book focuses primarily on cinema, which in the main has addressed the big stories rather than the little ones. In order to give a broader picture of national media at the moment, this book also makes small forays into television and advertising.

THE HIGH AND LOW ROADS OF CINEMA

Cinema has addressed the big stories rather than the little ones. For example, the eyes of the South African state and the global world have been glued to stories of the South African transition: the TRC with its litany of abuses, its reversal of roles (perpetrator as defendant, silent victim now giver of testimony, policeman now criminal), its courtroom drama, its high tragedy, and its moral aspiration; the HIV/AIDS pandemic with its dramas of death and destruction; the urban nightmare of inequality, failed aspiration, crime, and violence; the excitement that volcanic changes in city and geography produce in short periods of time; and for once, the celebration of individuals. Cinema has also provided entertainment and relief from the burdens of society through the usual kind of zany/parodic comedy that allows peoples to laugh at exaggerated images of their own foibles, even as they reinforce racial and cultural stereotypes from the past. The three highest-grossing South African films have been slapstick comedies produced by Videovision, South Africa's largest and most successful production company. *Mr. Bones* (Gray Hofmeyr, 2001), *Mama Jack* (Hofmeyr, 2005) and *Mr. Bones 2: Return from the Past* (Hofmeyr, 2007) all star the well-known comedian Leon Schuster, whose brand of slapstick comedy and impersonation recalls Jim Carey in his Ace Ventura role. Both *Bones* films play on reversals of racial stereotypes to create the film's jokes and funny moments that are then elaborated through a chain of actions and reactions. The narrative of *Mr. Bones* pits African "tradition" (prophecy, magic) against postmodern ambition and greed in a "post-racial" South Africa.

Schuster is Bones, the adopted white son of an imaginary black tribe, having been raised by the Kuvuki Tribe. Like Tarzan, he was found as a baby (the only survivor of a plane crash that killed his parents) and has the gift of prophecy. He throws the bones, hence his name, and is able to tell the future. His quest is to find the male heir to the throne that he has prophesied exists. A good deal of the chaos that ensues as Bones tries to fulfill his

goal occurs at a casino-resort modeled on the real Sun City, a luxury resort two-and-a-half hours from Johannesburg in the former homeland of
Bophuthatswana. The film's primary representation of Africa derives more
from the colonial period than the present one: tribally clad Africans, drums,
divination, huts, and an autocratic king. In true postmodern fashion, the
Kingdom of the Kuvuki Tribe and the casino-resort share a boundary, allowing Bones to cross over from one world to the other, although his passage is characterized by a great deal of cultural confusion.

Bones is a white version of black stereotypes such as Sambo, the magical negro and the hapless savage. Technology confounds him. He is easily
confused like a child, thus he mistakenly identifies the African-American
golf professional who is taking part in the resort's golf tournament as the
heir to the throne (clearly, he does not recognize the difference between
African-Americans and Africans) and pursues him doggedly, importuning
him in pidgin English to return to the tribe and assume the role of prince
and future king. It is possible to read the ethnic and racial reversals in the
film subversively as working to undermine the longstanding idea that racial
and ethnic differences are articulated through biological markers such as
skin color and that what is being represented is a post-racial, hybrid South
African space. Such a reading, however, ignores that the film constructs the
new space of South Africa from the shards of old tropes and images taken
from the colonial archives, thus reanimating old, racist ideas. These are national stories, even if, as we shall see, they are sometimes told as stories that
seem invented in Hollywood rather than Johannesburg.

What cinema has not done during the first ten years of the democratic
transition is focus on the ongoing poverty and homelessness; lack of educational resources; fierce, unyielding strife and hatred between peoples;
and complex questions of identity at moments when the children of traditional peoples are turning into twentieth- and twenty-first century subjects,
and the rise of intergenerational conflict grows as the youth move beyond
the "struggle" narratives. Television, more truly the mirror of ordinary lives
than film, has taken up some of these issues.

Most significant of all has been the unwillingness or inability of state-
subsidized film to critique the state or to address ongoing white racism and
black rage as conditions of society and subjectivity. It is worth pointing out
that these two failures are not restricted to cinema. It has taken South African universities some time to work out how to frame their critiques of the
state, so accustomed were they either to apartheid complicity (as in the case
of certain Afrikaans universities during that period) or Marxist and liberal

critiques of a state which in every way was their moral and political enemy. To find a language for critical partnership with a state whose democratic formation they are in alliance with has taken some doing. Universities, however, were stimulated to action by the HIV/AIDS denialism of the Mbeki presidency and really did spring into critical action. Cinema has not done this. What it *has* done is to take both a high road and a low road.

The high road can be seen in the films that speak from the pulpit of the nation, from an omniscient point of view, addressing subjects such as the TRC, as in *Zulu Love Letter* (Ramadan Suleman, 2004), *Forgiveness* (Ian Gabriel, 2004), *In My Country* (John Boorman, 2004), and *Red Dust* (Tom Hooper, 2004); history, as in Zola Maseko's *Drum* (2004), *The Promised Land* (Jason Xenopolous, 2002), and Darrell Roodt's *Cry, The Beloved Country* (1995); crime, as in *A Reasonable Man* (Gavin Hood, 1999) and *Tsotsi* (Gavin Hood, 2005); and HIV/AIDS (*Yesterday*, Darrell Roodt, 2004). This presumption of universality is well known in the history of thought and culture generally (e.g., law, civil-society ethics). It is the central characteristic of classic Hollywood's textual form, which creates a world of verisimilitude as opposed to one of documentary realism. Within this classic mode of cinematic representation, framing, montage, and other stylistic devices are subdued, subordinated to the creation of a coherent and unified fictional space in which the story unfolds. The low road can be seen through mostly state-funded projects that encourage the telling of individual stories from all manner of perspectives, such as the films in *Real Stories from a Free South Africa* (2004). Here the theme is not a national story, but the boisterous voices of a diverse colloquy suppressed under apartheid. New forms like the biopic—*Letter to My Cousin in China* (Henion Han, 1999) and *My African Mother* (Cathy Winter, 1999)—and the short film (exemplified by M-Net's 2005 New Directions initiative, *South Africa—Ten Years On*) have emerged. Equally significant have been those films funded outside of the state, by public broadcasting systems such as the STEPS for the Future series.

If the first decade of post-apartheid South Africa did not produce a cinema capable of critiquing the state or responding to the hatred, violence, and rage in the country, it did produce a genuinely post-apartheid tapestry of voices. In its own way, this has been a contribution to the democratization of the public sphere.

In the chapters that follow, we will travel along both the low and the high roads of cinema. Chapter 1 is about the race to begin the race, which started off with a spate of policy papers, white papers, documents, project reports, five- and ten-year plans, and proposals for restructuring, reorganizing, and producing everything, in short, but film. Chapter 2 examines how the new proposals have been implemented and delivered by the state and the film industry. Chapter 3 considers how the cinema has dealt with the TRC, one of the most visible forums that South Africa constructed to come to terms with the most brutish part of its apartheid history. Chapter 4 focuses on what one might call a cinematic counter-telling that begins when film-makers from South Africa and its neighbors attempt to come to grips with the HIV/AIDS pandemic. In particular, it foregrounds films made under the STEPS for the Future initiative, positioning them as evidence of cinema's capacity to participate in the reanimation of civil society. In a similar vein, chapter 5 examines what an oppositional or counter-cinema could mean in South Africa today, given that in the past, it meant a cinema of op-position to apartheid. Chapter 6 explores the ways in which two films of-fer strategies for national reconciliation by appropriating specific historical events. *De Voortrekkers* (Harold Shaw, 1916), made six years after South Africa's unionization, uses two events from eighteenth-century South Af-rican history, The Great Trek and the Battle of Blood River, to forge a rec-onciliation between the English "race" and Afrikaner "race" after the Boer War (1899–1902) to produce a "white" race. *Come See the Bioscope* (Lance Gewer, 1997) appropriates the story of Sol Plaatje, thus reconstituting an earlier moment of black modernity that was betrayed by segregation and apartheid, but has miraculously arrived again for both cinema and the na-tion in the new South Africa.

A BRIEF HISTORY OF CINEMA AND THE NATION

In outlining the dissemination and exhibition practices of early cinema in South Africa, Gutsche states,[17]

> By the end of 1910, there were scores of bioscopes (a British term for a mo-tion picture theater) scattered throughout all the larger towns of South Africa, which, except for a few, led a precarious existence, frequently closing and re-opening under different management.[18]

This situation ended with the formation of African Amalgamated The-atres' Trust, Ltd. in 1913 by I. W. Schlesinger, an insurance and real estate magnate. While Gutsche credits Schlesinger with saving the industry from chaos and bankruptcy, his takeover heralded the death of the independent exhibitor, an outcome very much in line with global patterns of cinema's industrialization and rationalization in the major film-producing countries such as France and the United States. In four short years, 1910–1913, the film

industry was reorganized along global lines in terms of production and exhibition to take advantage of the growing popularity of feature films engen-
dered by their increasing length. In historical terms, this period coincides
perfectly with the first of three great moments in twentieth-century South
Africa that frame the century with an almost perfect symmetry. This was
the birth of the Union of South Africa in 1910, when the nation formed as
a result of a British initiative that joined the two conquered Boer republics, the Transvaal and the Orange Free State, to the two British colonies,
Natal and the Cape of Good Hope. This period has been called the era of
segregation, as it sought to draw firm lines between the white "race," comprised of the English speakers and the Afrikaners, and the black "race,"
comprised of the various African societies present within the borders of the
new union. Schlesinger's formation of the Trust, African Film Productions,
Ltd., and Killarney Studios (Africa's first motion-picture studio, located in
Johannesburg) is a reflection of his confidence in the viability of a South
African film industry that proposed to make "South African films for South
African audiences"—words that could be spoken today by the current government.[19] The early years before 1913 had been desultory in terms of local feature-film production despite a robust documentary and newsreel industry that had begun with the filming of the Boer War at the very birth of
cinema in 1895. The first feature film produced by an overseas production
company in South Africa was *The Great Kimberley Diamond Robbery* in
1910, and the first sound movie, *Sarie Marais* (Joseph Albrecht), a love story
between a Boer prisoner of war and his girlfriend back home, was produced
in 1931. Given the coincident timing between the development of South African cinema and the South African nation, it is hardly surprising that the
most notable feature film produced by African Film Productions was a nationalist allegory, *De Voortrekkers*, highly imitative of D. W. Griffith's *The
Birth of a Nation*.[20]

Production tapered off during the thirties, another result of global trends
such as the rising hegemony of Hollywood product. The thirties also saw a
rise in Afrikaner nationalism that resulted in the establishment in 1940 of
RARO (*Reddingsdaadbond Amateur Rolprent Organisasie*, or Rescue Action League Amateur Film Organization), an organization geared toward
the production of Afrikaans-themed films in Afrikaans. Thus began the
second stage, a stage born from the resentment of the Afrikaans community suffering under "poor whitism" as it was called in South Africa to distinguish the condition from the poverty of the Africans. The fight over who
were the real South Africans among the whites gathered force after 1948
with the coming of the apartheid state. Cinema history saw the introduc-

tion in 1956 of a subsidy scheme favoring Afrikaans film production and resulting in a predominance of Afrikaans feature films.[21] It saw a drive by the
state to inculcate, through cinema, radio, and newspapers (there was no TV
service in South Africa until 1975), the ideology of apartheid and the mythic
force of Afrikaans culture.

The legalization of apartheid ideology occurred with the passing of
three parliamentary acts that built on the structures of segregation. The
first, the Group Areas Act of 1950, established spatial segregation of the
population defined into racial groups under the Population Registration
Act. The second, the Natives Registration Act of 1954, gave the state the
right to transfer residents to racially zoned areas—"homelands," or segregated satellite townships. Finally, the Urban Areas Act of 1955 permitted the
removal of black people who were living as servants in white areas and in
the central cities to the townships. This last act had a profound effect on the
racial geography of South Africa's cities, a legacy that urban planners are
grappling with today.[22] These three acts substantially increased the state's
control, which was already considerable, especially in the urban areas, and
allowed for a definition of South Africa as a white nation, not only legally,
but also spatially. Citizenship for black people was moved outside of the national borders to "proto-nations" or Bantustans.

Fueled by outrage against the situation, a small oppositional cinema
began in the late seventies and eighties with the production of a small
but significant number of anti-apartheid films by independent filmmakers
funded by overseas money. Mostly operating outside of state funds by necessity, these films sought to produce a critical cinema that "documented"
the perversities in South African society through the codes of cinematic
realism. Ironically, it was also in the seventies that the state subsidized a
"black film industry" composed almost entirely of white directors making
films for black audiences.[23] Needless to say, the films were little more than
propaganda for apartheid ideology. With the end of apartheid in 1994, the
industry faced a crisis of legitimacy.

The attempt to build a national culture that would be legitimate in
every sense is at the heart of the changes being sought by the state and by
the state-driven media in post-apartheid South Africa. In 1994, for the first
time in 350 years of conflict and oppression, a "common South African
citizenship" (to quote point 3 in chapter 1, "Founding Provisions," of the
constitution) was extended to all irrespective of "race, gender, sex, preg-
nancy, marital status, ethnic or social origin, colour, sexual orientation, age,
disability, religion, conscience, belief, culture, language [or] birth."[24] After
1994, the new government generated a slogan, "one nation, many cultures,"

to legitimize the idea of a unified yet culturally diverse nation.[25] This moment of rapture for the majority of South Africans had ripples that extended beyond the continent. For the first time in many years, Africa appeared to have done something right, something that the developed world could emulate and learn from. Knowledge flowed from the south to the north as the "South African miracle" accrued global cultural capital. In 2004, Kofi Annan began to talk of Africa entering into a "third wave" (this just ten years after the Rwanda genocide), following on the first one, which was decolonization, and the second, which was black authoritarianism/tyranny.[26]

Since the new millennium, however, the patina on the new South Africa has become tarnished. Despite the ANC's restructuring of the economy in accord with global capitalist demands, investment has not flowed into the country. As a result, growth has been slow to stagnant. One million workers have lost their jobs, and unemployment is at catastrophic levels. The Department of Labor recently put the figure at 32 percent, while other counts put it as high as 42 percent. Privatization has diminished the power of the state to provide a safety net for the poor and the sick. Along with Brazil and Guatemala, South Africa is one of the most unequal societies in the world. In addition, the HIV/AIDS pandemic has devastated the most active segment of the population, those between 18 and 40.[27] There are claims that those at the top of the ANC have become like a cabal, inhospitable to criticism and public debate. Intellectuals who formerly might have taken up the cudgels against the inequities of the society are cowed, unwilling to lose their state patronage, or have thrown in the towel in exchange for high-paid consultancies.

The picture painted by *Cinema in a Democratic South Africa* should be read against this background. Cinematic restructuring since 1994 embodies, reflects, and dramatizes the state of South Africa's momentous change to democracy; a transformation that altered the continent because of South Africa's status as Africa's economic superpower. Within South Africa, the first democratic, non-racial elections that brought in the ANC in 1994 were a moment of nationalism when both television and cinema were called upon to perform in the name of the nation, to address the nation as one within a multicultural diversity, and to bring about healing and oneness between peoples by preaching diversity as central to human equality. Hence the popular media jingle of those times: *simunye* (we are one).

It was also a continental moment. Thabo Mbeki preached an African Renaissance with South Africa at the helm, a rhetoric that was designed to totally blow away the former apartheid claims that because of its European heritage, South Africa was the only state in Africa worth considering. But Mbeki's desire to rejoin the continent in a celebration of first-generation post-colonial optimism has had, it turns out, disastrous political results, such as his unwillingness to criticize Robert Mugabe as Zimbabwe, South Africa's main trading partner, has collapsed under Mugabe's paranoid, authoritarian mismanagement. But in 1998 when it was first sounded, Mbeki's trumpet call was one seeking postcolonial legitimacy: the legitimacy of a friend among friends, a just ruler among the just, a decolonizing hero among the mighty. South African cinema had as one of its aims the desire to draw close to larger trends in the cinema of Francophone Africa. But South African cinematic desire has also, when it has looked toward the African continent, begun to replace that first generation of Francophone films with a newer one. With the largest economy in the region, it is sufficiently industrially developed to make the dream of an African film industry—the production, processing, distribution, and exhibition of local films—a reality for the first time.

Currently, there is no shortage of cinematic images of Africa and Africans. There is only a shortage of African filmmakers providing those images, despite the long fight waged against the hegemonic industrial practices and transnational domination of "Hollywood" by filmmakers in Africa and rest of the postcolonial/developing world. Postcolonial filmmakers have fought to gain control over their own representations, to rewrite their own histories, and to counter old narratives steeped in colonial prejudice. As the first rush of nationalist fervor abated, postcolonial filmmakers began to explore and critique the new nation through gender, sexual orientation, and ethnic and class differences. There is no way of talking about African cinema or African filmmakers as having produced a cohesive set of thematics or a stylistic continuity in their struggle against Hollywood, but they are united in their desire to generate images of Africa on the global and local screen, and this is not happening. *Blood Diamond* (Edward Zwick, 2006), *Catch a Fire* (Phillip Noyce, 2006), *Hotel Rwanda* (Terry George, 2004), *In My Country, The Last King of Scotland* (Kevin Macdonald, 2006), and *The Constant Gardner* (Fernando Meirelles, 2005) are all "Hollywood" in their funding and in their choice of stars and directors. Zwick is from the United States; George, Boorman, Macdonald, and Hooper hail from the United Kingdom. Meirelles comes from Brazil, but has been taken up by Hollywood since the success of *City of God* (2002). The same is true of Noyce, who made the leap from Australia to Hollywood thirty years earlier.

And the trend continues: South African Nobel prize-winning author J. M. Coetzee's novel, *Disgrace,* has been adapted for the screen starring Ralph Fiennes (British) and John Malkovich (American). The director, Steve Jacobs, is also American. Hollywood's Weinstein Company has just completed, in Botswana, the filming for TV of bestseller *The No. 1 Ladies' Detective Agency* by Alexander McCall Smith (Zimbabwean/Scottish) with Anthony Minghella (British) directing and Jill Scott, an American R&B Grammy-award winner, as Precious Ramotswe, the heroine of the series. Aired on the BBC in March 2008 (a week after Minghella's sudden death), the film attracted 27 percent of the British viewing population.[28]

It appears that the big producers automatically snap up those African and South African stories that gain international status. Where does that leave South Africa's "national cinema"? Some of these global Hollywood films are excellent; others, which invoke old colonial stereotypes and tropes, are not. It is the balance that matters: many films about Africa are written, produced, exhibited, and owned outside Africa, with relatively few inside. In that balance, the power of Hollywood's screen culture and its influence in the world is reflected. What gets produced and circulated and how films are received and understood are related processes that require explanation and, if possible, remedy, which is what countries like South Africa, are attempting to do. But the fight is difficult and probably cannot be won. Cultural diffusion has long been an unequal process flowing from the West to the rest, but when it comes to the cinema, it has been particularly so. Hollywood is central to the global mediascape, or as Toby Miller puts it, "Hollywood both animates and is animated by globalization."[29] He explains,

> The source of Hollywood's power extends far beyond the history of cinema, to the cultural-communications complex that has been an integral component of capitalist exchange since the end of the nineteenth century. In the second half of the twentieth century, Third World activists, artists, writers and critical political economists nominated that complex as cultural imperialism. By the late twentieth century, it became fashionable to think of this power in terms of globalisation, a maddeningly euphemistic term laden with desire, fantasy, fear—and intellectual imprecision. "Hollywood" appears in nearly all descriptions of globalisation's effects—left, right and third ways—as a floating signifier, a kind of cultural smoke arising from a US led struggle to convert the world to capitalism.[30]

THE QUESTION OF CIRCULATION

Different kinds of media produced in different institutional contexts will have quite different ways of reaching or failing to reach the public. Post

1994, film was thus called on by the South African state to play a role in representing the nation because of its potential to reach millions of people. Yet, while it is well known that cinema has the capacity to reach mass audiences in ways that other media, such as painting, do not, cinema is not always successful in this regard. South African cinema, for example, has never reached wide audiences locally or globally. Hence, this book deals with a particular kind of media, with its own circulation and production patterns, and these have to be read back into the analysis. The story of post-apartheid cinema in South Africa thus requires writing in a certain dialectical way. Although film and media have had profound effects at all three stages of South Africa's history, in many ways, these effects have been limited, occurring in a kind of bubble, because in some respects, this developing country has lacked the mechanisms of circulation required to broadly disseminate its cinema- and media-generated representations, never commanding, in practice, the wide social publics these media claimed to address and, indeed, to construct. From the point of view of a race to wide social dissemination, the story of South African cinema is, like most African stories, one of mixed success. In fact, this is true of many developing countries. So writing the story of cinema in South Africa's first decade of democracy is writing about a partial disparity between intention and performance.[31]

The race to build a cinema is going in many directions. At the level of intention, it is spurred on by many desires:

- to represent tumultuous events like the TRC proceedings
- to help with the process of resolution
- to provide justice
- to entertain
- to rewrite, rediscover, and resurrect history
- to mimic Hollywood
- to reject Hollywood
- to break into the global market
- to find an authentic or new voice/aesthetic/language
- to overcome stereotypes
- to create new ones, and thus mediate between languages in an African Esperanto

None of these goals can come about without access to filmmaking by diverse groups of people and circulation of films to vast populations. In both respects there is a pervasive sense that the cinema of post-apartheid South Africa has hardly begun. Fifteen years into the new nation, after a spate of state pronouncements, ideologies, policies, funding, co-production treaties, comparisons, research, idealization, and utopianism, its role remains weak and fragmented.

In terms of the industry, certain provinces—like Gauteng and the Western Cape—are performing well, while others are not. The disenfranchised have not found a strong voice in the industry, which is still in the hands of an elite, mostly male group, and the vast majority of South Africans can't even go to the cinema.[32] They are denied the pleasures of spectatorship, let alone the agency of production. Soweto, a sprawling conglomeration of different townships estimated to have a population of over a million people, had no functioning cinemas until September 2007, when Ster-Kinekor, South Africa's largest distribution and exhibition corporation, opened an eight-screen multiplex in the new Maponya Mall.[33]

Post-1994, the perception that the cinema offered a unique forum in which diverse creative projects would find shape and be projected to the nation was at the basis of its development. That perception is now under scrutiny.[34] And for those that have found a way into the industry, the standard of training is tremendously uneven, given that film departments are still barely present at South African universities and technikons (technical universities), and commercial film schools are very expensive. Improving training standards is a matter of obtaining and better allocating funding for film instruction. Francophone cinema was heavily funded by the French government, and when French funding collapsed, so did the industry. South African film instruction is underfunded by everybody, from philanthropists to foundations to government organizations. And it is hard to justify such funding in the face of ongoing crises of health, education, crime, housing, and employment.

A DIVERSITY OF READERS

Any book such as this one encounters the problem of multiple readerships. Many readers will be unfamiliar with South African history, which, like every specific history, is complicated. Others will be all too familiar. South African history and society do not reduce to simple iconic images—police brutality in Soweto, "Whites only" signs on benches and doorways, the body of Hector Pieterson draped in his brother's arms, Nelson Mandela's long walk to freedom—that have made their way onto the front pages of the international media.[35] Nor is South African history an African version of the civil rights movement in the United States, although it is often framed in those terms for American audiences. This book tries to set a middle path between a diversity of readers.

My own reasons for writing this book are many. First and foremost, I am a South African who has spent most of my life oscillating between the United Kingdom, the United States, and South Africa. Each time I left South Africa, I thought it would be forever. But I was wrong. I kept returning, unable to find a replacement home for the one I had left. The last time I returned, however, was different. The unimaginable had happened: apartheid had ended, and ended well, given the horrific scenarios of the last forty years. As I sat in Los Angeles and watched Nelson Mandela being sworn in as president outside the Union Buildings in Pretoria on CNN, I felt South Africa pulling me back again, and in 1996, I went back with my adventurous American husband and my eighteen-month-old child, who was, thankfully, too young to argue. I taught first in Johannesburg at the University of Johannesburg and then in Durban, at the University of KwaZulu-Natal. There, I organized an undergraduate media and film studies program as part of the university's post-1994 transformation project, which allowed me to develop and research the main ideas for this book.

Looking back over the years of democratic rule in South Africa, I feel that the South African experience holds important lessons for anyone interested in social transformation and the role of the cinema in that process. This holds true even though, and indeed partly because, the role of cinema in South Africa has remained attenuated and problematic. The democratization of cinema has taken place within many contexts:

- a context of global dependency
- a lack of institutional excellence
- a lack of wherewithal
- a lack of interest in capital investment from abroad
- a lack of media training
- a lack of audience (especially of color)
- an excess of revolutionary proclamation
- an oversimplified ideology
- a utopian fantasy
- a governmental high handedness

But, and this must be emphasized, there has also been a genuine concern for the importance of cinema in the achievement of social justice, a genuine desire for the representation of diversity over the airwaves, and a give-and-take about the autonomy of the cinema from the state. These conditions and questions are specific to South Africa—couched in its particular history, geography, economy, and population—but they are also not entirely unlike the problems and prospects of cinema which have been faced in

Chile, Canada, Mexico, Cuba, Mozambique, Iran, Spain, Australia, Egypt, and so on. What follows in the ensuing chapters cries out for comparison and contrast with the processes of media institutionalization and democratization in other places.

1

The Burdens of Representation

Now is our time to sing, to dance, to paint, and to create. This is our right as citizens of South Africa. There is so much to look forward to, and so much work to be done. I trust we can do this as a united community with a common goal in mind.

White Paper on Arts, Culture and Heritage, Department of Arts, Culture, Science and Technology, June 4, 1996

Each time the South African nation has formed or reformed itself, a profound break with the past has occurred, requiring that new structures be created, new modes of imagination be cultivated, and new social roles be disseminated and grasped. This statement does not mean to suggest that the three "moments" that frame twentieth-century South African history—union, apartheid, and post-apartheid—are completely separated from each other. Each follows from the social formation or formations that preceded it, and each draws on past templates. However, in terms of social formation, each is fundamentally different from the others, and in some way new to history. It is this newness to the past and to history per se which imposes an immense burden on representation: to rapidly construct new terms and images of state, society, citizenship, and identity—in short, of life. Time is of the essence, since each grows out of a crisis and seeks a solution that would require massive changes in population and its allegiances. Every major re-imagination of the nation generates malcontent, and in the South African case, this generates violence, not simply ill will. South African union followed the Boer War in which Britain invaded Afrikaner terrain (the Transvaal and the Orange Free State) and decimated Afrikaner populations. The apartheid state replaced segregationist liberalism with a proto-fascist state

founded on an architecture of racial division (racism) and a bureaucracy designed to replace the English with a new Afrikaner middle class that would
populate it. The state was not simply there to repress Africans, it was there
as a paternalist force for dispossessed Afrikaner peoples, who associated liberalism with English repression. The end of apartheid in 1991 brought vast
violence in the Province of Natal (the traditional Zulu homeland), then the
miracle of reconciliation between warring parties, a miracle because no
one believed it possible, and the threat of total conflagration and collapse
was felt to be imminent. Given the problematic character of each of these
changes of state and the chaos, systemic contradiction, and malaise of national reconstruction (for good, bad, or ugly as the example proved), representations that would utopianize, stabilize, and harmonize were of the essence. No delay was possible.

In analyzing this race to representation, there is a useful lesson to
be drawn from Homi Bhabha's scenario of the process-oriented nature of
nationhood and the role of performance in constructing national identity.[1]
Benedict Anderson has been criticized for exaggerating the speed with
which nation building historically occurred, and for concentrating only on
origins and not on maintenance.[2] Once imagined, Anderson seems to suggest, the nation is finalized: there to stay. Bhabha's focus on process is a way
of addressing its ongoing emergence and change. Process is dialectical, involving a relationship between pedagogy (state-driven stories of the nation)
and practice (the lived reality of social life that is constantly changing).

Moreover, the signs by which a nation is projected and known are ambivalent, the product of pressures moving in various and contradictory directions. The race for representation is motivated by the inner ambivalence
of the very representational signs themselves. Such representations are often
so dramatically split, and sometimes so dramatically splitting of public consciousness, that they immediately demand their own forms of reparation.
In apartheid South Africa, for example, the relation of the state ideology to
lived experience was ambivalently concordant: the state brought about lived
experiences, but also continually misrepresented the reality of things, including and especially the things it had brought about. Human consciousness was similarly split, filled with a mix of sympathies and ideas that did
not compute. A filmmaker like Jans Rautenbach, who made films in the fifties and sixties, was at once critical of racism and sympathetic to people classified as non-white, but at the same time, argued that people can only be
true to themselves by embracing their racial identity (or rather, the identity

assigned to them by the state) and living in their own, racially defined communities.

In *Katrina* (1969), one of Rautenbach's most popular films (I remember being taken to see it with my school class), the renunciation of one's race and one's family, and the two are the same in the film, leads to a disintegration of the self that is ultimately suicidal. A melodramatic story of a woman who lives a life away from her "coloured" (mixed-race) community by passing for white in Cape Town, Rautenbach is deeply sympathetic of her motives, but passes this judgment upon her: leave your race and you leave your people; this is an act that will end in your death. The film probes and "proves" that unraveling. Katrina's blonde son, recently returned from England where he has qualified as a doctor, has no idea that he is "coloured," yet he feels an unexplained affinity for the coloured community and hesitates to accept a position at the (then) elite Groote Schuur Hospital in Cape Town because he feels drawn to practicing medicine among that community. Katrina's trajectory is escape; his is return (albeit unknown return). Katrina's love affair with a white pastor is doomed to failure. Despite being an alcoholic, defrocked priest, the pastor refuses to marry Katrina when he discovers she is "coloured," even though he despises himself for his racist feelings. Katrina's alter ego is her brother Adam, a proud leader of the coloured community. It is Adam who gives the long pedagogical speech straight out of the apartheid bible on the rightness of equal but separate development. Katrina, who rejects this view, commits suicide, while her son, on learning of his "race," accepts his position and becomes the doctor that "his people" desperately need. Race finally trumps Oxford education and elite profession; its chorded call is as deep as the sea into which she jumps. The film almost tells the viewer that she is trapped by racism, but does not: rather, race is home, not simply prison. This duplicity cannot be worked out in the film, because the two positions are flatly contradictory. To believe both is the result of, and accommodation to, a racist and tribalist society.

Rautenbach's other notable films (*Die Kandidaat*, 1968; *Jannie Totsiens*, 1970; and *Pappa Lap*, 1971) are concerned with this Afrikaner tribe and its discontents, pathology, problems, and archetypes; the question of who is a true Afrikaner, or who is the truest Afrikaner, is always central. Such a way of posing the question of cultural truth is the evident and obsessive result of essentialist and racist identity politics: the demands of the master to remain himself, pure and separate from all others. "Truth," having been set forth in this anxious way, is in constant danger of fragmenting, both in its ideological function of propping up a tenuous social order and in its function of generating a new epistemology. Hence, the race for representation becomes a *compulsion* motivated by a deep and justifiable anxiety about *instability*, a way of regulating ambivalence through repetitive gestures, as well as through new inventions of gesture.

The race for representation is about things in constant danger of falling apart. As such, it is a race without a finish line, an infinite task, complete only at the moment of exhaustion, when all the runners give up or die—as happened in both segregation and apartheid when the center could no longer hold. Each moment of national formation (union, apartheid, democracy) is hardly the same in moral value. The exact opposite is true: these are the bad, the ugly, and the good. But each of these propels a race: a race to stabilize fragmentation, assuage difficulty, bind ties between people and the state (and between each other), and render the moment of change as one of "truth." The truths could not possibly be more different, nor the issues of human decency, but in each and every case, Rautenbach's example holds: he is uneasy with the regime, up to a point deeply critical, furious at its failures of sympathy and so on, but finally of it in its claims of truth, claims about essential differences based in the property of "race," a property so pervasive that it can take hold over a son who has no idea it applies, charging his every desire with its communalist pull. Race is therefore not a sign for inequality, but for human belonging: this in spite of the coloured people being as lacking in homogeneity as can be imagined (Hottentot, Afrikaans, Indonesian, etc.), there being no "racial unity" in their hodgepodge of intermarriages, only a shared condition of racism (applied to them) and a shared culture of Cape village life. What appears critical in the film ends up being a demonstration of the regime's deeper, ideological "self-truths," reinforced through superficial criticisms of the regime.

The race over the past decade and a half has been toward equality and equity and away from the tribal reconciliations of the South African past. The problem of these years, 1994–2004, has been, above all, getting out of the starting gate. There has been a rush to make policy, produce working papers, instruct formations and formulations, define and plan institutional growth, bring about a "South African media" through these thoughts and agreements, debates and their documentation, on paper. There have been white papers, green papers, five- and ten-year plans, South African Broadcasting Corporation proposals, film-board review evaluations, and so on, all of which indicate that the race for representation in the new South Africa is not simply a race to make movies, documentary films, television programs, and the like: it is also a race to generate plans and policy reports about media.

The phenomenon is radical and revealing: the desire for a new state to think itself into existence, to plan its future in the rush and tumble of its actual making. Order is the desire of societies in transition, societies that seem to be particularly beset by what Bhabha has called the "double time of the nation": furious ambivalence and contradiction between the nation as a state pronouncement from above and a lived reality from below.[3]

There are many reasons why the South African state has rushed into print and pronouncement and not into image. Both the Mandela and Mbeki governments are marked by the pro-Soviet history of the African National Congress (ANC) which grew to maturity on the Russian idea of the five-year plan and planned economy. If, in terms of the economy, the government has made a neoliberal turn toward structural adjustment (World Bank style) and corporate investment, in the cultural sector, it has retained a more Socialist line, at least for the first ten years of its existence. Second, the post-apartheid state inherited a calcified, bureaucratic, and completely undemocratic set of media institutions: SABC, the film board, the censorship board, and the film subsidy system. This legacy has required remaking, and in many respects the new state had to begin from scratch. Third, the post-apartheid nation was born of crisis. Many South Africans, lining up to vote on that momentous day in 1994 when the first truly democratic elections took place, didn't really believe they were actually going to succeed. As little as a week before the election date, Inkatha, the "Zulu nationalist" party of KwaZulu-Natal, which had waged bloody war with the African National Congress in the early 1990s, was still boycotting the election, something the Pan African Congress, with its more radical and violent platform, actually did. Prior to the election, South Africans stocked up on long-life milk, canned goods, and bottled water, believing that major shutdowns might take place when the results were announced. Separatist threats from members of the Right, who were dressed in fascist khaki uniforms, were hurled in every direction. This was the third time in the history of South Africa that a race for representation was taking place.

Each race was a radical break with what had come before in a number of moral, political, and economic respects. Each jockeyed new constituencies into power, and from comparative obscurity or marginality. The moral dimension to each of these moments could not have been more different. Yet each, formed out of and in the manner of crisis, required rapid representations to generate the sense of order, the shaping of plans, and the activity of movement that the fragile unities, each in its own way, required.

In this third race, the goal was set at its highest point, for what was at stake was radical democracy and genuine populism. To think through the putative role of media in bringing good citizenship about, in allowing mass participation and representation by the peoples of South Africa, was no easier a task than to create, or to negotiate, the interim constitution of 1994, with its image of reconciliation, its mandating of elections, and its procedural concepts of how to write a final constitution. The final constitution was written in 1996 and was firmly rights based, beginning with an image of human dignity defined through the right to health, shelter, economic and political and civil rights, and liberty, including freedom of sexuality.

The issue of diversity was raised and highlighted through the idea that human beings can only become free and live dignified lives if their cultural heritages are maintained. In the law, for example, the issue became one of incorporating customary law and tradition into the legal framework and acknowledging it in the constitution. Where conflicts arose between Western/national law and customary law, the matter was mediated through the constitution's Bill of Rights. In other words, the courts would judge a case to be constitutional or not based on the principles of human dignity, quality, and freedom enshrined in the Bill of Rights and not on whether the accused person was acting according to customary law.[4]

In terms of language, always a thorny issue given the elevation of Afrikaans to an official language over other indigenous ones during apartheid, eleven languages were deemed official and instruction was mandated in all of them, as was cultural activity, including media representations by the state broadcasting system.

Media was part of the thinking of democracy, and crucial to its constitutional formation.

> Open debate and transparency in government and society are crucial elements of reconstruction and development. . . . The democratic government must encourage the development of all tiers of media—public, community and private. However, it must seek to correct the skewed legacy of apartheid where public media were turned into instruments of National Party policy; where community media were repressed; where private media are concentrated in the hands of a few monopolies and where a few individuals from the

white community determine the content of media. New voices at national, regional and local levels, and genuine competition rather than a monopoly of
ideas, must be encouraged.[5]

But terms of citizenship, freedom of expression, diversity of representations,
populism, and the question of a plethora of new voices having access to
media making had to be reconciled with a Socialist legacy of state-driven
media organizations. Hence the need for plans, for sharp definitions of the
state's role, which generated the kind of ambivalence Bhabha points to between radical populism (let a thousand voices, most formerly consigned to
silence, now sing with cameras) and state desires for control. Democracy sat
radically, but uneasily, in the ANC-governed state.

The size of the demand must be measured against the size of the actual
content—the lack of television networks except for a very few, the lack of
major film companies, the absence of film studies from university curricula,
the failure of any film school to have emerged as yet—all of which was the
sad legacy of an isolated, boycotted apartheid past and also of a country
with vast corporate resources (gold, diamonds, platinum, and sugar) owned
by an oligarchy, but a small middle class. And herein lies the difference between South Africa and Brazil or Australia. Both Brazil and Australia have
achieved major film cultures: Brazil because (although the country has a
similar Gini coefficient, a common measurement of inequality, to that of
South Africa) its middle class has been growing bigger since the 1970s; Australia because although of comparative size, it is a middle-class society.[6]
Brazil shares with South Africa a post-fascist background, Australia a colonial inheritance. But even if one cannot produce cinema, one can still produce documents about it. The word serves as a proxy for the filmic product.
Herein lies the other reason for the rush to plan the future of media and not
simply produce it. These actions were not merely guides, but compensation
for its absence and for the fact that it wasn't going to suddenly spring up in
large quantity in a month's or a year's time.

DOCUMENTING THE CINEMA

In 1994, the Human Sciences Research Council (HSRC) issued its Report on Restructuring Film Industry. The report recommended the formation of a statutory body known as the National Film and Video Foundation
(NFVF) to support the local film industry, subsidize a diversity of films irrespective of commercial viability, and fund training and education.[7] In the

same year, the Arts and Culture Task Group (ACTAG) formed to advise the Department of Arts and Culture (DAC) on how best to restructure the film and television industry so as to realize the goals outlined in the Reconstruction and Development Programme, the leading policy document of the ANC. The Group's final report was published in July 1995.[8] Four months later, the DAC appointed a reference group to draft the White Paper on Film based on the ACTAG report. In 1995, the Triple Enquiry Report of the Independent Broadcasting Authority (IBA), which dealt with the protection and viability of public broadcasting through SABC, the provision of local content for broadcasting, and cross-media ownership, also appeared. The local content mandates set out in the report were important to the future of the film and television, since the bulk of film production in South Africa has been and continues to be television production.[9]

In 1996, the DAC published the White Paper on Arts, Culture and Heritage, with the subtitle "All our legacies, our common future," which laid out government policy for establishing funding mechanisms and institutional frameworks to support the arts, museums, libraries, archives, and monuments. Also in 1996, the first draft of the White Paper on Film appeared and later in the year was published.[10] The paper recapitulated most of the ideas first promulgated by the HSRC report and then taken up by the ACTAG report. It recommended the formation of a film foundation (which later changed its name from the South African Film and Video Foundation to the National Film and Video Foundation) to oversee the industry and promote it abroad; support the production, distribution, and exhibition of films; facilitate training and education; and provide seed money for projects and funds for developing scripts, experimental films, bursaries, and scholarships through a finance division within the foundation.[11] The National Film and Video Foundation Act passed into law in 1997, and the Foundation was inaugurated two years later.[12] The Cultural Industries Growth Strategy (CIGS) document, a research report commissioned by the DAC, offered an industry strategy analysis of the current economic and social contribution of the film and television industry (as well as the music, publishing, and craft industries) and appeared at the end of 1998.[13] In addition, the NFVF has put out two influential reports, NFVF Film Indaba 2001 and NFVF Film Indaba 2005. *Indaba* is a Zulu word much in use today that means a conference or consultation between different indigenous tribes to discuss something of import to the group. In this case, it means a meeting convened by the NFVF of public and private film and television industry stakeholders. The reports contained the results of the two meetings, where the participants brainstormed constructive solutions to the industry's problems.

LEGITIMATING THE CINEMA

The state can't simply make pronouncements; it must legitimate them in some kind of bigger discourse about the new nation, its forms of equity, and its place in the world. The reigning discourse of these acts is that of "Renaissance." This means the African Renaissance, that return of South Africa to its continental brotherhood and its mytho-poetic *présence africaine*, something deeply connected to racial unity but now rewritten as social diversity. The goal is to culturalize the new South Africa as a central cog in the new and glorious rise of post-colonial Africa, to make myth, and history, of this moment. Through the mechanisms of the African Renaissance, mere policy documents become cultural poems to the continent. And so they are legitimated. The African Renaissance is also about making a "cinema of one's own," which is understood as black empowerment. "Black empowerment" is, in fact, President Mbeki's term for a continental African social and economic renewal. The concept of an African Renaissance at that time (the mid to late 1990s) captured the imagination of many since it offered a way of connecting the new modes of political assertion within the country to a larger discourse involving the continent at large. Through it, the South African miracle could become the African miracle, reversing the feeling of Afro-pessimism that had settled in across the continent fueled by thirty years of despotic military coups, internecine fighting (the Congo, Angola, Sierra Leone, Burundi), incredibly violent wars (Ethiopia and Eritrea, Sudan), genocide (Rwanda), and the ever-increasing poverty faced by most Africans today.

The idea of an African Renaissance draws on the heritage of *negritude* and pan-Africanism—two powerful anticolonial discourses which emerged from the intellectual fervor of the sixties, certainly a more optimistic era for the continent than the ensuing three decades—without inheriting all the Marxist baggage that went along with them. In short, it is a useful term that has found much use in industry and in the politics of culture. It is a call to arms without arming anybody, a legitimizing ideology for cultural change, a poetic vision for the continent at large, and a self-help program for the individual. It is also a saleable slogan for attracting Western funding since it draws on the heritage of liberalism—a Western heritage—and uses a word that evokes a historical period that arouses intense pride in the Western cultural imagination. The term allays deep-seated Western fears that African nationalism is not an exclusive term based on that old specter of reverse racism, but reaches out to all those who live on the continent and seek to participate in its development.

We might at this point return to Frantz Fanon and recall his distinction between nationalism and "national consciousness." In his celebrated dialectic of the deficits and benefits accompanying the idea of nationalism, Fanon preferred to speak of a national consciousness that formed the grounds for an international one. This distinction is very much in place when Mbeki states, "I am an African," in his speech on May 8, 1996, to the Constitutional Assembly.[14] For with that remark he claims to speak on behalf of all of Africa in the name of South Africa's constitution, which defines "Africanness" as a concept not defined by race, color, gender, or historical origins,[15] but through experience and assent. Africanness is not assigned by others from the outside. It lies in the capacities demonstrated by all the people of Africa. The national aspirations embodied in cultural forms have been of pivotal importance for theorists of the neo- and postcolonial, from Fanon's famous paper, "On National Culture," to the work of Edward Said and his followers, often to the point where such theory has run the risk of Hegelianizing the postcolonial field as a single, homogeneous shape defined in terms of this aspiration. Such theorizing has not been without its reasons, however, for the question of what kind of nations would emerge out of their transitions from colonies to independent states has been a crucial one, and postcolonial thought has opened up creative ways for considering it.

Despite the passing of more than a decade, the original moment of change in South Africa is still very present and there are substantial continuities with the past in maintaining social and political structures and policy orientations.[16] Those on the left interpret this as failure on the part of the ANC to effect real change, resulting in "the constitution of new elites that largely recycle old ones."[17] There has been a strong call by the ANC's alliance partners, the Congress of South African Trade Unions and the South African Communist Party, for a greater concentration on the material needs of the country, to eradicate what Patrick Bond terms the "persistent uneven development in social and economic arenas marked by huge areas of local, social, gendered and racial exclusion."[18] Faced with the enormous social problems present in South Africa today, Bond's frustration at all this "cultural talk" is understandable and opens up a number of related questions: Are cultural renewal and its products really that essential right now to a people who do not have bread, houses, jobs, or adequate health care? Is it not a luxury, a cover-up, or worse, evidence of the government's despair at not being able to solve the country's real problems?

These questions are all part of the critical debate by intellectuals and activists surrounding the term "African Renaissance." The left wing accuse it of being obscurantist, a term that "serves to obscures the class contradictions between them and their imperialist masters and the African masses who need a revolutionary renaissance, which seeks first and foremost to fundamentally change their terrible conditions by challenging the forces largely responsible for them: The World Bank, IMF and WTO."[19] Democratic analysts fear that if wrongly interpreted, the word "African" could be taken as meaning that only black people are entitled to be part of the renaissance, resulting in an intolerant future for the growth of a human-rights culture in South Africa. After all, as Mahmood Mamdani in his observation on the South African decolonization process noted, South Africa is "the one place where yesterday's colonizer is making a claim to common citizenship."[20]

The most pessimistic and certainly poignant attack on the idea of an African Renaissance was made by playwright and poet Wole Soyinka. Speaking at the University of Cape Town in 1999, Soyinka talked of "a permanence of violence" to describe the indiscriminate slaughter and systematic dehumanization that has become the norm in many parts of the continent.[21] "How," he asked, "does a sculptor begin to carve with only stumps for arms? How does a village griot [poet, storyteller] ply his trade with only the root of a tongue still lodged at the gateway of memory?"

Does this pessimism apply to post-apartheid South Africa, where many see the move to democracy as the path to Utopia, in much the same way as the newly independent African countries in the post-war period viewed Socialism? There is no clear answer to be had, but there is an implicit warning sounded by the critics on the illusory nature of talking in terms of a pending renewal. Warning words as powerful as these should leave one either silent or, at the very least, cautious of enunciating anything at all, let alone a renaissance. Yet people do continue to speak of it, not only as a potential on the horizon, but also as something that has already arrived, something in which one can participate. It found its way into the media as the title of a thirteen-part series, *The African Renaissance*, produced by Ice Media, one of the most prolific South African production and distribution companies with transnational connections.[22] The press release issued on March 17, 2000, billed it as the "first Pan-African television and radio documentary series to capture the vision that lies behind the new wave of democratization in Africa."[23] It has been used to describe the Dv8 project, which has proven to be a prolific digital-film initiative, started by Joel Phiri (who produced the *Renaissance* series) and Jeremy Nathan, vital forces in the industry. Using high-resolution digital technology combined with training in script development and production plus a secure funding base, the project speaks of "a renaissance in South African film production, distribution and marketing, offering local filmmakers the opportunity to make their film without having to worry about finance, but rather [with the ability] to concentrate on writing and directing the best possible films."[24] Aspiring filmmakers are invited to join "the new wave of Electric African Cinema and stand a chance to tell your story on digital film."[25] Working with the NFVF and the SABC2 channel, films that have emerged from the Dv8 stable include *Bunny Chow* (John Barker and Dog Pack Films, 2006), which was the Official Selection at the Toronto Film Festival in 2006; *Forgiveness* (Ian Gabriel, 2004), which was in the main competition at Locarno in 2004 and won the Best South African film award at Sithengi in 2004; *Max and Mona* (Teddy Mattera, 2004), which won Best First Film at FESPACO in 2005 and Best Script at Sithengi in 2005, and *The Flyer* (Revel Fox, 2005).

The word also popped up at the inauguration of the NFVF, when the minister of the Department of Arts and Culture talked of the NFVF's role in enhancing an African cinema aesthetic that would "lend further credence to the renewal of the African continent, our African Renaissance."[26] On the same occasion, the first CEO of the Foundation's board drove the point home by promising the Foundation would "embrace the challenge of the African Renaissance" in carrying out its work.[27] Clearly the efficacy of the term lies in its mutability, which permits application and redefinition as circumstances require.

PUTTING FILM ON PAPER

> [Our vision is] a South African film and video industry that mirrors and represents the nation, sustains commercial viability, encourages development and provides a medium through which the creative and technical talents of South Africans are able to reach the world.
>
> *National Film and Video Foundation Value Charter*[28]

The politics of cultural ownership in South Africa post-1994 rapidly spawned a series of intense battles along the fault lines of race and class. Despite the government's effort to emphasize the healing role of arts and culture in the reconciliation process, it was clear that the new transfer of power underway would be filled with conflict and rancorous rhetoric. Former elites who had defined what was and was not culture were being ousted, and in their place, argued the newly created Department of Arts, Culture, Science and Technology (DACST) (now the DAC), should be "the community." State funding of the arts would confer, "cultural capital," to use Pierre Bourdieu's phrase, on those who had been excluded under apartheid.[29] Responses from the former cultural custodians were predictably negative with accusations of "cultural hegemony" being leveled at the government. White academics charged the government of deliberately sacrificing the "high arts" because they had been used by apartheid functionaries to deny South Africa's African (black) roots and claim a European (white) heritage. The government countered, arguing that its aim was to institute a new vision based on inclusion and rooted in freedom of thought, creative expression, and creativity. It stated, "Culture should not be used as a mechanism of exclusion, a barrier between people, nor should cultural practices be reduced to ethnic or religious chauvinism."[30]

It was against this rancorous background that the DAC published the White Paper on Film in 1996 after a protracted period of consultation and debate between stakeholders, politicians, cultural workers, and filmmakers. The paper embodied the country's fledging cultural policy of restructuring the film industry, which it deemed "integral to the success of the democratic project," which was to take place as part of the general transformation of what was termed "heritage."[31] What strikes one in reading the paper is the fluidity with which it combines the "fighting rhetoric" of postcolonial discourse with phrases that could have emerged from a reader on neoliberal economic policy. No distinction is made, for example, between the concept of a national cinema that "will enable South African audiences to see their own interpretations of their experience and stories reflected on local screens" and the creation of a film industry based "on a sound commercial footing in order to enable it to become internationally competitive."[32]

Chapter 2 of the White Paper opens by positing cinema as "an important dimension on the terrain of cultural expression and the exploration of social meanings," while also calling it a way to "generate significant employment, income and investment opportunities" in the turbulent global media markets.[33] In a later paragraph, the industry is credited with the potential to promote South Africa as both tourist attraction and location for international film and advertising production due to the low costs in comparison to production in the European Union and the United States.[34]

What kind of cinema do these remarks envisage? Is it one that reflects the "petty bourgeois nationalism" that Frantz Fanon warned led to a "false decolonization," or a "combative" cinema (to use another Fanonian expression) that speaks to its own nation irrespective of whether the outside world can understand it (and be likely to buy it)? The answer is neither. The White Paper is not a manifesto announcing a position, although at times, it masquerades as such. It is a state paper, and as such must satisfy diverse constituencies: the industry, the state, the disempowered majority (at least it must talk on their behalf). In its rhetoric, one can see an attempt to solve what Thomas Elsaesser called, in his analysis of New German Cinema in the seventies, the "incompatible objectives of national cinema," economic viability on the one hand and cultural motivation on the other. According to Elsaesser, the reconciliation of cultural and economic priorities in Germany's film subsidy bill of that period leaned heavily on a particularly German concept, something Kluge characterized as *brauchbarkeit*.[35] Roughly translated, it means "usefulness"—that is, useful for the nation, for the industry, and hence for the general good. Enter the concept of African Renaissance on which the White Paper relies to reconcile the ideals of reconstruction, development, and culture with the need for economic growth. The concept of *brauchbarkeit* answers to both the private and public sectors, providing them with a meeting place. In time, the marketplace will overwhelm the public sector, a process that we see happening right now to the NFVF, the child of the White Paper.

TRYING TO PUT FILM ON A FIRM FOUNDATION

The White Paper mandated the creation of a film foundation which would oversee state funding for promoting local film and video, producing education and training, a diversity of film genres and types without regard for commercial value, and a growing cinema culture in South Africa. The foundation would be at arm's length from the government, a vitally important condition considering the horrible history of film subsidy in South Africa.

Former schemes under apartheid (an "A" scheme from 1956 for films in English and Afrikaans and a "B" scheme from 1974 for "ethnic" or black films) had been incoherent, corrupt, and racist.[36] Cloaked in the language of cultural preservation against the predations of Hollywood and a concern for a sustainable local film industry, they did little else than prop up Afrikaans as *the* language of "South African" cinema, comply with the censorship laws of the day, and foster "conservative populist themes."[37] The result was a racially marked cinema circulating in a closed and internal space. Of the 604 films produced from 1956 to 1984, only 16 were sold abroad.[38] Apartheid ideology and the desire to support Afrikaner ethnonationalism (films made in Afrikaans received a higher subsidy percentage than those made in English) drove the scheme, and without state subsidy, the majority of films during this period would not have been made. (As we will explore later, this state of dependency is still in play in current film-funding practices.) "Almost overnight," the chair of the South African Film and Theatre Technicians Association remarked, "butchers, bakers and candlestick makers were becoming filmmakers."[39]

In the mid-eighties, corruption exceeded even ideology. Producers exploited a government tax break (known as the double deduction) to fuel not a film industry, but a "monumental tax avoidance scheme."[40] As international producers like Golan-Globus and Cannon used over $36 million of South African's taxpayer dollars to produce more than 600 Hollywood clones—mainly for the video market—the South African landscape became the generic backdrop for films like *King Solomon's Mines* (1985), *Allan Quartermain and the Lost City of Gold* (1985), *American Ninja 2: The Confrontation* (1987), *American Ninja 3: The Domination* (1989), *American Ninja 4: The Annihilation* (1990), *Africa Express* (1989), and *Mercenary Fighters* (1989). Local filmmakers protested the waste of tax dollars on films that had nothing to do with South Africa and that privileged major global film companies. At a meeting between filmmakers and government bureaucrats in 1990 on the question of state subsidy, David Bensusan, the director of *My Country, My Hat* (1981) argued:

> You can only claim subsidy if you're making a film that has some relevance to the society you live in, some notion of culture or history or what South Africa is all about. I have no problem with commercial films, but it's important to draw a distinction between private and public interests. People keep talking about the South African film industry, but they are really talking about an American film industry, which has set up its little base here. There's no reason why the South African tax payer should pay for that.[41]

By the end of the decade, the government closed the tax gaps and the binge collapsed. The old system was back in place, but in effect, it was eviscerated. Years of systemic abuse had left investors with little confidence in the industry. Outside of production subsidies, there had been no support for the development of markets, talent, and circuits of exhibition and distribution. Nothing had been done to develop a sustainable film industry. What remained was a strong infrastructure of technical skills (in the white population) and production facilities that met international standards.[42] The system's implosion reflected the general sense of crisis in a country staggering toward apartheid's end.

This was the situation the Interim Film Fund (IFF) inherited when it was put in place to bridge the gap until the NFVF could be inaugurated. The IFF met with criticism in the areas of transparency and infrastructure. Local filmmakers complained about the absence of official application procedures or administrative principles. Novice filmmakers felt that the IFF should be more open about their judging criteria, the logic behind success and failure, and the different amounts awarded in each case. They also suffered from the lack of a supportive infrastructure and the industry contacts and expertise needed to realize their projects. The situation was exacerbated by the lack of formal film training in the country, and the pervasive idea in the existing industry that filmmakers were technicians, not artists or cultural critics. Although plans in the White Paper had emphasized the importance of training and recommended the establishment of a national film and television school, this had not happened. The few training institutions that did exist offered a variety of courses at differing levels and tended to reinforce the "technicity" approach to film by employing people from within the industry to "train" their students, thereby splitting theoretical and critical skills off from technical ones.

By the time it ceased to function in 1999 with the NFVF's inauguration, the IFF had infused $3.3 million into 206 films. The funds were allocated as follows: 43 percent went to production and post-production, with documentaries taking 49 percent of that total, features 29 percent, and television the remainder; content creation (scripts, treatments) received 22 percent of the total, with 48 percent allocated to features, 23 percent to TV, and 21 percent to documentaries. Training received 21 percent split between institutional training (54 percent) and on-the-job training (46 percent). The remaining 14 percent was spent on promotions at film markets and festivals locally and abroad.[43] In this way, the IFF kept cinema and film production alive for four years.

CONTINUING PROBLEMS

Most of the problems that had dogged the IFF—lack of experience and appropriate training, lack of transparency in funding procedures, lack of funds for research and development, lack of distribution and exhibition possibilities for local film, and lack of black production companies—have continued to plague the NFVF. There is still no national film school; the industry continues to be fragmented, offering few opportunities for mentorship and on-the-job training; transparency in the allocation of funds is insufficient; funds available for developing and producing projects are inadequate; and local films cannot find distribution and exhibition (in South Africa, the two are the same). These facts and more emerged at the 2001 Indaba. The Indaba's final report described an industry that had the necessary infrastructure for success but was fragmented in the private sector and hampered by a lack of professionalism, a climate of mistrust and suspicion, a lack of transparency, and insufficient knowledge of industry practices.[44]

The film industry had shown little growth since 1997. Production of feature films was at an all-time low, with private-sector investors very wary of investing in the industry due to its bad history and the closure of a number of production companies' filmmaking units. The one exception to the bad news was Videovision, a production company headquartered in Durban and owned by Anant Singh, South Africa's most successful producer, which was breaking box-office records with its comedy, *Mr. Bones* (Darrell Roodt, 2001).[45] The number of production commissions had not kept pace with costs due to an increase in labor costs and inadequate state support. The effect of increased labor costs was only felt the local level. South African labor was still 20 percent cheaper than EU or U.S. labor and 30–40 percent cheaper for international producers when compared to filming costs in Australia.[46] The private sector needed a federation of some kind to help it negotiate with the National Association of Broadcasters, as communication between the broadcasters and the independent producers had broken down. There was a dearth of provincial film industries outside of Gauteng (Johannesburg) and the Western Cape (Cape Town) and also a lack of black-owned companies due to unfair (some said racist) commissioning procedures on the part of the broadcasters, lack of training for black commissioning editors and producers, inadequate marketing and distribution circuits, and lack of investors. International co-production treaties were in process or had been negotiated with France, Ireland, and Canada, but not with any African country. Local co-productions did not exist due to unfair commissioning practices and an inherited culture of secrecy and clannishness.[47]

The industry needed two kinds of money: development funds and project finance. Development funds operated like grants, with no expectation of return on the money. They were only available through the NFVF as part of its mandate to create cinematic diversity in content, genre, and points of view and to bring new filmmakers and production companies, especially black ones, into the industry. Project finance was business oriented and sought a return on investment. It did not draw on state funds, but sourced funds from private investors: the banks and, most notably, the Industrial Development Corporation (IDC), a self-financing, state-owned national development institution providing financing to entrepreneurs and businesses, which opened a Media and Motion Pictures Strategic Unit in 2001.

Both types of funding were in short supply, a fact that weakened the NFVF given its dependency on government support and the unlikelihood of it being able to find other sources of money.[48] Its objectives, formulated during the utopian years of transition, were filled with the kinds of hopes and dreams that seem plausible at such moments: to develop and promote the film and video industry; to provide opportunities for people from disadvantaged communities to get involved in the film and video industry; to encourage the development and distribution of local film and video products; and to address "historical imbalances in the infrastructure and distribution of skills and resources" in the film and video industry.[49] To achieve such objectives requires a leap of faith into the cinematic beyond, as one is talking about something that is, to plagiarize Marx, a "vague immensity." Yet as the somewhat utopian pronouncements of all national cinemas tell us, part of what the project entails is not to sit back and take a retrospective view, but to make an announcement. Talk of what an "indigenous" cinema" might or should be is always a discourse that contains within it an insecurity, an imaginative content, a dreaming of possibilities that may or may not be there and may or may not be realized.

A BREAK FROM THE "DEPENDENCY SYNDROME"

The NFVF was just such an announcement. It was framed in the terms of the Reconstruction and Development Programme (RDP), the ANC's first economic program (1994–1996), which emphasized the need for the government to bring about a more equal distribution of income:

> [T]he RDP takes the view that neither economic growth by itself [n]or redistribution on its own will resolve the serious crisis in which South Africa finds itself. . . . [Government policy] will involve the promotion of a more equitable pattern of growth, an equitable distribution of assets . . . [as well as] the maintenance of macro-economic stability.[50]

The goal for redistribution was radical: to double the national income share of the poorest 20 and then 40 percent of households by 2005, which received

9 percent of national income at the time. To achieve this, the incomes of the poorest 40 percent would have to grow at almost double (7.2 percent) the percentage per annum in comparison to the incomes of the other 60 percent. This would require a profound shift of investment to the poorest sector as well as a large increase in the progressivity of the personal income tax. The important point was that redistribution was a principle and would not be held hostage to growth.

Economic policy changed in the last quarter of 1996, with the coming of GEAR, orchestrated by Thabo Mbeki, South Africa's current president, which turned the RDP on its head by placing (G)rowth first, (E)mployment second, (A)nd (R)edistribution last. Reducing inequality was not a policy over and above all others for GEAR. It concentrated on decreasing unemployment through growth, something that the RDP also considered important but not sufficient in terms of equitable distribution of income.[51] To achieve growth, certain "reforms" had to take place:

> [G]overnment consumption expenditure should be cut back, private and public sector wage increases kept in check, tariff reform accelerated to compensate for the depreciation and domestic savings performance improved. These measures will counteract the inflationary impact of the exchange rate adjustment, permit fiscal deficit targets to be reached, establish a climate for continued investor confidence and facilitate the financing of both private sector investment and accelerated development expenditure.[52]

Such "reforms" are not kind to non-profit organizations such as the RDP. It is sad to see the Foundation struggling to reformulate itself in accordance with GEAR, urged to be more proactive in fundraising, more concerned with marketing the film industry, more interested in product than cinema, and in particular, the kind of product that will attract international co-productions. Earlier in this chapter, we saw this same disciplinary process overtake the White Paper's recommendations, which were reformulated in the RDP era and ended up being completed and adopted into law under GEAR. Like the Bill's language, The NFVF's stated mission swings between idealism and pragmatism, searching wildly to find a middle position. It describes itself on its website in the following terms:

> The vision of the NFVF is to strive for a quality South African film and video industry that is representative of the nation, commercially viable and encourages development.[53]

Suggestions made at the first Film Indaba to help the Foundation increase funds involved state interventions. The value-added tax (VAT) could be collected on cinema tickets, there could be a withholding tax on foreign films screened in the country, a withholding tax on royalties paid to foreign film distributors, and a clear monitoring of investment companies to prevent abuse of South African incentives to produce films of benefit to the industry (as had happened in the eighties). None of these options were implemented. By the 2005 Indaba, it was clear that a business mode had set in. The charter, which had articulated its mission and values, had transmuted into a "value chain," an organogram that looked more like a business plan for the industry than a developmental strategy for an emerging film industry.

The process for getting funds moves from concept to distribution to financing to manufacture to marketing, which means that funding is dependent on getting distribution. In order to get distribution (which need not mean distribution only in the classic sense of a cinema chain, but can also involve video, broadcasting, or non-conventional sites such as schools, halls, churches, universities, and festivals), the project must be defined and targeted at a viable audience. "Viable" here does not necessarily mean financially viable. If the project is developmental (say, concerned with health issues) and aimed at a specific audience, then profit is not a concern. What *is* a concern is the difficulty in defining the audience, since that usually requires quantifiable data. Without some way of quantifying the target audience, no distributor (conventional or alternative) will invest time and money in distribution. Projects that fall outside of the usual fare are thus unduly compromised, since measurable data is hard to obtain. Also, researching an audience and coming up with measurable data takes funds and skills, which new filmmakers and producers may not have. Furthermore, if one seeks to develop an audience for alternative cinematic projects (to develop a more diverse cinema culture, which is meant to be one of the NFVF's objectives), there is no way to measure the audience potential for projects that do not yet exist.

All these points are not symptoms of what the NFVF terms a "dependency syndrome, where people have waited and even expected government to act on their behalf," but obstacles in the way of empowerment.[54] Without funding upfront, one cannot research an idea or who would be the target audience. Lack of experience and professional training hamper filmmakers because private capital, being risk aversive, is not available to new filmmakers and producers. The problem is exacerbated by the shortage of black capital that might be persuaded to take a risk. Distribution (which includes exhibition) circuits are conservative and committed to the bottom line. Since local films have done badly at the box office, they are not willing to take a risk unless forced to do so as in the case of local content mandates for broadcasting. The NFVF is the only advocate for the disempowered (in terms of film and filmmaking), but it appears to have abandoned that role, acting instead on behalf of the industry as a "service deliverer to the broader industry," a "strategic partner in the industry."[55] Martin Botha, head of the HSRC report that had mooted the idea of a film foundation way back in 1994 and one of the writers of the Film Bill, spoke of a "crude commercialization" taking place at the NFVF. In an interview in 2005, he told of applicants being asked for "rushes," "pitches" for new projects being reduced to 25 words or less, and projects being rejected as non-commercial (Ross Devenish's inability to get funding for a film version of Zake Mda's novel, *Ways of Dying*, 2005) or politically incorrect (Gavin Hood's Oscar-winning film, *Tsotsi*, 2005, which was initially refused funding because it did not project positive images of black people). Non-mainstream cinema, he said, was being marginalized and a new avant-garde (short films, critical films, experimental films) was needed in the name of progressivity.[56]

No support for films outside of the mainstream could be expected to come from the IDC's Media and Film Development Unit, created in 2001. Working on a business model, the Unit aims to stimulate production and develop an export market by financing the development of competitive industries in South Africa. It bankrolls small and medium-sized budgets ($155,000–$6,000,000), and, depending on the assessed risk, invests up to a maximum of 49 percent of the deal value on a project that must secure significant theatrical release or television airing.[57] Currently, the IDC has co-produced over 30 films with international companies, including *Hotel Rwanda* (Terry George, 2004), *Red Dust* (Tom Hooper, 2004), *Tsotsi, Catch a Fire* (Philip Noyce, 2006), and *Wah Wah* (Richard Grant, 2006).[58] It has spent over $6 million in the process and, it claims, created over five thousand jobs, which are more than just a paycheck. Specialist skills learned on the job are transferred to "home-grown films," thus raising production values and viewership, since research has shown that South Africans see local films as shoddy in comparison to imported ones. The IDC's partnership with the Department of Trade and Industry (DTI) has introduced another incentive to attract international co-production, a tax-rebate scheme that offers $1.5 million cash back on budgets of at least $3.8 million. The tax rebate is credited with bringing in around $76 million worth of production during 2005.

TELEVISION AND ADVERTISING TAKE UP THE BURDEN

Early representative signs to the nation of how it might view itself did appear in television and advertising—watched by more South Africans than movies. Marginal groups in the society often feel recognized and expressed by being included into the dominant culture, which to the postcolonial theorist is best explained by Anthony Gramsci's concept of cultural hegemony. As Gramsci theorized, cultural hegemony worked to obscure the differences between people's individual existences and the social and economic oppression that structured their lives in a fundamental fashion. For a poor, black South African from Soweto to see someone like him or herself in the local soap opera *Generations*, which played out the usual fare of crises, melodramas, attempted suicides, and excesses of consumption within the setting of a hip, black Johannesburg advertising company, would be, for Third Cinema's foremost theorists, Fernando Solanas and Octavio Getino, a subversion of his or her representational rights, since it encoded him or her in "First Cinema's" world of manipulation and critical annihilation. Yet in post-1994 South Africa, the *Generations* narrative was also a sign to that viewer that the nation was, at least in principle, a place where he or she, too, could end up on top of things rather than back in the kitchen cleaning up for the white "madam" and "master." So just possibly the *Generations* model was the right way of utopianizing the poor, black South African into an image of the new nation and its possibilities. Whether these were genuine possibilities is another question. The question is certainly related to the question of ideology, as Gramsci noted, but it is not quite the same question as the one of cultural rights, for that individual's right is also to be recognized in his or her aspirations, however unreal they may be. Or so it might be argued.[59]

CAMPAIGNING FOR THE NATION

The race for representation is also, parenthetically, a race from all parts of society to provide and capitalize on new images and brands. While the state pronounces from above, the work of reimagining often starts from below in practice, as Bhabha has pointed out. A specific example here was the "What makes you black?" campaign created by Net#work BBDO in the late 1990s for Metro FM, the largest national urban commercial radio station in South Africa. According to its current website, Metro FM has around six million adult listeners. It regularly reaches 19 percent of the total market of listeners of all races, and it has a 43 percent reach in the 16–34 age group. In its own words, "it epitomizes Black success and leadership with attitude."[60] The "What makes you black?" campaign was aimed at increasing listenership across all racial categories. To achieve this goal, the advertisers came up with a series of images, which they placed on billboards along the M1, the main motorway leading to and from Johannesburg's central business district.

The images turned being black into a consumer choice as opposed to a racial category. Apartheid's obsession with racial classification had inevitably placed great emphasis on a person's visual appearance. No one from that period can forget the ugly scenes of officials in the 1950s combing people's hair as a test of whether they should be classified white, black, or colored based on how firmly the comb stood up in their hair. The ideology behind such actions lay rooted in the nineteenth century's conviction that race was determined by a morphology of primarily skin color, hair type, and eye color. What lay beneath the visual structure of these specific parts (which at times included other parts than those mentioned above, such as the shape of the eye or the structure of the sexual organs, as was most famously demonstrated in the case of Saartje Baartman, the "Hottentot Venus") was irrelevant, which is why Fanon used the word "epidermilization" to describe this visual regime.

The images for the Metro FM campaign directly countered that regime and offered a new vision of what it meant to be black. It showed black female models with long, straight blonde hair and blue eyes and sexually ambiguous (they could be read as either "metrosexual" or homosexual) black males, including one who was albino, all with slim, non-traditional African bodies, all in hip, contemporary, exclusive designer wear and accompanied by the tagline: "What makes you Black? It's the radio station you listen to." The conjunction of image and text opened up a series of questions for the viewer: If black people could look white in the sense of having straight blond hair, blue eyes, and even a white skin and the body shape associated with white models, then what had made black people different in the first place from their white counterparts? If difference was no longer marked by skin color, eye color, hair texture, and body shape as it had been under apartheid, then where did it reside under the new dispensation?

The answer to the question resides in what Fredric Jameson has called, in his classic work on postmodernism, the "cultural logic of late capitalism."[61] Jameson points out that one fundamental task of postmodernism is to combine new habits of thought and behavior with new forms of capitalism so as to produce new subjects or people. Jameson casts postmodern subjectivity in a negative light as schizophrenic, affectless, and fragmented.[62] Subjects do have reactions and feelings, but they are surface emotions stimulated by images severed from that which they represent in the real world. The image stands for nothing but itself, a perfect example of commodity fetishization. In fact, that is the only reactive possibility open to the subject under postmodernism, and thus the desire to shop, to consume, to fashion new identities from commodity objects, to try them on for size, and then to discard them in favor of the latest style is emblematic of the nature of postmodern subjectivity.

Through the Jamesonian lens, the "What makes you Black?" campaign positions blackness as a subject position that can be constructed through props, cosmetics, and listening to the right radio station. Being black is allied with a whole set of brand values, or "core concepts," articulated on the Metro FM website as follows: quality, cosmopolitan, stylish, progressive, attitude, and proudly black.[63] The racial discourses of apartheid have disappeared, or, as Eve Bertelsen notes, been redefined under the logic of the market. She explains,

> On the one hand progressive forces set about the task of 'undoing' the discourses of the apartheid era and naturalizing in their place ideas of non-racism and equity. But as quickly as this is achieved, we observe a contrary movement, as the vigorously propagated discourses of consumerism and the 'free market' in their turn move in to displace the quasi-socialist . . . terms of inherited discourses of struggle, redefining democracy as individual freedom, and, especially, the freedom to consume.[64]

In contrast, the Castle Lager beer campaigns of the 1990s, crafted by Ogilvy and Mather, South Africa did not challenge the epistemology of face, but instead offered up a heady brew of nationalism, colorblindness, and male bonding. South African Breweries, which owns Castle Beer, had been targeting black consumers since the 1970s. But only in the nineties, when it became clear to the business sector that apartheid was falling apart, did they produce multiracial commercials. The campaigns from this period are examples of how a well-known consumer brand can be redeployed so as to construct a changing sense of how people should act and of the kinds of relationships they should have with one another. The brand had lost its position as leader in its category because it no longer reflected the changing South African racial landscape. To restore that position, the company had to expand its market, which meant reaching the black consumer, and in particular, the black male. At the same time, they had to avoid losing two of the brand's important attributes: "heritage" (the beer had been going since 1895) and "tradition. Castle Lager was perceived to be a beer consumed by a working-class, white male constituency. It was the beer of choice for bonding at rugby matches and around the *braaivleis* (South Africa's version of the barbecue). The problem was how to reach the black men (and to a lesser extent, black women) who now generated more than 80 percent of total beer consumption in the country without alienating its established white consumer base. The solution they chose was to craft a campaign around the concept of friendship. Television commercials for the urban market and radio and outdoor ones for the rural and media-poor areas showed young black and white males socializing in bars and at sports events in an atmosphere of warmth and expansiveness. The advertisers used South Africa's readmission to the global world of sports, which permitted tie-ins and sponsorship with major sporting associations, to create a multiracial world in which the consumption of Castle Lager promised friendship, popularity, and, above all, uncomplicated relationships.[65] South African Breweries had always been a major sponsor of sports, which under apartheid had been a very vexed category. In the new multiracial South Africa, however, the trope of sport could now be coupled to nationalist sentiment. South Africans could play on the field together and drink beer together and support the national team without problem. Nowhere is nationalism stronger than in the international arena, where even the most skeptical South Africans feel a surge of pride on hearing the new anthem played and seeing *Bafana-Bafana* ("the boys," the nickname for the South African national soccer team) in action.

In 2007, Castle Lager showed a commercial set in New York City. It began with a white man pushing a huge case on wheels through the crowded streets. There was no dialogue, just ambient street sound and the song lyric, "I bless the rains down in Africa."[66] Dragging the case with great difficulty up the stairs, he entered a building and took the elevator to the roof where his multiracial buddies, dressed in South African rugby uniforms, greeted his arrival with enthusiasm. The case was opened to reveal bottles of Castle Lager stacked up on each other. Within seconds, meat was thrown on an open flame, beers were cracked open, and a traditional South African *braaivleis* (barbecue) commenced. In one shot, the men lined up as if they were a rugby team about to go on the field, saluting the South African flag with bottles of Castle Lager. In the last shot, the skyline of New York was framed as if from their point of view, and over it was superimposed the label of the beer and the slogan, "the taste that's stood the test of time." At the same moment, a deep male voiceover says, "All over the world, the South African's home is his castle."

Cultural critics have excoriated commercials such as these for their consumerist, macho values, their superficial representation of race relations, and so on. But that is really not the point. Commercials are indicators of the zeitgeist, multilayered, highly ideological texts that organize what Judith Williamson has called "structures of meanings," which rely on the conventional codes and myths at play in the society.[67] Of course, no advertiser can be sure that the reader or viewer will interpret the meaning as intended. Advertisements are polysemic texts and can be read against the grain. As Jean-Luc Comolli and Jean Narboni demonstrated, even a text as tightly encoded as a Hollywood film could be read for internal flaws and deconstructed accordingly.[68] But that requires critical skill and awareness. Like most genre films, commercials use an iconography that places severe limits on meaning, resulting in a "modestly plural text."[69]

The discipline of cultural studies has taught us that commodities, even if they change and alter endlessly under the logic of advertising and marketing, play an important role in identity construction. National sentiment does not play well when it comes to the "Born Frees," also known as Generation Y, the descriptor given to young South Africans aged 13–25, who came of age after the end of apartheid. Their rejection of national appeals shows that the splits between populations in South Africa are not always along ethnic, racial, or gender lines. Unlike the youth of the former generation who were radically political, these youth find organized politics boring and non-relevant, a "nonevent."[70] Like their global peers, they are interested in brand-name clothes, music, cell phones, shopping, and dancing, but not in politics. "Born Frees" have the lowest voting percentage in a country where 20.7 million out of 27.5 million eligible voters cast their ballot in the last election. Their interests are personal and social. However, if one looks closer at the some of the products that the "Born Frees" or Generation Y embrace, it is clear that there is a political message to be seen. It just does not take the familiar forms of resistance politics from apartheid South Africa. In fact, scholars draw a distinction between the old politics of resistance and what they term a "politics of the emergent."[71] Joining the ANC Youth League has been replaced by the brand names of their clothing, the sound of their music (known as *kwaito*, a South Africanized version of hip hop), and the places where they hang out. Sarah Nuttall calls this a stylization of the self, in which people

> seek to transform themselves into singular beings, to make their lives into an
> oeuvre that carries with it certain stylistic criteria. . . . [and] the emergence
> of explicit forms of selfhood within the public domain and the rise of the first-
> person singular within the work of liberation.[72]

The name "Generation Y" is a global one, and Nuttall is careful to explain that she is not equating the South African "Y" generation with all of the others in some general amorphous group. She examines how the global and the local interact with each other in constructing this urban youth culture, which has its own name taken from a fashion label: Loxion Kulcha (a corruption of the words "location culture"), which expresses a mix between the culture of the location (another word for township) and that of the city. Since the two spaces were separated and racially coded under apartheid, the latter being white and the former black, the phrase implies a racially mixed state. One of the most important points emerging from her analysis is the way in which the racial identities from the old South Africa (black, white, coloured, and Indian) have taken on a new taxonomy poached from the media, fashion labels, rock bands, sports, and advertising. Depending on one's age, and the median age in South Africa is 24.1 years, the objects of consumption play a large role in reimagining the nation.

Achille Mbembe talks of the "chaotic plurality of the postcolony," a space in which signs are mobile and ambivalent allowing the people, both the powerless and the powerful, to improvise and continually reshape themselves.[73] The daily circumstances, which could provide opportunities for resistance and counteraction, become instead sites for the reproduction of power. Yet we cannot stop there. Mbembe's analysis is specific to the particular political conditions of post-coloniality in Togo and Cameroon. It is not wholly applicable to contemporary South Africa, which is trying, with its magnificent constitution, to introduce a democratic modern state as opposed to an all-embracing regime of power. Still, his picture of a polysemic realm in which signs are under contestation and constantly changing, be it on billboards, in shopping malls, in the cinema, or in the boardroom, evokes the chaos following apartheid's collapse and the difficulties of integrating into one space all that which had been deliberately fragmented.

Nothing is simple when it comes to the issue of rights and representations, especially style and content. There is no longer any single image of "the people" which in these post-national, post-Marxist, transnational times can be relied upon to frame the question of national cinema in relation to cultural rights (that is, representation). A diverse group of South Africans with diverse cultural backgrounds, distinct languages, and astonishingly different historical trajectories cannot be assimilated into any single picture of how cinema might best "express" their right to representation, and their larger cultural rights generally. Even if one is clear on what a cultural right is, one will still remain unclear about their content. Hence, one of the first images in South African cultural theorization was that of a rainbow nation, which projected a group characterized by unity through diversity in virtue of a common project, a common landscape, a common history, and a common requirement (to bind themselves into a new whole while remaining diverse).

The image has become something of a joke as the utopian moment of transition has faded into the reality of the present, but the desired ideal is still one of a harmonious refraction of color bands, each into the others, to produce a beautiful thing while each retains its own color properties. This is the aesthetics of multiracialism, a harmony of types, each formerly at war with the other, and now, glowing in the light of the other. How Technicolor can achieve this rainbow effect while also catering to a variety of quite distinct audiences is the central theoretical problem in South African cultural pronouncements. For, as Anderson has noted, "nation-ness" is the most universally legitimate value and provides the framework for all kinds of political activity, and yet its terms of representation tend to be homogenizing, taking disparate texts and bringing them together as one under the auspices of an imagined community. How to do that while focusing on what is distinctive and different, especially given the overwhelmingly homogenizing fare of globalization, is the South African problem in a nutshell.

2

State and Market
Enter the Race

This is not an apathetic industry. It abounds with passion and aspirations. However, it is one where individuals pursue survival instead of growth. It is fragmented, ill informed and in need of training and development.

National Film and Video Foundation

The previous chapter dealt with the avalanche of documents, acts, reports, inquiries, and the like that followed the end of apartheid as the state raced to instantiate a new vision for South African culture. This chapter focuses on how the state and the private sector (the film industry) have implemented and delivered on those plans.

The state's mission is to produce a contemporary South African cinema under the sign of the nation through structures such as the NFVF and the IDC. Its activities must be seen against the context of South Africa's global dependency and general lack of local institutional excellence evidenced by the recommendations and statistics garnered at the 2001 and 2005 film *indabas*. Many companies from the private sector, partly due to pressure from the state and partly driven by corporate public relations, have made positive contributions to the film industry. The South African Screenwriters Lab (SCRAWL) has sponsored script-writing laboratories, and New Directions, a developmental film initiative begun in 1993 by M-Net, South Africa's largest private subscription television service, has funded short films and features in an attempt to develop new filmmaking talent. Ster-Kinekor Cinemas has opened a new multiplex in Soweto and promises to develop more sites for marketing and distribution of local product. These gestures all seek national legitimacy in different ways, by appealing to reconciliation, nation building, and Pan-African development beyond the boundaries of the nation.

State and market drew closer over time as the Mandela presidency segued into the Mbeki one and the focus on reconciliation ("the rainbow nation") was replaced by the notion of "two nations." The phrase comes from a May 29, 1998, speech by Thabo Mbeki in Parliament where he described South Africa as a country comprised of "two nations," one relatively wealthy and mostly white and the other relatively poor and overwhelmingly black. The only way to bridge the gap was through economic empowerment of the poor nation, not through a process of reconciliation that required symbolic acts.

One can see the effects of this new social prognosis in the state's turn from idealism toward a more market-driven program. Gone is the rhetoric of an indigenous cinema. The historical imbalances will find redress through the building of infrastructure, which takes the form of developing small, medium, and micro enterprises (SMME) for the effective growth of the industry. Nonetheless, the embrace of the business model has affected many aspects of the cinema. There is less funding for short films, experimental films, alternative cinema, and training and education—in short, for a more progressive approach to cinematic production, exhibition, and distribution. This is the state of cinema at the time of writing. An examination of the past will reveal how we arrived at this point.

BROADCASTING COMPLAINTS

Film has never been considered much of an art in South Africa in comparison to literature, music, dance, opera, or theater. At best, it has been an industry (a rather unsuccessful one), and at worst, it has been one of the old regime's propaganda tools. Even the anti-apartheid films (those that weren't banned outright) that challenged the regime garnered most of their attention and praise on the international, not domestic, scene.

Television only came to South Africa in 1975 after a long struggle to keep it at bay by the apartheid state, which feared losing control of information flow. Dr. Albert Herzog, the then-Minister of Posts and Telegraphs, puritanically dubbed TV "the evil box" and vowed to keep it out of South Africa. He failed. The desire for the medium, coupled with the feeling that the country was falling behind the rest of the world in communication technology, forced the state to accede and a state-controlled service came into being.[1] The mix of local and imported shows seemed to satisfy people's appetite for local product.

All of this explains why the state's new film policy raised few hackles among the custodians of culture. Indeed, the use of quotas to protect local audiovisual production is a common practice throughout the world even though it runs counter to existing international trade regulations. The practice is justified under the idea of preserving cultural diversity, and consequently, special treatment is granted by the World Trade Organization to film, radio, and television products.[2] The broadcast industry, however, vociferously protested the local content mandates outlined in the Independent Broadcasting Authority's (IBA) Triple Enquiry Report, which came out in 1995 and passed into law two years later. Twenty percent of all content broadcast on both private and public channels had to be commissioned from local producers. This requirement would rise to 50 percent for the public broadcaster and to a lesser 20 percent for the private ones by 2000.[3] In addition, commissions had to be (where possible) evenly spread between the various genres, with at least 20 percent going to drama, the most expensive genre. When the broadcasters failed to meet the target by the required date, the regulators met again and lowered the requirement to 40 percent (to reach 50 percent in the near future). The protests from the broadcasters grew even louder. Costs would increase, they claimed, since it was cheaper to import productions than to commission them locally, especially since the local product was so specific to South Africa as to make it non-exportable.[4] In addition, they were being asked to shoulder an unfair amount of the burden. The mandates reflected the state's belief that broadcasting had a central role to play in the growth of the film industry. This was true, but evidence from other countries' experiences showed that no film industry could survive and grow solely on commissions from local broadcasters.[5] More state support in the form of tax incentives, training, and funding were needed in addition to broadcast commissions, the broadcasters correctly claimed. The film industry (which in South Africa means both television and film) generates over $200 million per annum, but is only funded by the state at a ratio of 2.6 percent. Countries that have been successful in growing a local cinema, such as Australia and Canada, fund at a ratio of 19 percent. Based on the size of South Africa's industry, funding of at least $38 million per year would be necessary to meet international benchmarks.

State funding was not only inadequate; it was too centralized, which conjured up echoes of apartheid's emphasis on a centralized media economy.

South African film policy appeared to be following what Richard Maxwell, in his description of Spanish broadcasting policy in the seventies, called a "high-policy" phase of democratization, or "democracy bestowed from above."[6] In response, the Department of Arts and Culture (DAC) pleaded poverty. Its resources were too limited to increase funding for production and regional initiatives, but by not promoting regionalism, the DAC and its creation, the NFVF, were going against one of their own mandates: to increase access and representavity by extending the industry beyond the two provinces in which it was concentrated, Gauteng and the Western Cape, to the other seven provinces. This was a highly utopian goal given the state's unwillingness to allocate more money to the growth of the film industry and the lack of education and skills in the poorer, more rural provinces.

Once more, Australia appears to have gotten democracy culturally right. Its film commission acts as a core funding body and facilitator in alliance with other government agencies, including those dealing with telecommunication and broadcasting, to create a strong, interlinked federal matrix that works to support regional film initiatives. In the late nineties, the NFVF brought in consultants from the Australian Film Foundation and one can see their influence in the subsequent partnering of the NFVF, the Department of Trade and Industry and the IDC. But the economic and social conditions in Australia are quite different from those in South Africa. Australia implemented broad-based economic reforms at both the macro and micro levels in the mid 1980s. A more competitive climate for industry was created through deregulation, and capital controls were relaxed. Inflation was brought under control, allowing for better medium-term planning for businesses and greater purchasing power for consumers. With lower interest rates, investment increased and productivity improved. A productivity surge followed, and per capita income grew.[7] By the mid 2000s, the economy had recorded nine years of straight growth averaging 4 percent a year. At its highest, in the mid 1990s, unemployment was just over 11 percent.[8]

South Africa's economic reforms started after 1994 against the backdrop of a system that actively restrained "participation of the entire population in the market economy and constrained the development of human skills to participate competitively."[9] Because of its late start, South Africa did not benefit from the strong growth in international trade during the 1990s. The official unemployment rate in 2008 was 25 percent, but unofficially, the figure was closer to 50 percent. South Africa's economic growth rate is far below what is needed to stop that rate from increasing, let alone reduce it. Unlike Australia, South Africa's reforms came about in response to crisis conditions: enormous poverty, inadequate human development, and the HIV/AIDS pandemic. These conditions are more like the situation in Malaysia than in Australia, so it is unlikely that the NFVF and its partners can build the type of infrastructure that allowed Australia to diversify film production beyond metropolitan limits into other areas.[10]

In the meantime, both Gauteng and the Western Cape, which means Johannesburg and Cape Town, have jumped national borders and set up their own film commissions to market themselves as strategic arenas for international film producers, thus joining a global network. Now in competition with Toronto, Sydney, Prague, and other cities for "runaway" or "flyaway" productions (films not set in South Africa, but produced there because of lower production costs or other incentives), the Gauteng Film Commission (GFC) and the Cape Film Commission (CFC) play up the advantages of their respective cities. The CFC touts Cape Town's extraordinary natural beauty, its history as a stop on the trade route from Europe to the East Indies, its colonial connections to Britain and Holland, and of course, its filmic infrastructure and skills base. With 150 production companies, the industry contributes 4 percent of gross regional product and 45 percent of total film industry revenues, mostly due to commercials.[11] To use an America analogy, Johannesburg, with its economic clout, is to Cape Town, with its beauty and history, what Los Angeles is to San Francisco. Like Hollywood, "Gaullywood" is the center for 70 percent of all South African TV productions, which are worth more than $100 million, and is the corporate headquarters of the three major broadcasters, SABC, e.tv, and M-Net. Seven out of the top ten South African TV dramas are based in Gauteng.[12] It offers access to major financial institutions, over 900 registered production companies, the best weather in the country (a dry sunny winter in comparison to the Cape's wet one), and a world-class infrastructure.[13] Major international films such as Ali (Michael Mann, 2002), Catch a Fire (Philip Noyce, 2006), Blood Diamond (Ed Zwick, 2006), Red Dust (Tom Hooper, 2004), and Hotel Rwanda (Terry George, 2004) have used Gauteng film crews, which speaks to their skills and expertise. Like many institutions in the global mediascape, the GFC and the CFC operate both locally and globally, connecting with bodies like the NFVF and the IDC in their immediate locales, and fostering unilateral relations from a distance.[14]

MORE FILM PRODUCTION DOESN'T MEAN
MORE FILMS FOR THE CINEMA

In South Africa, film production includes production for television, commercials, and the cinema. Documents and reports from the government and its institutions show an apparent confusion in the minds of state planners, present from the very beginning in the language of the National Film and Video Foundation Act (1997), which equated cinema and television as one and the same entity all rolled up under the label of "film production." One can only attribute this misrecognition to the thinness of cinema culture in the country and to the fact that the majority of film production is television production, a fact that has influenced independent filmmakers in terms of the genres and styles they choose, since they see television as the most lucrative and least risky market.[15] Television *is* a crucial component of film production, but it is only part of the story. The cinema is still there and waiting: for funds, development, nurturance, definition, exhibition, and distribution. A television commissioning editor who develops and supports projects is not the same as a film producer. He or she has different requirements and needs, answers to a different boss, and serves an audience with different expectations regarding production values, narration, genre, performance, narrative development, and filmic form. Expectations apply regardless of the mode of exhibition (e.g., in a cinema theater or on TV), which is not to say that the experience of watching a movie on the big screen with Dolby surround sound is not vastly different from watching it on the small screen at home, just that the mode of exhibition does not define it as either a television program or a film. Therefore, mandating local content on television on the assumption that it will help grow cinema (as opposed to the generic term "film industry") is misplaced if one is talking about the cinema specifically. This may seem almost too obvious a point to make, but it is one that appears to have been overlooked by the state's planners.

The majority of television projects, particularly in drama, are supplied by independent producers (both national and international) as opposed to in-house ones, and in many cases, film directors cross over and work for television as writers, directors, or co-producers. Gray Hofmeyr, one of the most established and successful directors with films such as *Mama Jack* (2005), *Oh Shucks—I'm Gatvol* (2004), *Murmur* (2004), *Mr. Bones* (2001), *There's a Zulu on my Stoep* (1993), *Jock of the Bushveld* (1992), and *Schweitzer* (1990), has also worked as a writer for SABC's popular sitcom *Suburban Bliss* (1996), and was then co-producer of 90 *Plein Street* (1997), a political drama series from SABC on the clash between personal ambition and public good among South African politicians as they struggle to meet the demands of democratic governance. So too with Dumisane Phakathi, one of the most talented and prolific filmmakers of the new generation, best known for his documentaries, *Wa n Wina* (*Sincerely Yours*) (2001), *Ha Ea Rona* (2002), *Don't F*** with Me, I Have 51 Brothers and Sisters* (2004), and the short films *Waiting for Valdez* (2002) and *Christmas with Granny* (1998). Phakathi has directed episodes for *Jozi-H*, a Canadian Television production on the gritty world of a fictional Johannesburg hospital, and for Mtunzini.com, SABC's weekly murder mystery about a group of friends in a small coastal town who work for an internet magazine and inadvertently end up solving murders. There is movement in the other direction as well. Franz Marx directed numerous movies under apartheid with little fame before switching to television in the 1980s, where he became famous for his soap operas, particularly *Egoli: Place of Gold*, the longest running soap in South Africa, carried on M-Net during its "open hour" so the whole country can tune in without subscribing.[16]

In terms of enabling the production of films for the cinema however, South African television has done the minimum.[17] Consequently, it has not shaped cinematic production in the same way as happened in Britain, Germany, and other European countries. Driven by commercial concerns, broadcasters have shown little confidence in the business ability of the industry. There are no made-for-TV movies, although producers have called upon the NFVF to use its influence to push broadcasters in this direction. There is limited co-production of feature films with the exception of the Dv8 Project, an initiative brought to SABC by two major forces in the private sector, Jeremy Nathan and Joel Phiri, with the goal of increasing the number of South African (and, in the future, African) feature films through the use of digital technology.[18]

As a public broadcaster, one might assume that SABC would feel able to be more adventurous and less prosaic than the private broadcasters, of which there are two: e.tv, a free-to-air channel that anyone can access without paying for a subscription, and M-Net, an encrypted channel for subscribers that has a daily, free "open window." But SABC has made no attempt to take risks, search for first-time directors, or structure special "slots" for showing their work, as happened in the seventies with New German Cinema.[19] When it comes to moving outside of the institutionalized cultural forms, SABC is as timid and concerned with the bottom line as the commercial broadcasters.[20] It turned down Helen Noguiera's proposal for a documentary on the life of Ingrid Jonker, a forgotten Afrikaans poet from the 1960s, who found new fame when Nelson Mandela opened South Africa's new parliament in 1994 with lines from her poem, *"Die kind wat doodgeskiet is deur soldate by Nyanga"* (The child who was shot dead by soldiers at Nyanga), and *Tsotsi* (Gavin Hood, 2005) which went on to win an Academy Award the following year and smashed local box-office records, outperforming other Academy Award nominees *Ray* (Taylor Hackford, 2004), *The Constant Gardner* (Fernando Meirelles, 2005), *Hotel Rwanda*, and *Yesterday* (Darrell Roodt, 2004). In 2007, SABC made its first significant gesture toward local cinema with the announcement of a $6 million film fund for the co-production and production of feature films. A series of documentaries on famous South Africans called *Icons* is planned. These documentaries will be made into feature films for the local and export market. The directors chosen for both stages of the project are Zola Maseko, Mickey Dube, and Khalo Matabane, three filmmakers who have made a large impact on post-apartheid cinema.

Maseko has won twice at FESPACO, first with his short film, *A Drink in the Passage* (2002), which won the Special Jury Award in 2002, and then with his feature film, *Drum*, which took the Golden Stallion in 2006. Dube returned to South Africa in 1994 after training at the University of Southern California's School of Cinematic Arts. His film, *A Walk in the Night* (1998), an updated version of Alex LaGuma's classic novella, shifts the setting from apartheid-era South Africa in the 1960s to present-day Johannesburg. Using a highly subjective camera, Dube explores the themes of alienation and violence. In this universe, the type of redemption seen in *Tsotsi* is not possible, but a more nuanced view of race is offered. Things are less black and white than before, as evidenced by the actions of the white cop who shoots his black partner, who is about to kill Mikey, a young coloured man that has murdered his white neighbor. Despite the fact that SABC partially funded the film, but did not air it, Dube has been extremely critical of the broadcaster, describing it as "nepotistic, corrupt and racist."[21] Matabane's *Conversations on a Sunday Afternoon* (2005), which starts as a work of fiction and turns into a documentary, is closest in style to David Bordwell's definition of the Art Cinema from the 1960s in its stress on visual style and character as opposed to plot and action.

SABC's unwillingness to take risks is partly due to its peculiarly hybrid configuration: part public service, part commercial. The public commercial division is mandated to support both the public service division and itself, yet receives only 2 percent government funding. Some revenue comes in from license fees, but the majority, 76 percent, comes from advertising. Of all three channels across the two divisions, SABC 3 receives the greatest share of advertising money (or "adspend").[22] While both divisions carry advertising, the commercial division (SABC 3) broadcasts mainly imported programs in English in an effort to attract viewers the highest Life Style Measurement (LSM) groups (LSM 7 and LSM 8). The LSM index is the most widely used marketing research tool in South Africa, developed to cut across race and other demographic data as a way of categorizing the market. Instead, it groups people according to their living standards using criteria such as degree of urbanization, ownership of cars and major appliances, and use of media services. But given South Africa's past, the people with the highest living standards in terms of possessions and services are mostly white, and studies have revealed that advertising in all major media is skewed toward that population, which is small in number but has the largest disposable income. By having to rely on advertising in competition with the private broadcasters, SABC is caught between its public-service interests and commercial concerns, which always win out in the end. The result is a conservative public broadcaster, frightened to lose market share. So untenable is the situation that the ANC has called for state funding to be increased from 2 percent to 60 percent, an inexplicable figure which could be dangerous for the autonomy of SABC since it would magnify the power of the state over the broadcaster.[23] But it would also reduce SABC's reliance on advertising revenue, bring it more in line with the concept of public broadcasting as a state-funded entity, and increase advertising revenues to the private stations, all of which might improve conditions for creating a more progressive broadcasting environment.

LOCAL IS *LEKKER* (NICE) WHEN IT COMES TO TV

One of the challenges that the NFVF faces is creating demand for film products. At a micro-economic level, the need is to stimulate the culture of film appreciation and cinema going, which will ensure growth within the sector.

National Film and Video Foundation[24]

Going to see SA cinema is at the moment a patriotic duty rather than what it should be—entertainment, fun, exciting.

Bata Passchier, film teacher

One of the major problems facing the film industry in South Africa lies in attracting local audiences. Is it that South Africans just do not go to local films, having "grown up on American taste" as Anant Singh, CEO of Videovision and South Africa's only major international film producer, asserts,[25] or are the films just not reaching the right audiences due to distribution and exhibition constraints? Then again, perhaps it is a question of content. Whatever the reasons, the problem is not new. From the predominantly whites-only, Afrikaans-speaking cinema of the fifties and sixties to the anti-apartheid films of the late seventies and eighties, the audiences for local product have been as small and fragmented as the industry itself. What *is* new is the desire to home grow a cinema for the majority.

There are many issues involved in trying to sketch an adequate response to the public's rejection of local films. In the first place, Singh is right in that South Africans have grown up on a diet of American movies and imbibed along with that the idea that movies are international commodities as opposed to national cultural products like dance, theatre, or even literature. Against this perception, the use of patriotism or national feeling as a marketing strategy seems woefully inadequate.

Interestingly enough, the perception of movies as global products does not seem to hold when it comes to the television, that arch symbol of global enculturation, where local content is not only popular with viewers, but in many cases, outperforms imported product in audience ratings. Nowhere is this trend more marked than in the "soap wars." In the 1980s, soaps from the United States dominated the ratings, but post-1994, the profound changes that took place in the mediascape challenged commissioning editors to think local in their use of the genre, and the challenge has paid off. Four out of five of the top soap operas are South African. *Generations* (SABC 1), set in an advertising agency and aimed specifically at the new and aspirant black middle class, is the most popular soap in the country, attracting 4.674 million viewers per week. Second is *The Bold and the Beautiful* (SABC 1), with 2.574 million viewers. Then comes *Muvhango*, which attracts 2.432 million viewers with its slew of characters struggling to resolve the conflicts of township life and rural traditions in Venda. *7 de Laan* (SABC 2) has been on the air since 2000. Written in Afrikaans with English subtitles, it has a crossover appeal for a variety of language groups and attracts 1.775 million viewers weekly The last soap, *Rhythm City*, a youth drama that revolves around the music industry, has only been on the air since July 2007. It airs on e.tv, the free-to-air commercial channel, and has been very successful in attracting 1.721 million viewers, which is just under the figures for its competition, *7 de Laan*.[26] While local soaps seems to have found ways of satisfying an enormously diverse viewership both locally and across the continent (for example, *Isidingo* is popular in Zambia, Malawi, and Uganda and *Generations* is a hit in the Caribbean), local film production is still struggling to find its place in the economics of culture as a viable commodity on the local cinema circuit.

In South Africa, television is growing its viewership, while the cinema is losing it, but it is impossible to say whether the growth is due to local content. South Africa has a population of around 42 million people, but only 5 million of them go to the cinema.[27] Meanwhile, 48 percent of households have one or more television sets, and television reaches 80 to 90 percent of the population in a given week, but film reaches only 1.5 percent of the population per week. Since 2001, cinema attendance has declined at a rate of 2 percent per year, forcing the closure of cinemas, particularly in the townships.[28] Until the 2007 opening of Ster-Kinekor's eight-screen multiplex in the new Maponya Mall, Soweto had had no functioning cinemas for half a decade. The decline was unexpected given that cinema audiences had increased 5.5 percent per annum from 1990 to 1995. In addition, 1996 had seen a growth of 36 percent over the 1995 figures in the number of black people going to the cinema, leading to an assumption that there was a large additional market just waiting to be tapped.[29] A sharp increase in crime in 1996, the increased penetration of television, the rise of DVD rentals, and competition from other forms of entertainment, such as rock concerts, were all blamed for the decline.

No doubt these are relevant factors for South Africa, but declining movie attendance is also a global matter, affecting Germany, France (that bastion of cinema culture), and the United States, which experienced the greatest increase in screen closures. The only exceptions in Europe have been the United Kingdom and Italy, mainly driven by multiplex growth.

A global survey conducted by PA Consulting Group, a management and market-research firm, and the Motion Picture Association of America on movie theater attendance in 2007 across three European capitals and seven American cities indicated that consumers were not dissatisfied with the content of films but with the experience of going to the movies: the food, the lack of reserved seats, the ticket price, the travel time. Of the 2,028 consumers surveyed, people indicated that moviegoing no longer satisfied their needs for socialization, which suggests that changing lifestyles and work habits have changed their social needs. The survey also revealed that movie attendance and home entertainment sales (including DVD sales) will go down as entertainment options increase.[30] Whether a similar mood applies to movie-goers in South Africa is difficult to say, but the survey suggest that patterns of movie consumption cannot be reduced to questions of content or distribution, but must be seen as part of a larger matrix of people's desires and needs.

FILMS AREN'T GETTING TO THE RIGHT PEOPLE

In terms of the distribution explanation, it is true that while many local films such as *Kini and Adams* (Idrissa Ouedraogo, 1997), *Fools* (Ramadan Suleiman, 1998), *The Sexy Girls* (Russell Thompson, 1998), *Zulu Love Letter* (Zola Maseko), *Max and Mona* (Teddy Mattera, 2004), and *Hijack Stories* (Oliver Schmitz, 2000) have a predominantly black cast, provide spectatorial identification through black role models, and employ narratives that have historical and contemporary appeal to a black urban audience, they are mostly shown, if they are shown at all, in predominantly white areas due to the lack of transformation in the distribution and exhibition networks. Consequently, the films do not reach the audiences for which they are intended, which was the reason given by Richard Green, the producer of *Chicken Biznis—The Whole Story* (Ntshaveni Wa Luruli, 2000) for the film's box-office failure.

Chicken Biznis follows the fortunes of Sipho, a small-time entrepreneur who has resigned his job as a messenger at the Johannesburg Stock Exchange to enter the business of selling chickens. With an all-black cast using the liveliness of township slang, the film depicts a slick, small-time operator trying to make it big in the new South Africa, where the streets are not lined with gold but with foreigners and locals selling their wares in the informal sector. By concentrating on the small details of the ordinary and the everyday and by refusing to treat township life as a political spectacle ("I hate this affirmative action bullshit," Wa Luruli said when questioned on his political position), the film manages to avoid the usual dose of polemics so typical of many South African films. Instead, it treats the dilemmas of post-apartheid township life with humor and good nature. But despite being praised by the local critics as "a charming feel good picture that for once doesn't treat South Africa as a landscape solely made up of politics" and winning awards at festivals in Milan, Montreal, and FESPACO, the film was seen by only 800 people in South Africa.[31]

How could this happen? The answer lies in the way South African distribution and exhibition circuits operate as an oligopoly of two companies, Ster-Kinekor (now part of the multinational conglomerate, Primedia Group) and Nu-Metro (formerly CIC Warner). The same companies who controlled the circuits under apartheid continue to control it today.[32] They have restructured in response to government's affirmative-action objectives and taken black board members, but their close alliance to Hollywood's conglomerates is the same as always, as is their risk-aversive business model. They continue to pursue a rigid bottom-line mentality when it comes to local products, citing statistics that show that only 1 percent of South African movies shown each year are financially viable. With the exception of slapstick comedies, *Mr. Bones, Mama Jack,* and *Tsotsi,* local films lose money at the box office.[33] A recent report put out by the NFVF on box-office performance for local films revealed that most films failed to recoup 50 percent of their production costs. According to Helen Kuhn, head of Ster-Kinekor's local content division, the outcome was to be expected. Kuhn's pessimistic view of the financial viability of local films within the country is at odds with the idea that South Africans deserve and expect to have a home-grown cinema, something that is reiterated by the NFVF on a constant basis. Instead of assuming a defeatist attitude from the start and hoping to recoup losses through marketing the films in other territories, it would be better to search for local solutions.[34] Part of the problem is marketing costs. Local films don't have marketing budgets and cannot get funds for them from the NFVF. They siphon off money from the production budget and/or rely on free publicity unless they can find distributors willing to invest in packaging and promoting them, which is beginning to happen. Ster-Kinekor has invested in marketing campaigns for a number of local films produced by the Dv8 Project.[35] But in the main, both Ster-Kinekor and Nu-Metro remain wedded to prepackaged Hollywood films ready to go on the screen and into the commercials without any extra investment.

In addition, local films have to cover their own print costs. With shares of the profits going to the producer, the distributor, and the advertisers, the film must earn four times its budget on the circuit before breaking even.[36] *Max and Mona,* an offbeat comedy about a young man who wants to be a doctor, but is forced to use his talents as a professional mourner in the townships in order to save his feckless uncle from being "iced" by gangsters, won international recognition on the film-festival circuit. It opened in 32 local theaters and took in $46,000 at the box office. But with the cost of publicity and prints amounting to $145,000, the distributors lost almost $100,000 on the deal.

There are other distribution practices more supportive of local film. In Australia (the Land of Oz for filmmakers), distributors have an interest in the film's financial outcome from the beginning because they are involved in pre-financing and securing distribution before production. South Africa could also handicap imported films as they do in England, France, and Ireland by imposing a levy on cinema ticket sales, which could then be used to defray local distribution costs. But little has been done to push the distributors in that direction and the state has no instrument for regulating their activities outside of appeals to national pride.

South Africa once had a flourishing feature-film industry, but it folded in 1923 when Hollywood flooded the global market with cheap products, a practice today called "dumping."[37] Since then, South Africa has been a profitable relay point—it is the eleventh-largest market—on Hollywood's distribution circuit. Ninety-two percent of screen time is dominated by mainstream Hollywood fare through contractual agreements between exhibitors and distributors, with the remaining 8 percent hotly contested for by European cinema (which includes Britain), independent and "art films" from the rest of the world, and local cinema.[38]

THE SANKOFA PROJECT: AN EXERCISE IN
ALTERNATIVE DISTRIBUTION AND MORE

Like most exhibitors in the developed world, South Africa replicates Hollywood's model of film exhibition. Movies are shown in expensive luxury buildings, today usually part of a mall complex, with air conditioning, expensive sound equipment, comfortable seating, and a lobby that sells snacks and drinks at inflated prices. Any other exhibition model, such as building low-cost multiplexes or complexes with low-cost screening and sound facilities, is rejected, probably due to pressure from Hollywood distributors as well as from their own boards.[1] There has been no attempt to think outside of the Hollywood box, to try to come up with solutions that take into account the fact that mainstream cinemas are not accessible to the majority of the population. Of course, commercial distributors are not trying to reach a "population"; they are trying to reach an economically viable audience. On the other side of the theater sits the Film Resource Unit (FRU), a non-governmental organization (NGO) whose goal is to distribute African and South African films to as broad an audience as possible irrespective of their economic viability. If this means growing an audience through education, lectures, free screenings, and showing films in non-traditional sites, so be it. These two visions—

audience as consumer versus audience as public—are irreconcilable, but they can be brought together in partnership if there is enough push from the cultural activists' side, and enough political clout behind the push to have it taken seriously.

In November 2002, FRU, backed by the DAC, the NFVF, the European Union, and the Prince Claus Fund, a Dutch fund that supports cultural activities in the developing world, launched the Sankofa Project, a high-profile theatrical release accompanied by an innovative distribution, exhibition, and marketing campaign for Haile Gerima's film, *Sankofa* (1993), which had never been released in South Africa before. The film is about the Atlantic slave trade. It tells the story of Mona, an African fashion model on a shoot at the Cape Coast Castle in Ghana, one of the sites from which the slaves were sent to the New World. Mona is shown frolicking in the surf in a scanty bikini, while a young, white, male, photographer takes endless shots of her half-naked body. An old man, a spiritual leader, who accuses the mainly white tourists of profaning this sacred site, breaks into the scene of commerce and spectacle. He implores Mona to "return to her past," and through some magical condensation of time and space, she does. And her past is terrifying: She is captured, endures the horrifying trauma of the transatlantic passage in a slave ship, and ends up as a house slave named Shola on a Caribbean plantation. There she meets the rebel, Shango, the matriarch, Nunu, and the Creole, Joe.

Sankofa is not only about enslavement; it is also about resistance rebellion. There are secret meetings under a tree at night with free blacks about the possibilities of rebellion, and a number are attempted and fail, with terrible punishment ensuing. Nonetheless, Mona/Shola begins to realize how important resistance is to her spiritual survival. When Joe finally breaks through the religious propaganda that has persuaded him to kill his mother, and in an act of revenge kills the priest, the community is re-energized and once again, the slaves rise up and, this time, manage to kill their most heinous tormentors. Except for Mona/Shola, who is transported back to the present day, this act of resistance ends in their deaths, but in the process they and Mona/Shola discover their true African identities. Gerima calls the film a "turning point and an amalgamation of everything he has done to date," by which he means that in the process of making it, he discovered a language, a way to empower his voice and register his accent.[2]

The Sankofa Project was ambitious, far reaching, intensive, and costly, involving high-profile film launches in the four major cities (Johannesburg, Pretoria, Cape Town, and Durban), numerous facilitated workshops and discussions on the key themes of the film, block bookings (an arrangement to reserve the cinemas ahead of time) for screening at relevant theaters to ensure audiences, and an extensive promotion and publicity campaign on behalf of the independent theaters participating in the project. At the premiere and launch of *Sankofa* in April 2003, Eddie Mbalo, head of the NFVF, spoke of the distribution and exhibition difficulties that African and South African films face. The Sankofa Project was an attempt to create an "enabling exhibition environment for African film." Of course, it was more than that. FRU's hope was to show the commercial sector that there was an African audience out there for African and South African films, if they were promoted and distributed in the right way. Forcing them to compete with Hollywood products and screening them in mainly white and affluent areas was a recipe for failure and worse, reinforced the old stereotype of African films as box-office poison. By using independent theaters, FRU was also creating an alternative distribution network that could become a platform for independently produced African films.

What were the factors involved in creating this "enabling" environment? FRU designed a multifaceted urban and township marketing plan that included a convergence of print, radio, and television at both the national and provincial levels. Instead of the usual top-down approach taken by the commercial distributors, FRU got people involved at the local level. Project and regional managers were allowed considerable input into the design of the marketing campaigns in their local areas. Publicity began two months before the release date of the film and included the deployment of eighteen FRU-associated agents who promoted the film at schools and universities in their own locales.[3] In addition, 600 educational booklets were produced and distributed as complementary learning aids to provide a better understanding of the transatlantic slave trade and African history. Conventional advertising began three weeks before the release date. Based on All Media Product Survey (AMPS) figures from Radio Metro, SABC, and the *Sowetan* newspaper, the estimated reach was 4,300,000 people.[4] The media campaign set a new benchmark for African film with each media channel reaching well over one million people during the four-week campaign. Preview screenings for the media were held a week before the premiere in Johannesburg, Durban, and Cape Town.

A key tactic in the campaign, according to FRU, were the workshops hosted by Gerima and Mutabaraka (a lead actor in the film) at twelve tertiary institutions across the nation. Over 5,000 school children attended school screenings and discussions. At both workshops and screenings, the topic of African film and media was discussed, and the specially prepared booklets containing information on the transatlantic slave trade, the history of Cape slavery, and film material were distributed.

Poetry, music, and dance evenings were held in addition to a symposium ("Slavery: Umbilical Cord or Chains") at the Apartheid Museum, one of the campaign's partners. The program included a "dialogue event" where Gerima and Mutabaraka conversed with African National Congress officials, the Senegalese Ambassador, the UN Commissioner for Refugees, and community leaders from Soweto and Sebokeng.

DIFFERENT STORIES CAN UNITE US

Sankofa's story of slavery has little in common with the historical facts of Cape slavery, which started in 1658 with 228 slaves from Angola being brought to the Cape by the Dutch East India Company (VOC). Six years earlier, the VOC had chosen the Cape as the site for a refreshment station for its shipping fleet on its way to the Indonesia and on its return from Batavia (Java). Slaves were bought from four regions: 26 percent from Mozambique, 25 percent from India and Ceylon, 25 percent from Madagascar, and 23 percent from Indonesia. Their cultural and linguistic diversity made it difficult for them to form a homogeneous community.

Slavery in the Cape was far more widespread in than other slaveholding societies. By 1693, the Cape had more slaves than free people, but by the mid 1700s, the two populations were roughly equal at about 6,000 each.[5] In 1834, the slave trade was abolished in British colonies and liberated slaves fell into the category of "free blacks." About 39,000 slaves were freed on Emancipation Day in 1838 (the year which marked the end of the four-year apprenticeship system imposed on the freed slaves).

History, not cinema, tells of two slave rebellions in the Cape: the *Koeberg* rebellion in 1808, led by Louis of Mauritius, which resulted in the capture of 300 farm slaves, and a second one at a wine farm named *Hou-den-Bek* that was crushed in 1825. Most incidents of insubordination were individual cases of slaves turning on their tormentors in rage. Despite minimal resistance considering the number of slaves, a great uneasiness on the part of the masters regarding the dangers posed by their slaves prevailed, particularly after the British took over the governance of the Cape and made the recording of punishments mandatory in 1826. These fears were cited as grounds for not complying with government orders.

Recent historians have described Cape slavery, particularly slaves owned by Afrikaans farmers, in terms of the concept of paternalism, which was used to reconcile slaves to their fate. Owners propagated the myth that slaves were members of the household--an extended family of sorts. The master called the slaves and servants his *Volk* (people) and invited them into the inner sanctum of his family to attend prayers. This model of paternalism accompanied the *trekboers*—those Afrikaners who left the Cape and journeyed into the interior in search of a land free from British interference. Their journey, known as the Great Trek, became the national narrative under apartheid and is the subject of the film *De Voortrekkers* (1916), discussed in detail in chapter 6.

Despite the differences between the representation of slavery in *Sankofa* and the actual history of Cape slavery, the booklet put out by FRU during the campaign used the film's narrative as an occasion to draw parallels between the two, thus sketching a narrative that sutures South Africa into the dominant history of Africa by presenting Cape slavery as another example of, and not an exception to, the history of African slavery in Africa (and we might add America), making their history, ours. We have just been late in arriving, that is all. Hence the special place given to American slavery in the African Renaissance and the historical importance of a film like *Sankofa* for linking South Africa's past to its present through the past of "Africa."

Sankofa challenges what is known as South African exceptionalism, the idea that South Africa has had a different historical trajectory from the rest of black Africa and therefore does not belong. South Africa has often been presented as unique and "somehow able to evade the pressures experienced by the rest of Africa."[6] This myth is currently being dismantled in scholarship, now that the walls that South Africa created between itself and the rest of black Africa have come down. It is clear that South Africa is very much part of the region, that it is a developing country, not a first-world one somehow "stuck" at the end of Africa. As such, it suffers many of the same problems faced by other developing nations. The booklet also mapped the history of colonialism in Africa and the fight for independence by various countries onto apartheid and the struggle against it, placing Nelson Mandela, Steve Biko, and Robert Sobukwe as freedom fighters alongside Jomo Kenyatta, Kwame Nkrumah, Samora Machel, and Amilcar Cabral. Hence the historical importance of a film like *Sankofa* for linking South Africa's past to its present and to the story of Africa as a whole.

CONCLUSION

The Sankofa Project was a one-off gesture, never to be repeated, and characteristic of the country's first five years of democratic rule, when people reveled in constructing postcolonial identities. In the heady days of liberation immediately following the formal collapse of apartheid, the "culture industries" reflected a kind of utopian excitement. Fueled by vast quantities of liberated desire—the desire for a better society, for a new set of social relations, for fun and play, for experimentation—few felt the need to agree with the stylistic choices of everyone else or, for that matter, to respect the sanctity of others' styles. The work of Francophone filmmakers trained in quite different traditions and schools was suddenly seen as possibly pertinent to South African cinema. Finally the dream of pluralist toleration and the pan-availability of diverse cultural styles had become a possibility. In this state of what the South African art critic Neville Dubow called "cross-pollination," it is not farfetched to think that what was

being sought were the utopian aspirations and dreams of a new nation in which the principle of diversity would not only be respected,
but also become an invitation for playing at hybridity. The cinema
could reflect the progressive imagination of a nation of difference,
unified nonetheless through patterns of shared mutual interest and
socioeconomic and political goals. Using the idea of a diaspora not in
its usual sense of meaning peoples scattered from an original homeland, but in the sense of recognition of history, Stuart Hall talks of
an identity constructed through and within difference.[7] This seems
to capture the mood of the project and the times, the feeling that African filmmakers could negotiate a collective identity without imposition, repression or appropriation. I am not talking here of truth or
fiction, falsity or genuineness, but of an explicit process, a search (in
the case of cinema) for a set of styles that can be put to use in imag-
ining, but not obscuring, the nation. Hall calls this search the "vo-
cation of modern Black cinemas."[8] It is *this* search, not just a search
for an alternative distribution circuit, that lies at the bottom of the
Sankofa Project.

Unfortunately, it is a search that seems to have been abandoned.

NOTES

1. South African Cultural Observatory, http://www.culturalobservatory
.org.za/p_ff_fsal.html.
2. Frank Ukadike, *Black African Cinema* (Los Angeles: University of
California Press, 1994), 184.
3. According to FRU estimates, each agent ensured direct reach of up to
500 people, resulting in a total of 7,200 people.
4. The breakdown of impressions for the *Sankofa* trailer, which ran for
two weeks, was as follows: *Sowetan* newspaper, 1 million impressions; Radio
Metro, 1.2 million impressions; Rabk TV, 1.5 million impressions.
5. Alistair Boddy-Evans, "African History," About.com, http://www
.africanhistory.about.com/b/2004/08/24/timeline-slavery-in-the-cape-colony.
6. Hein Marais, *South Africa: Limits to Change: The Political Economy
of Transformation* (Cape Town: University of Cape Town Press, 1998), 125.
7. Stuart Hall, "Cultural Identity and Diaspora: Identity, Community,
Culture and Difference," in *Colonial Discourse and Post-Colonial Theory: A
Reader,* ed. P. Williams and Laura Chrisman (New York: Columbia University
Press, 1994).
8. Ibid., 402.

A WEAK CINEMA FOR A WEAK STATE

Almost half a century of subsidy and tax incentives under the apartheid regime had failed to produce a cinema or film industry. The Film Bill, along with Parliament's adoption of the Triple Enquiry's recommendations, gave the impression that South African cinema was on the brink of a new and potent beginning. It also reified the state's power to initiate a national cinema irrespective of South Africa's position as a developing economy in the fiercely competitive global cultural economy. All these factors fed into the euphoric interlude following the end of apartheid, which set up a series of expectations on the part of filmmakers and policy makers that failed to materialize.

It was not surprising then, when in 1997, Mandla Langa, CEO of the Independent Communication Authority of South Africa (ICASA), charged the industry with an "unbearable Whiteness of being."[39] It favored, he claimed, those who already had training, resources, and access to the medium, which inevitably meant whites; was hostile to the tradition of oral culture; and was unfriendly to black would-be filmmakers. Quoting Haile Gerima's words, he complained of the lack of "image equity in representations of and access to the means of production by Black practitioners." Langa advocated that the industry's top players be chastised and, like naughty puppies, "taken by the scruff of their collective neck, and brought into the new millennium" so that a decolonization of the imagination could take place.[40] In the same vein, William Makgoba, professor of science and chancellor of the University of KwaZulu-Natal, labeled the industry Eurocentric, insensitive to the complexities of a transforming society, subliminally racist, insufficiently African, and an obstacle to transformation.[41]

The level of anger expressed by Langa, Makgoba, and others must be seen as driven by a deeper emotion, a feeling of compulsion, which comes from the transformative, reconstructive character of South African society. Post-1994, a national industry rapidly arose to proclaim, regulate, and utopianize the new state schemes in the name of development, democracy, and the "African Renaissance." Underlying many of the attacks on parastatals like the NFVF and SABC was a deep sense of disappointment at the small gains made by the black majority in the country, not only in the media, but throughout post-apartheid South Africa. After such a bitter and lengthy struggle, South Africa's "miracle" seemed an empty one for former activists, like Langa and Makgoba, who were schooled in the culture of resistance.

Political enfranchisement has failed to translate into material improvement for the black majority, making them citizens in name only. After a decade in power, the African National Congress has failed to deliver the whole array of social, cultural, civil, political, and economic rights necessary for substantive citizenship. South Africa is not unique in this aspect. Jim Holsten and Arjun Appadurai note that "a condition of formal membership without much substantive citizenship characterizes many of the societies, which have experienced recent transitions to democracy and market capitalism in Latin America, Asia, and Eastern Europe."[42] Increasingly the nation appears less as a community, which despite its inequalities, is linked in what Benedict Anderson called a "deep horizontal comradeship," and more as a corporate state that has so far failed to deliver a good life for the majority of its workers.

AN INCOMPLETE TRANSFORMATION

How can we begin to understand this failure, which has occurred across the board despite a strong affirmative action policy enforced by the Labour Relations Act (1995), the Skills Development Act (1998), and above all, the Employment Equity Act (1998)? Legislated racial apartheid may be a thing of the past, but class apartheid is very present and can be seen in the widening gap between rich and poor. Affirmative action policies have done little to close that gap. Instead, they have widened it by advantaging people who already have jobs and job skills, which in a country with South Africa's high level of unemployment, are already an elite group. In short, it benefits a minority group: the black petite bourgeoisie who aspire to rise up into the middle class. Affirmative action policies as they are currently conceptualized and applied are an inadequate remedy in circumstances such as these because they take but a small percentage of the disadvantaged population and make them new elites. That is Neville Alexander's argument.[43] The act, he notes, was designed to ensure that "suitably qualified people from designated groups have equal employment opportunities and are equitably represented in all occupations and categories in the workforce of a designated employer."[44]

This model of affirmative action comes from the United States, where it was designed to incorporate an excluded minority into the mainstream of economic life. But South African history is different than that of the United States. A generation of black South Africans abandoned formal education completely for the struggle against apartheid, while those who did attend school remain undereducated, lacking the skills needed to succeed in a capitalist society thanks to Bantu education, the system of education for blacks under apartheid. Thus, affirmative action in its current formulation, even when applied with the best will in the world, cannot achieve the stated objectives of the post-apartheid government. There is a strong call by the Left (to which Neville belongs) for the state to abandon the model and replace it with a state-driven program of mass empowerment, a Roosevelt-style "New Deal," that would create broad structural changes in education and training so that the unemployed and the underemployed could enter the workplace and earn a decent wage. Only with major reforms can one speak meaningfully of affirmative action policies as a means toward progress.

Applied to the film industry, Neville's analysis offers a trenchant way of understanding the conditions that have disabled transformation in the industry. No doubt white racism, nepotism at SABC, and insufficient state funding for the NFVF impede progress, but they are not decisive in shaping a national cinema. What *is* decisive is a commitment by both state and industry to invest in education and training at whatever level is necessary in order to reverse the inequalities of the past. There have been gestures in this direction with the establishment of the Sector Education Training Authority (SETA) that offers job training, capacity building, and the development of research and technical skills in a variety of areas including media, but the entire enterprise has been unsuccessful due to corruption, the length of training time required, a lack of worksites, and poor communication.[45] Suppose the state were to radically increase the NFVF's budget—would that make a difference to the black South Africans who desire to be in the film industry but lack the relevant skills and education to do so? The answer is no, since the film industry requires highly skilled people and there is a tiny pool to choose from in the black communities.[46] Consequently, black players in the industry are so rare as to make their presence remarkable. The only people who would benefit from an increased NFVF budget are those who already have the skills and are already in the industry. On the other hand, if the state mandated that the extra funds were to be used for establishing a national film school or schools to train students drawn from the poorest communities and women, then real change would be a possibility. Of the 55 feature films produced by South Africans between 2000 and 2007, only 6 were directed by women, and of those, 2 were black and 4 where white. Aside from gender and looking only at race, only 2 out of the 55 films were directed by black directors.[47] The recommendation for the establishment of a national film school for training and education was raised as far back as 1994 in the first report on the restructuring of the film industry by the Human Science Research Council and then written into the Film Bill.

The idea was revisited at the 2001 and 2005 film *indabas*, where delegates recommended that the government be lobbied for funds to develop a national strategy for film education which would include a school, or at least, a study on the feasibility of a school.[48] There have been no further developments. In the meantime, commercial film schools are a lucrative business given the high demand for training and education in the field, but only those who can afford the expensive fees can get the training. Once again, the same problem that Neville highlighted surfaces: one must have the skills to find a job in a highly skilled industry (the issue of creativity only comes into play after the craft is mastered) before one can benefit from affirmative action policies. Learning on the job is a tradition in the film industry (although it is one that is fading fast even in successful industries like Hollywood), but it requires mentorship and is not a viable scenario for training large numbers of people.

The mandating of local content quotas in broadcasting is another example of state intervention in the name of transformation and redress that "failed" to bring about structural change. The quotas were an attempt on the part of the Independent Broadcasting Authority to satisfy two constituencies: the independent producers and the state. Their pro-competition stance pleased the independent producers, who saw it as an opportunity to finally break the monopoly and nepotism of SABC. The state operated on the assumption that increased commissions for local product would open up the industry for black people to become producers, screenwriters, filmmakers, and more. A greater number of commissions meant more production companies and these, in turn, meant an expansion of the industry beyond the confines of Gauteng and the Western Cape. These assumptions did not prove true even though local content quotas were generally adhered to. Without funds for developing provincial film offices or even film co-ops, without training and support for small indigenous companies in any of the provinces, and without rewards for broadcasters who awarded commissions to small companies (especially black production companies), the structures needed for transforming the status quo were missing. A research report from 2001 revealed that 86 percent of all production companies were located in Gauteng close to the commissioning agencies of the three broadcasters, and that of the registered film production companies in the area, 10 percent got 90 percent of the commissions. Little has changed judging from the figures produced at the 2005 Indaba. The state's involvement in film production has to find another model for cinematic financing, production and training if it is going to live up to its aims.

THE FILMMAKER: CAUGHT BETWEEN SUBSIDY AND SELF

Any discussion of subsidy in whatever form it takes must be followed by a caveat: there is always a partial contradiction between the projection of state or industry planning and the subjectivity of the individual filmmaker. One of the difficulties of being progressive in a newly forming and progressive nation whose first president was Nelson Mandela and whose constitution is universally considered to be the model for democratic governance is to remain autonomous from the dictates of social and cultural policy—or, in the case of industry initiatives, to avoid giving in to market dictates. Filmmakers may well agree with and benefit from the structures and ideologies put forward by the state or industry, but their autonomy will nevertheless lie in the way they resist subjugation by both. It is not easy to reconcile one of the major principles of cinema as an art, the right to self-expression and personal vision, the idea of art for art's sake (and not for the sake of the nation) with the complexities of a state subsidy system conceived under the sign of cultural and economic renaissance or with the demands of industry conceived under the sign of a free marketplace of goods.[49] Since cinema is still so new, we may look to the position faced by the universities in South Africa, particularly those which opposed apartheid and fought to operate outside of its laws, as an excellent example of this unstable position. As one enters the main hall of the University of the Witwatersrand, one is confronted with a relic of apartheid in the form of a plaque which declares, in ringing tones, the university's autonomy from the dictates of the former regime. However, despite the introduction of a government that now shares its internal goals and mission, the issue of autonomy has not gone away. Indeed, it has resurfaced with enormous vigor and acrimony as South Africa struggles to come to terms with the deficiencies of the democratic process, a process that cannot please all of the people all of the time. Such debates, however painful and disappointing to some, are of course a recipe for, and a sign of, a healthy public sphere. And therefore, we may conclude that one way in which South African filmmakers will remain progressive, innovative and independent within institutional and market controls is to avoid giving into both the dictates of political correctness and the hegemony of the market.

PRIVATE LESSONS

Of all the industry initiatives that emerged in mid nineties as part of the transformative push of the period, SCRAWL and M-Net's New Directions Film Initiative are the most enduring. SCRAWL, with funds provided by M-Net, media consortiums, and the British Council, offers a screen-writing laboratory modeled on the British Performing Arts Lab (PAL) and the U.S. Sundance Institute. It recruits screenwriters and brings them to-gether with actors and directors (people like Alan Rickman and Anthony Minghella have provided their services) with the aim of producing profes-sional scripts able to attract local investors. For lab director Liza Key, the emphasis has been on professionalism in comparison to what she calls the "missionary kind of funded courses" available in the townships in the eight-ies.[50] SCRAWL has been going since 1998, and the roster of film directors and screenwriters (which are usually one and the same person in South Africa) who have attended is comprised of many of South Africa's new-est film directors and screenwriters (usually one and the same). These in-clude Ntshaveni Wa Luruli (*Chicken Biznis—The Whole Story; The Wooden Camera*, 2003), Helen Noguiera (*Quest for Love*, 1988; *The Good Fascist*, 1991; and *Ingrid Jonker: Her Lives and Time*, 2007), and Tim Greene (*Twist*, 2004). With good scripts in hand, it is hoped that investors will overlook past failures and see local cinema as commercially viable. This has happened, but rarely at the local level.

Of all the broadcasters, M-Net, an encrypted subscription television service, has done the most to encourage and promote local film produc-tion with its New Directions initiative. Launched in 1993, the initiative is one of the longest-running film projects on the continent. It holds an an-nual competition for novice directors and screenwriters, mentors the win-ners, and broadcasts the completed films on its network that reaches over forty countries in Africa. Initially open only to emerging South African di-rectors, in keeping with the idea of an African Renaissance, it has expanded beyond national borders to include Zimbabwe, Tanzania, Kenya, Ethiopia, Ghana, and Nigeria (hence its new name, New Directions Africa). Almost all of the New Directions productions have been short narrative films; in-deed, the short film has become quite prolific in South Africa, with New

Directions producing only two full-length feature films to date: *The Sexy Girls* and *Chicken Biznis—The Whole Story*.[51] Of the short films, two stand out, and both are by Dumisane Phakathi, a local filmmaker from Soweto. *An Old Wives' Tale* (1998) is a comedy about an Afrikaans farmer who decides that equal rights in the new South Africa mean that he, too, is entitled to have more than one wife like his worker, Lucas, a Xhosa who has three wives. *Christmas with Granny* is a journey of self-discovery on the part of a young boy on his way to being baptized into his grandmother's religion, an event that he dreads and resists. In both films, Phakathi's style—an expressive camera that remains truthful in its depiction of everyday life—is already evident. It returns, deeper and richer, in *Wa n Wina*, his documentary on life and its problems for young people in Soweto today.[52]

MARKETING SOUTH AFRICAN CINEMA GLOBALLY

International film festivals play a crucial role in establishing the identity of a national cinema, especially in the case of marginal filmmaking nations such as South Africa. This fact seems counterintuitive at first, but once we realize that international is not the opposite of national but rather a gathering together of the nations, it becomes clear that the festivals are representations of national culture. The fact that the films are not submitted by nations but chosen independently by festival directors (global tastemakers) does not make them any less national in the eyes of the audience. In fact, it increases their validity as examples of the nation's best and brightest. The inclusion of South African films in major international festivals is a source of national pride, and read in relation to its history as world pariah, an indication of its new moral status which permits its re-entry into global culture. After years of exclusion, South African films are being snapped up by festival directors searching for a new product. International film festivals are in competition with each other and other cultural festivals, and they have to attract consumers while at the same time promoting the idea that they are exclusive sites and that entry is competitive.

At the Toronto Film Festival in 2004, there was a special focus on South African cinema, and the lines to get into the films stretched round the block, even for documentaries. Officials from the NFVF attended, giving it the official stamp of approval, as did Hollywood glamour in the form of Hilary Swank, the star of *Red Dust*, Videovision's production of Gillian Slovo's novel on the Truth and Reconciliation Commission. At Cannes in 2008, special permission was given by executive director Jérôme Paillard for the

Deputy Minister of Arts and Culture to lead the South African delegation attending the festival up the famous red carpet at the *Palais des Festivals*, something usually reserved for star actors, filmmakers, and producers. This was an enormous promotional highlight, not for the country's films, which had not been invited for screening, but for its film industry, which was the focus of the South African pavilion. Under the tagline, "South Africa: Your co-production partner of choice," the delegation was taking advantage of the global platform to push co-production treaties (by the end of 2008, the NFVF had co-production treaties with Ireland, New Zealand, Australia, France, Canada, Germany, and the United Kingdom) and tax-incentive rebates. International film festivals are as much about economics as art, operating as marketplaces, cultural showcases, and often political arenas as well. As Thomas Elsaesser notes, they offer an alternative network to Hollywood in terms of offering production, distribution, and exhibition opportunities functioning in much the same way as Hollywood. But, as he goes on to say, they are not really in opposition to Hollywood: they "interface" with it.[53] The NFVF used Cannes as a platform to showcase successful film and television co-productions like *The World Unseen* (Shamim Sarif, United Kingdom–South Africa co-production, 2007), *Goodbye Bafana* (Billie August, Germany–South Africa co-production, 2007), *Jozi H* (Alfons Adetuyi and Thabang Meleya, Canada–South Africa co-production, 2006), and *Molo Fish* (Clarence Hamilton, Canada–South Africa co-production, 1997), thus merging cultural and economic objectives.[54]

One way of breathing life into what is a fragmented and mostly profitless film industry in search of both a cultural identity and a market niche is to look beyond the economics to the art, which means moving from market to festival. The move paid off in 2005, which proved to be a good year for South African festival cinema. "I think that history is going to look back at this time and say that there's a South African genre, a South African aesthetic," said Zola Maseko upon winning FESPACO's highest prize, the Golden Stallion of Yenenga, with *Drum*, making South Africa the only Anglophone country to win since Ghana's Kwaw Ansah's *Heritage Africa* in 1989.[55] Set in the 1950s, a fabled period in South African cultural history known as the Sophiatown Renaissance, the film deals with the life and death of journalist Henry Nxumalo, nicknamed "Mr. Drum" for his hard-hitting reportage on black convict labor and prison conditions for *Drum* magazine. The film is striking, following a classic narrative structure that reflects Maseko's formal film training at the National Film and Television School in England before returning to South Africa in 1994. Mark Dornford-May's *U-Carmen e-Khayelitsha* (2005), which offered a version of Bizet's opera transplanted to Khayelitsha Township in the Cape sung and spoken in isiXhosa, won the Berlin International Film Festival's Golden Bear for best film, another first for South Africa. *Yesterday*, Darrell Roodt's film about the stigma of HIV/AIDS in South Africa and the terrible suffering endured by a rural woman who is HIV positive in KwaZulu-Natal, was nominated for (but did not win) an Oscar in the Academy Awards' Best International Film Category. Finally, Gavin Hood's film on gangsterism and redemption, *Tsotsi*, won both the People's Choice Award in Toronto and the Audience Award at Edinburgh before going on a year later to win the Oscar in the same category at the Academy Awards.

MARKETING SOUTH AFRICA REGIONALLY

South Africa has its own market and festival circuit, the most important of which is the Sithengi Film and TV Market in Cape Town, held in conjunction with the Cape Town Film Festival. With considerable support from the government, the larger players in the film industry, and the Rockefeller Foundation, the Sithengi market began in 1995 as a regional initiative for southern African film and television products and has been a successful site for the film trade, attracting African countries from the north (such as Ghana, Nigeria, and the Francophone contingent) and international delegates, mainly from the EU. Recently, it fell prey to bureaucratic incompetence and mismanagement with the result that Sithengi 2007 failed to take place. It has since been taken over by the NFVF, which is a clear sign of its significance to the industry.

But more than business is at stake in the Sithengi market's continuation. The market is an acknowledgment of South Africa's reconnection to the African continent in terms of shared histories of culture, struggle, expropriation, misrepresentation, and resurrection, the kind of connection proposed by the idea of an African Renaissance. It is a recognition that cinema in Africa and South Africa share common challenges and problems:

- the cultural dominance of mainstream narratives
- the lack of an audience
- distribution and exhibition problems
- the lack of local funding, and concomitant reliance on foreign (Western) funding

· a pervasive sense of cultural inferiority (especially in the arena of filmmaking)
· a widely held concept of films as global commodities

Africa and South Africa should seek common solutions to these problems, solutions which do not always try to produce "Africa" on film solely as a saleable commodity to the West. In many cases, this desire to be successful in international markets is not just a matter of profits, but one driven by deeper perceptions of cultural and national identity and of belonging. As Marsha Kinder argues in her work on Spanish cinema, "every national film movement seeks to win legitimation as the valid representative of its culture by striving for international recognition—the way revolutionary governments seek to be recognized by other nations."[56]

A second recognition that has emerged in tandem with South Africa's embrace of its African past is the industry's acknowledgment of Africa not as an appendage to the "real" markets in Los Angeles, New York, and London, but as a true part of the global market, a part that offers a viable commercial network of television and radio broadcasters, satellite broadcasters, video distributors, mobile video networks, and production houses which can be used to produce, exhibit, and distribute films across Africa for both profit and prestige. From this acknowledgment emerges a third recognition: that South African cinema is part of the global media and entertainment industries and cannot be bracketed off, even if it chooses to label itself in national terms, just like that unmistakably global medium, television. But as Philip Rosen convincingly argues, this distinction between the two does not hold up.[57] The history of cinema is part of media history, "just one historical stage," in Rosen's words, "in a world-wide proliferation of technological media."[58]

The internationalizing character of cinema need not automatically spell the demise of local production. The technology that helped to create the global can be used just as easily on behalf of the local. Take Dv8, the film company started by Jeremy Nathan and Joel Phiri that is dedicated to providing a flow of South African feature films, as opposed to the isolated few that emerge each year. With the use of digital technology, not only can films be produced less expensively and therefore more often, but they can be distributed more easily and at a lower cost, which has given rise to far-reaching distribution sites, particularly in Africa.[59] The films are broadcast on SABC, and those that warrant theatrical release are distributed and marketed by Ster-Kinekor. *Forgiveness* (Ian Gabriel, 2004), *Max and Mona*,

Straight Outta Benoni (Trevor Clarence, 2005), and *Bunny Chow* (John Barker, 2006) are all Dv8 productions. The company has attracted both established filmmakers—such as Darrell Roodt, whose film, *Zimbabwe*, was released in 2008—and younger filmmakers like Khalo Matabane, whose film, *State of Violence*, is the second part of a planned trilogy, following *Conversations on a Sunday Afternoon*.

THE LAST AFRICAN CINEMA

European critics label African cinema as if it was from one country. It's a continent of 54 countries with loads of different dialects. They'd never do the same thing in Europe. After all, Danish cinema has nothing to do with British Cinema.

Ramadan Suleman[60]

In its previous incarnation, South Africa thought of itself as a Western outpost at the bottom of Africa, an accident of geography that should find reflection in its cultural forms. It sought validation from the only world that mattered—the Western world—with which it continued to maintain, despite economic sanctions and moral rejection, an imaginary bond. Now those bonds of commonality have been redrawn, as evidenced by *Sithengi* and also by South Africa's large presence at FESPACO in 2003. South Africa still seeks validation, but this time from a different source. As the Deputy Minister of Arts and Culture stated,

FESPACO is an important event in the calendar of African cinema. In recognition of the role that cinema can play in the African Renaissance it is crucial that South Africa as one of the African countries should be present at such an event, to contribute to the development and growth of the film industry within the continent, to encourage and foster partnerships, share experiences and strengthen relations with one of the most prolific countries in the history of African cinema.[61]

Will South Africa's inclusion back into black Africa result in the kind of pan-African film industry originally envisioned by the Pan-African Federation of Filmmakers (FEPACI), or just a South African one? It is impossible to predict, but South Africa's presence cannot help but change the dynamics of FESPACO, which up until now has been dominated by Francophone Africa. Already there have been resentful eyes cast at the "rich" South Africans and complaints that the country has become the bullyboy on the block—predictable criticisms, perhaps, considering South Africa's domination in terms of GDP, economic institutions, and investment flows, and considering the recent move of FESPACO's headquarters to Johannesburg.[62]

African cinema has not been frozen in time, like a fern in amber, since its incarnation. In the early 1960s, Ousmane Sembène described it as "night school."[63] For Sembène, the cinematic utterance was vital in the battle against colonial thought and domination. Taking his cue from Fanon's argument that colonialism sought to deform the psychology of its subjects through cultural denigration, Sembène saw the cinema as an antidote to that process. Cinema could not only rewrite the suppressed history of the colonized, but help them develop a fighting consciousness that would overcome their introjected sense of abjection. Cinema should be overtly didactic and polemical, as evidenced by his use of Wolof in *Xala* (1975) and *Le Mandat* (1968), his attack on neocolonial dependency *in Guelwaar* (1992), his exposé of patriarchal imperialism in *Ceddo* (1977), and his powerful critique of female genital mutilation in *Moolade* (2004). But for many filmmakers in Africa, profound changes have taken place in the way they defines themselves, their audiences, their films, and their positions in the global mediascape.

Profound changes are at work in the way filmmakers in Africa define themselves, their audiences, their films, and their position in a global entertainment industry. I deliberately use the term "filmmakers in Africa" rather than the more commonly accepted one of "African filmmakers" to signal this new attitude. Many of the leading filmmakers in Africa are rejecting the concept of "African cinema" and, concomitantly, the label of "African film director." Even those who have made their names under that label argue that films made in Africa should not be placed in a box marked "African films" and separated off from the rest of the world's film output. To reject the label of African filmmaker is to reject being co-opted under the name of state nationalism, of being seen as important only in terms of one's contribution to the nation or the continent at large. It is also to reject the idea that each African filmmaker represents and speaks for the continent as a whole. As British writer and cultural critic Kobena Mercer and famed filmmaker Isaac Julien have argued, black British filmmakers bear a burden of representation that is not shared by their white counterparts. They have to speak for *all* black British filmmakers, an assumption that works insidiously to limit the possibilities of increasing their ranks—for if one can speak for all, then there is no need for more voices and visions to be added to the pool.[64] As Gaston Kaboré sharply comments, "just because you come from the African continent, why should you be expected to make films that represent the whole continent? Your film represents your own corner of life."[65]

This does not mean that films made in Africa do not draw heavily on their African context, or on a particular set of cultural modulations that inflect certain formal elements in the film—the sense of space and time, of rhythm, of language and gesture. But these particulars, even if they are recognized as African in the way that Japanese film is recognized as Japanese, should not be taken as representative of either a national or a continental consciousness. Africa is comprised, as Ramadan Suleman, has caustically noted, not of one nation occupying a huge landmass, but of an immense diversity of nations and cultures.[66] To view Africa and Africans as a unit is a continuation of the colonial mindset.

According to Kaboré, making films that mirror his African context does not make him an African filmmaker, but reflects his own individuality and personal history. He calls African cinema an emotional rather an ideological concept, emotional in the sense that it reflects, as do all art forms, the feelings of the filmmaker. Even Souleyman Cissé, who tends to be less resistant to the idea of an African cinema, talks of it as a pragmatic (by which he means marketing) position, as a form of leverage that can be used to force the industry to show African films or as the organizing logic behind a film festival (as is the case with the New York African Film Festival).[67]

There are two factors that are important to understanding filmmaking in Africa. The first is the filmmakers' desire to reach a transnational audience, both within the continent and abroad, and if that means making films that are audience oriented, relying on mainstream genres, using similar identification strategies to those of classical Hollywood cinema, and dealing with more layered and personal themes such as a boy's journey to discover the identity of his father (*Faro, La Reine des Eaux*, Salif Traoré, Mali, 2006), conforming to European ideas of your country (*Juju Factory*, Balufu Bakupa-Kanyinda, 2006), telling a family saga that highlights intergenerational conflicts (*Il va pleuvoir sur Conakry*, Cheik Fontamady Camara, 2006), or relating the story of a street child who writes to Santa Claus (*Dewenti*, Dyana Guaye, Senegal, 2006), then so be it. The second factor, which emerges out of the first, is the filmmakers' view of themselves as transnational as opposed to national. Most are independent producers as well as filmmakers who spend their time in the metropolitan centers of Western Europe and the United States in search of production funding and marketing and distribution deals. Many are graduates of prestigious film schools in the West, like Gaston Kaboré, who studied at the École Supérieure d'Études Cinématographiques (ESEC); Haile Gerima, who went to film school at the University of California, Los Angeles, and Safi Faye, who attended the Louis Lumière Film School after studying at the Sorbonne. Others are graduates of schools in the former USSR, the most famous example being Ousmane Sembène, who studied in Moscow at the Gorki Studios in the early 1960s.

South African filmmakers have also crossed national boundaries and received academic and/or on-the-job training. Ramadan Suleman majored in directing at the London International Film School in the late 1980s; Zola Maseko is a graduate of the National Film and Television School in Beaconsfield, UK; Gavin Hood graduated from the University of California, Los Angeles, film school; and Teddy Mattera worked in the United States and United Kingdom for the BBC and Channel 4 after studying at the London International Film School and at the Maurits Binger Film Institute in Amsterdam. There is a reciprocity now between filmmakers and audience that did not exist in earlier times, when African cinema was seen as a pedagogic tool and the filmmaker, the teacher. Even the more didactically inclined Francophone filmmakers (in comparison to their more pragmatic Anglophone counterparts) tolerate a greater divergence of styles and themes today in African cinema.

The acknowledgment of the transnational character of African cinema should not be translated as an abandonment, or selling out to the West, by filmmakers in Africa. Rather, it should be seen as a way of broadening film production in Africa, a way of claiming autonomy for the filmmakers of Africa outside of state regulations and the hegemony of nationalism. As transnational filmmakers, they can forge their own affiliations with other progressive cinemas irrespective of geography or nation or race. Gaston Kaboré put it well. Referring to British film director Ken Loach, whose powerful political films and social realist style have marked him as an auteur for the Left, Kaboré stated, "The independent film-makers of Britain are fighting like us to communicate how they see the world. We are happy if there is one guy named Ken Loach—his battle is the same as ours."[68]

3

The Moment of Truth: Screening the Truth and Reconciliation Commission

[A] commission is a necessary exercise to enable South Africans to come to terms with their past on a morally accepted basis and to advance the cause of reconciliation.

Can structures such as the TRC contain the psychic and cultural processes involved when far-reaching social change is underway? Might they not unwittingly encourage cultural and social amnesia?

In broad terms, this book is concerned with exploring the ways in which South African cinema attached itself to the nation and thought of itself in national terms by addressing the big issues of the South African transition. This chapter expands on that idea by examining a group of films that narrativize South Africa's Truth and Reconciliation Commission (TRC), the next big event on the national agenda after the drafting of the Final Constitution in 1996. No event consolidated the nation's democratic vision, offered a picture of the future, and trumpeted its triumph over the past in quite the same way. Yet despite its overwhelming centrality to the nation, the drafting of the constitution failed to capture the public's imagination.

This was clearly not the case with the next big event on the national agenda, the TRC. Mandated by the interim constitution of 1994, the TRC consisted of three different subcommittees—the Human Rights Violation Committee, charged with investigating gross abuses of human rights from 1960–1994 based on statements made to the TRC, the Committee on Am-

nesty, charged with judging applications by confessed perpetrators in exchange for amnesty against legal prosecution (most did not qualify), and the
Committee on Reparation and Rehabilitation, which meant to (but never
properly did) give financial reparation to victims and/or their families. It
had all the elements required to dominate the public's imagination, which
it did.[1]

Even though both the broadcast and print media were present at the
hearings, the avid attention paid to the proceedings by the public came as
a surprise to the Commission. Alex Boraine, Deputy Chairperson of the
TRC, commented,

> Never in my wildest imaginings did I think that the media would retain its in-
> satiable interest in the Commission throughout its life. Not a day passed when
> we were not reported on radio. We were very seldom absent from the major
> television evening news broadcasts, and we were, if not on the front page, on
> the inside pages of every newspaper throughout the two and a half years of our
> work. . . . Unlike many other truth commissions, this one was center stage,
> and the media coverage, particularly radio, enabled the poor, the illiterate,
> and people living in rural areas to participate in its work so that it was truly a
> national experience rather than restricted to a small handful of selected com-
> missioners.[2]

Boraine should not have been so surprised by its reception. Unlike previous
truth commissions, South Africa's TRC was a self-consciously public and
open performance, conducted in full view of the world's media on stages in
public venues (churches and town halls) and in front of an audience. Those
not present were able to hear the proceedings word for word on the radio
and television. This fact, plus the ability of the Commission to grant conditional amnesty to the perpetrators in exchange for full and honest disclosure of crimes committed as part of a political agenda, gave the proceedings the sort of drama one associates with cinema or the theater. It was, as
Catherine Cole points out in her analysis of the TRC's performative modes,
"like a traveling road show."[3]

The drama of the TRC began at the moment of its conception. It was
born from the Interim Constitution negotiations, itself a masterpiece of social transition completed only two years after the Kempton Talks between
Nelson Mandela (representing the African National Congress) and F. W.
de Klerk (representing the National Party). These talks set the train in motion for the writing of the Interim Constitution and for the first democratic
elections, open to all South Africans, which took place in that same year.
The buildup to the elections was precarious, threatened when Inkatha, the

ethnic Zulu party (Zulus being the largest ethnicity in the country), first refused and then consented to participate just one week before the scheduled date. Thousands of lives had been lost in the ethnic fighting between Inkatha and ANC in the Natal province, the traditional center of Zulu nationalism, and rumors of the role of a "Third Force" propelled by recalcitrant apartheid forces and fomenting violence in the region in concert with Inkatha against the ANC were constantly in the news. The country was on the verge of being torn apart, just at the moment of the election. To mandate a Truth and Reconciliation Commission in the face of failure was a bold and creative stroke.[4]

The provision of qualified amnesty was new to South Africa, adopted from the idea of blanket amnesty offered in the Chilean Truth Commission and adapted to the South African context. The commonly held belief that the ANC wanted outright punishment for perpetrators and "gave in" to the National Party's demand for a blanket amnesty with qualified amnesty is untrue. Although it was unpopular among the liberation movements, the majority of them realized that an amnesty process was necessary to a successful transition and signed on to the idea. The idea, however, remained controversial and contentious, a balancing act between redress for victims and reconciliation with old enemies, between the desire to create a better country and the need to discover what had happened under the old one. It appeared only as an appendage in the interim constitution, and few details were given of how the process would work. The idea was that the political process that followed would work out the details. In the ensuing months, negotiations took place and the details began to emerge. It was decided that all parties, not just the apartheid state, would be interrogated regarding gross human-rights violations between March 1, 1960 and May 10, 1994. The anti-apartheid movement was deeply resentful of the inclusivity of the arrangement, since it potentially put it on par, morally speaking, with the apartheid state. Those granted amnesty would be immune from criminal and civil prosecution. Amnesty would be conditional and the hearings would be conducted in open forum and not in secrecy.

The two major conditions under which amnesty would be granted were proportionality and full disclosure. As Daniel Herwitz explains,

> Amnesty would be granted in exchange for full disclosure of the truth and demonstration that the crimes committed were in proportion to the hypothetical goals that motivated the larger scheme of action of which the crimes were a part. Full disclosure would be measured by the Amnesty Committee

on the basis of the proceedings of the TRC hearings. Proportionality would
be decided on the basis of whether a gross violation of human rights could be
explained in terms of the larger political motive that compelled the perpetrator to act: a motive such as keeping the state intact or "winning the war against
the Communists."[5]

The issue of full disclosure, so central to the granting of amnesty, has remained one of the most controversial aspects of the TRC's amnesty process. Unlike victims, amnesty applicants appeared with their lawyers (if
they could afford them) before an amnesty committee comprised mostly of
lawyers and chaired by a judge. In this quasi-juridical procedure, the committee had to make a decision on whether full disclosure had taken place
based on the testimony given by the applicant. There was little opportunity
for the committee to investigate whether the applicant was telling the truth,
let alone the whole truth. Furthermore, the applicant only had to disclose
those facts that were relevant to the particular crime for which he or she was
applying for amnesty, which limited the amount of information that could
be garnered and comprised the whole idea of full disclosure. Many family
members felt cheated by the process, which they had initially hoped would
give them a full picture of what had happened to their loved ones.[6]

Around the proceedings of the TRC, victim testimony proved central,
providing a majority underclass with the public venue of a voice for the first
time in their difficult history. And although the biggest perpetrators, such
as ex-President P. W. Botha, Minister of Law and Order Adriaan Vlok, and
the heads of the Security Force were never prosecuted, the TRC, which
took place during the writing of the Final Constitution of 1996, was critical
in guiding the nation through its early moment of fragile transition. The
final report, released on October 29, 1999, listed more than 21,000 victims,
of which 2,400 gave testimony in public hearings held by the TRC from
1996 to 2002. Of the 7,112 appeals for amnesty received, 849 were granted.[7]
To date, no meaningful reparations have been offered to those victims or
their families who gave testimony apart from the experience of public acknowledgment so central to the TRC.

The TRC was critical to the transition from apartheid, under which
most victims and their families (largely people of color) had been consigned
to political silence as well as economic servitude. Equally central was the
power of the Commission to break the authority of the police state by com-
mandeering files, requiring officials to testify, and placing under its power
those who during apartheid believed in their happy, indeed smirking invul-

nerability. The victims' testimonies as well as those of the perpetrators (who were subpoenaed to appear) were summarized in the report, along with a chronology of the conflict both within and outside the country and the involvement of specific societal institutions such as media, law, education, business, and so on. Although the ANC was found to have committed severe human rights abuses in its training camps outside of South Africa, the report found the apartheid state and its functionaries to be the main perpetrator of crimes against humanity in South Africa.

A FLAWED BUT WORTHWHILE PROCESS?

> Victims of apartheid are now narrowly defined as those militants victimized as they struggled against apartheid, not those whose lives were mutilated in the day-to-day web of regulations that was apartheid.
>
> *Mahmood Mamdani*[8]

Despite its achievements, the TRC was the object of immense public criticism from its inception. Afrikaners claimed that they were being singled out from the rest of the white population for a witch hunt when all whites, covertly or overtly, had been complicit in the system. Many black South Africans felt frustrated by the fact that the perpetrators of horrific crimes, like murder and torture, would go unpunished if they gained amnesty. The family of Steve Biko, the Black Consciousness activist brutally murdered by the authorities in September 1977, refused to participate in a "show trial for TV" that offered freedom to the apartheid thugs who came clean and put on a show of confession. Thabo Mbeki entered the fray with the claim that the TRC was dignifying political liberalism by focusing exclusively on violence and ignoring economic servitude. This he called "the problem of two nations," the first, white and privileged with houses, bank accounts, and freedom to spend at will, and the second, black and still in economic chains. Academics, notably political scientist and public intellectual Mahmood Mamdani, then director of the Centre for African Studies at the University of Cape Town (now a professor at Columbia University in New York), argued that by focusing exclusively on victims of severe human rights violations the Commission failed to highlight the daily ordinary humiliations of the apartheid system faced by millions: restrictions on travel, forced removals, police harassment, inferior education, inadequate housing, pass laws, forced labor, humiliation, and poverty. Why should only the militant ones, who suffered jail or exile, but not the silent majority, who suffered the endless humiliations and hardships of the system, be heard? The Commission did not investigate the "social distribution of pain and suffering" caused by the apartheid system.[9] However, the TRC's mandate was to investigate the gross abuses of human rights that had occurred during apartheid in search of the truth, meaning the revelation of the facts surrounding the events, not to detail the everyday humiliations of black life under apartheid. The latter required a different mechanism—like the cinema, for example—one capable of capturing the "brute objects" of the world, to use Pier Paolo Pasolini's phrase, by which he meant that capacity of cinema to offer an unmediated vision of the world on top of which the filmmaker then builds his or her subjective, expressive language.[10]

Cinema has played this role to perfection in the past. Think of Italian neorealism in the immediate post-war period, a period of political and social turmoil out of which emerged a reformist aesthetic dedicated to a conception of realism rooted in the human condition. Thus the collaboration of Cesare Zavattini and Vittorio De Sica that produced *Bicycle Thieves* (1948) and *Umberto D* (1951), in which the characters are ordinary, small people crushed by the nature of their circumstances, and the *mise-en-scène* is humdrum and drab. The father in *Bicycle Thieves* is unemployed and desperate. No heroics save the day, and the message is that none can until conditions change enough to allow the characters to flourish as human beings are meant to. In *Umberto D*, the old man (Umberto), like his dog, Flike, does not even have a surname—and why should he? He is helpless and old, no longer of any use to a rapidly commercializing society eager to forget the defeats and humiliations of the war. Glauber Rocha's austere call for an "Aesthetic of Hunger" (1965) and Julio Garcia Espinosa's declaration "For an Imperfect Cinema" (1969) valorize a combative cinema that in its later post-Third-Cinema formulations produced films exploring the experiences of women, gays and lesbians, and interracial individuals who had been marginalized by the meta-discourse of the nation.[11] Some of the anti-apartheid films—*Jobman; My Country, My Hat; The Guest; Fiela se Kind;* and *Mamza*—were successful at breaking away from the grand narrative of opposition to the system and engaging life under apartheid at the individual level. Clearly there is a role for South African cinema to play here.

While many of the criticisms leveled at the TRC are trenchant, they do not destroy the Commission's accomplishments (one should not let, as the philosophers say, the perfect be the enemy of the good). Nor do they destroy the immense political importance of its prestige for the dignity of political transition to democracy both locally and internationally.

If South Africa and the "South African miracle" (a phrase which annoys South Africans intensely as they feel it elides the struggle for democracy that took place for forty years) have become an imaginary site for the West, a place in which the tired narratives of modernity can be replayed with different and perhaps more optimistic outcomes, this was in no small part due to the TRC. And although now tarnished by Thabo Mbeki's denialist stance on HIV/AIDS being caused by a retrovirus (see chapter 4), South Africa still has, as Marsha Kinder puts it, "considerable transformational capital" in a world hungry for modern success stories. The picture of a new moral regime and the idea of a "Road to Reconciliation" (the words emblazoned on the banner that hung above the commissioners each day of the proceedings) were critical to easing tensions and strife and to creating a vision at the fragile moment of transition, a vision also contained in the Final Constitution of 1996. Most importantly, in the history of a country constituted in the repression of debate, the TRC was a public event around which crystallized genuine public disagreement in which people of all "races" felt passionately assured of being able to speak their minds and were listened to intently. The TRC effected a sea change in the country. As Njabulo Ndebele puts it:

> It can be said that as a result of the TRC, South Africa has become a more sensitive and a more complex society. South Africans have been forced to confront the complex contradictions of the human condition, and the need to devise adequate social arrangements to deal with them. The healing that results will not be instant. It will come from the new tendency for South Africans to be willing to negotiate their way through social, intellectual, religious, political and cultural diversity. In sum, it will come from the progressive accumulation of ethical and moral insights.[12]

This "progressive accumulation" became a working recipe for the project of democracy itself: a project dependent on dissension over issues of public importance. Around the TRC, one can claim, a public sphere was reconstituted, and it became even more robust when the report was finally released.

SCREENING THE TRC: A MORAL URGENCY

Cinema immediately jumped onto the bandwagon of the TRC's representation, understanding the event's power to place South Africa at the center of the world's moral stage, changing its image from pariah to exemplar in a single stroke. If film suffered the seduction of the TRC's aura, adulating it in the manner of early silent films with their simple stories of good and evil, it is in part because this was how the world wanted to view this event. Cinema found itself blessed with a historical urgency and the kind of story it has always reveled in making, and these became the power, and limitation, of filmic narratives of the TRC.

Cinema has not (as yet) participated in any public criticism of the event. Rather, it has been drawn to the power and the glory of the event and the desire to propagate that on screen to the public gaze. Critical to cinema's representation of the TRC was the fact that the events had already been widely broadcast by both the national and international media, and further, that there had been a great deal of critical commentary along with the facts.[13] In the race to representation, TV, newsprint, and radio got there first, leaving cinema with a number of possibilities: It could perform the task of documentary work of a more complex order (one relying on TV footage itself) such as one sees in *The Gugulethu Seven* (Lindy Wilson, 2001), *Between Joyce and Remembrance* (Mark Kaplan, 2004), and *Long Night's Journey into Day* (Reid and Hoffman, 2000), or stoke up the dream machines of Hollywood and those of South Africa itself to produce the TRC as genre cinema as has happened in *Red Dust* (Tom Hooper, 2004), *In My Country* (John Boorman, 2004), *Forgiveness* (Ian Gabriel, 2004), and *Zulu Love Letter* (Ramadan Suleman, 2004). Let us begin with an examination of the former.

DOCUMENTING THE UNEXPECTED MOMENT OF TRUTH

The hard work of documentary filmmaking is evident in every frame of *Between Joyce and Remembrance*. Mark Kaplan, the film's director and producer, spent seven years following the case of Siphiwo Mtimkulu, a student activist who was tortured, poisoned, and, when that did not stop him, eventually murdered by (among others) Gideon Nieuwoudt, one of apartheid's most terrifying killers. Siphiwo was in a wheelchair due to the effects of thallium poisoning by the security police at the time of his abduction and murder in 1982. Fourteen years later, after years of frustration and lies and harassment by the people who had tortured and killed her son, Joyce Mtimkulu appeared before the Human Rights Violations Committee of the TRC to testify. Even then, she was constrained by a series of court rulings taken out by Nieuwoudt and others which prevented her from naming them in her testimony. The truth might never have emerged had Nieuwoudt, serving a long prison sentence for another apartheid-era human rights crime (the Motherwell bombing) not applied for amnesty in the case of Siphiwo and Topsy Madaka, the other activist abducted with Siphiwo.

The facts that emerged at the amnesty hearing were horrifyingly brutal. After the two young men were abducted, they were drugged, shot to death, doused with gasoline, and burnt. What remained of them was thrown into the Fish River. The full disclosure of the events, and the fact that it had been done in the name of a political cause, earned the perpetrators, including Nieuwoudt, full amnesty, but not, in his case, freedom. Nieuwoudt returned to prison to serve out his sentence for his other crime.[14] The story then took the turn that led toward what would become the most dramatic sequence of the documentary. Nieuwoudt had found religion in prison and wanted more than amnesty for his crimes. He sought forgiveness from the families of his victims and, in search of that prospect, asked Kaplan to arrange for him to meet the Mtimkulu family and allowed him to film it.

The first few scenes of the meeting show the failure of reconciliation. Sitting on a couch, face to face with their son's torturer and killer, the parents reject Nieuwoudt's pleas for forgiveness over and over again. Too much wrong has been done to them, to Siphiwo, to his teenage son, Sikhumbuzo, who sits in the background, a shadowy, inarticulate figure and all that is left of Siphiwo. Joyce's face is a study in stoicism and conviction. The father shows more anger, more willingness to engage only to reject. Nieuwoudt, used to getting his way with people in the past, presses his case, his eyes flicking from side to side, his voice insistent. Like any good filmmaker, Kaplan is more interested in the visual than the verbal and his camera dwells on the faces, then moves to the objects in the room, only to circle back incessantly to the face. It is necessary here to mention Nieuwoudt's face. Many of the killers who testified at the amnesty committee hearings were remarkable for the very banality of their appearance; ordinary men in ill-fitting suits that one might encounter in the street or at church. In Nieuwoudt's case, his looks matched his deeds. His face was reptilian, terrifying. It was the face of evil and Kaplan seems to have understood that he had a murderer who fit the part as if he had been cast for the role.

So when the unexpected happens while the camera is rolling, the viewer is both shocked and yet unsurprised, satisfied and even validated by the events. Sikhumbuzo (whose name means "remembrance"), leaps forward and hits Nieuwoudt on the head with a vase, fracturing, we learn later, his skull. As blood pours down his face and hands and he clutches his head in agony while still making his case, the parents rush to help him and the camera keeps rolling, recording this extraordinary moment of reversal when the victims come to the aid of the killer.

The reversal continues as we learn Sikhumbuzo has been punished for this "crime" by expulsion from school. His father's friends, however, put together a scholarship for him to continue his education. He receives nothing from either the state or the TRC to compensate him for his loss. Only his family and friends come to his aid.

The story in *Between Joyce and Remembrance* is not a large national story of the TRC's success, but it is a small personal one. Without the TRC, the facts of Siphiwo's death would not have been known, his mother's voice would never have been heard, and the last remains of Siphiwo, a little tuft of hair, would never have been buried. While we would all like to see someone like Gideon Nieuwoudt tried and punished for his heinous deeds, a trial might not have accomplished what the TRC did. Trials are not victim-centered or public hearings. The evidence given must be tailored according to the rules of criminal justice: the person giving evidence cannot simply tell the story from their own point of view. As Andre du Toit puts it,

> What is at stake when victims are able to tell their own stories is not just the specific factual statements, but the right of framing them from their own perspectives and being recognized as legitimate sources of truth with claims to rights and justice.[15]

THE GUGULETHU SEVEN: THE FACTS

On March 3, 1986, seven young activists from Cape Town's Gugulethu Township were murdered in a covert action by the Special Branch of the security police. All seven of the young men were shot multiple times; in one of the riddled bodies, eighteen bullet holes were found. The police claimed to have killed the men in self-defense after one of them exploded a grenade within three meters of the police van. The young men (Mandla Mxinwa, Zanisile Mjobo, Zola Swelani, Godfrey Miya, Christopher Piet, Themba Mlifi, and Zabonke Konile) were described as known terrorists, armed and dangerous. Photos and video taken at the scene showing guns perfectly laid across their bodies and a grenade between the legs of one man allegedly "proved" this version of the story.

Two investigations were held during the apartheid period, one in 1986 and another in 1989. Both upheld the original verdict that the men had died during a legitimate anti-terrorist operation. In addition, *Cape Times* journalist Tony Weaver was tried in 1987 on the grounds that he printed untruths about the incident (and most important, passed these on to the BBC). A decade later, this trial would provide critical evidence to the investigatory team preparing the evidence for the TRC. The team would use the testimony of Dr. David Klatzow, a pathologist hired by Weaver's defense lawyer who conducted experiments on dead pigs, shooting them at close range with the same weapons used by police, to show that the wounds on the victims matched those of pigs, which had been shot at very close range. The results challenged the statements of the police, who had claimed to have fired at long range.

Dr. Klatzow's evidence, along with testimonies from two eye witnesses, postmortem photographs of the deceased, and photographs of one of the policemen, Sergeant Sterrenberg, posing over a body and smiling as if a hunter over his kill, and of another stepping against the head of a victim in the mortuary, cast doubt on the police's story that they had killed dangerous terrorists in self-defense. One witness claimed to have seen three policemen attack one of the "terrorists," throw him to the ground, and shoot him at close range. The other told how he saw a policeman shoot one of the men who was lying on the ground in the head. These witnesses' testimonies directly contradicted those of the police and fed the rumors that accreted around the killings.

The truth remained secret, however, until uncovered by the TRC's investigatory team a decade later. The result of this investigation was proof of direct involvement of *Vlakplaas*, the government-funded hit squad, headed by notorious killer Eugene de Kock. De Kock was serving two life sentences for other murders and had to be brought from the prison in chains to give evidence at the TRC hearing. It became clear that the event was a complete setup, designed to ambush and kill the victims in the manner of lions in the wild, hence the image of man over kill.

During the TRC investigation into the deaths of the Gugulethu Seven, it emerged that *Vlakplaas* had used *askaris*, former liberation fighters who defected under the threat of torture into black security branch policemen. Posing as liberation fighters trained by the ANC outside of the country, the *askaris* infiltrated a group of young Rastafarian resistance fighters in the township of Gugulethu. They trained the unsuspecting men, supplied them with weapons, and planned with them an attack on a police bus. This provided the rationale for the police's "counterterrorist attack." In early January 1986, the local police drove to Koeberg, a suburb of Cape Town, in three vehicles. There they were briefed about the setup by members of the security branch. After the killing took place, a video was made of the aftermath and used by *Vlakplaas* commander Adriaan Vlok to persuade Parliament to increase the *Vlakplaas* budget. In short, the entire operation was staged to allow a video to be made in order to raise money for more "counterterrorist" insurgency and infiltration.

This dramatic story emerged only gradually during an investigation headed by black journalist Zenzile Khoisan and his colleagues while researching the case for the TRC in 1996.[16] The story broke the band of invincibility surrounding the security branch and erupted in a moment of truth so powerful that when the police video was shown at the proceedings, the mothers of the killed men were overwhelmed with grief and had to be carried out of the room. The truth was volcanic, erupting in the stories these mothers told to the Commission. Jabulani's mother spoke of watching the TV news that evening and seeing that one of the bodies, torn apart by bullets and twisted in the mud, belonged to her beloved son:

> Around two o'clock in the afternoon it was time for me to go home. I did my usual shopping. Then I went home with the train. We switched on the TV for the news, it's my daughter who did that—her name is Thombisodwa who switched on the TV. . . .
> The music started for the news. Then in the news I was told that these seven children were killed by the guerrillas from Russia. And one of the children was shown on TV who had a gun on his chest. He was facing upward. And now we could see another one, the second one, only to find that it's my son Jabulani.
> We were arguing, myself and my daughter. She said, "It's him." I said, "No, it can't be him, I just saw him this morning, it can't be him. I can—I can still remember what he wore this morning. He had navy pants and a green jacket and a warm—and a warm woolen hat." I prayed, I said, "Oh, Lord. . . . I wish—I wish this news could just rewinding . . . Why is it just him? . . . Why were the others not shown, why is it just him?"[17]

In this testimony given to the Commission, Eunice Miya, mother of Jabulani, speaks in the past, except at one moment: "He was facing upward. And now we could see another one, the second one, only to find that it's my son Jabulani." This burst of the present tense from the past is the way he lives in her, ever present and ever unreachable, a slice of TV video unable to be rewound. In the testimony to the TRC, the dead are shown to be un-buried for family and victim, specters haunting the present.

And then there is the process of uncovering that which was buried, the story of the investigation, which is also the story of Zenzile Khoisan, returned from years covering the tough city of New York to work for the TRC. The TRC gave Khoisan and his colleagues (mostly people of color) a mandate, authority, and power of inquiry for the first time in South African history. In the course of finding and following the evidence trail, he and his colleagues confronted the police, forced them to open locked chambers where the case dockets and many related documents were found, confronted the police without humiliation and reprisal, and forced them to comply. The case dockets were written in encrypted script, but through gradual deciphering (like Alan Turing and his colleagues deciphering the Nazi code at Bletchley Park) and forced testimony, Khoisan's team unlocked the extent of the collusion between police and anti-terrorist units. This unlocking of the gates of power was a victory for the TRC, for the archive, for the record, for the power of inquiry, and for people of color. And so in two ways the TRC dignified victims. First, it gave black mothers a place of testimony, lending precedence to their views and requests and treating them with dignity. Second, it gave reporters, judges, and researchers of color the rite of passage, the authority to challenge the systems of apartheid power, a power that had refused categorically to account for itself, especially to people such as these.

Wilhelm Bellingan and Thapelo Mbelo, both of the security branch in charge of the police actions, and a well-paid *askari* applied for amnesty under the provisions of the Amnesty Act. All were granted amnesty for their roles in the killings in 2002.

If one wants to call the TRC process a moment of truth, the truth is multiple, a way of bringing the trauma of the past to uncovering, eruption, archive, a way of reorganizing the domain of inquest, the domain of power. The TRC created many moments of unburial for the dead, resurrecting them on video, on TV, in the haunting presentness of the past to be faced in an explosive drama of address. Mothers collapsed, audiences were horrified, and all were shocked into silence. This silence of a past long buried, a trauma long unspoken and unregistered, created the perfect conditions for the medium of cinema, where what is past appears on screen as a continual present—especially in documentary, which takes actual footage and reweaves it into an evolving story.

DOCUMENTING THE MOMENT OF TRUTH
IN *THE GUGULETHU SEVEN*

Lindy Wilson produced and directed the documentary *The Gugulethu Seven* in 2000. It is a film made within the same dramatic and volcanic space as the TRC itself, almost, one might say, part of the TRC's long arm of propagation and circulation. Funded by the Kellogg Foundation, the film seeks to reveal the entirety of the TRC's investigative process: research, inquiry, interview, testimony, and interrogation of police by advocates and commissioners.

It begins on the scruffy plain of the Cape Flats. Then there is an image of a black man driving into a tangle of something uncertain. Cut to gunfire, a gunshot, running legs, and a first-person point of view as another dashes through trees, then a shot of a window and a body lying dead (the same?). Next, live-action cameras, testimony, and a description of the crime in Afrikaans by someone we can't make out. This seems to be the domain of re-enactment, of memory so strong it demands live action camera. In fact, it is not live re-enactment at all, but the live footage that the filmmaker got from SABC. The footage shows seven dead bodies on the ground, police wandering the "crime site" measuring distances between a body and a police van, the camera panning across drawings of the crime site, police drawings of the scene, and a panoply of evidence. Then SABC news footage, shown on the nightly news from March 3, 1986. The anchor describes how police foiled a terrorist plot to ambush and bomb a police patrol. The shot immediately cuts to a woman, who says, "I didn't believe it." The woman's voice continues. As she talks, we see a funeral for one of the victims, perhaps more. Crowds march and *toyi-toyi*, stamping their feet and chanting in the dance that had become iconic of the apartheid protest movement. "We were born in vinegar times and we are fed with lemons," someone says.

Then there is a subtitle: "Ten years later," and a tape played of a witness seeming to give testimony along with simultaneous translation. The testimony clearly comes from the Committee's investigation into the Gugulethu Seven, although the filmmaker has not explicitly told us so. A thin man in a tie, the first identified, speaks about the case. Is this happening during the events or later? We, the viewers, do not know. He says, "Weapons placed on them. Ambushed." Shortly thereafter the viewer learns that he is the head of the research unit appointed by the TRC to investigate the Gugulethu Seven "incident." Next, a South African journalist returned from New York with street smarts (his name, we learn from a subtitle, is Zenzile Khoisan) tells us with a canny grin that his team, the researchers, two former policewomen and two former journalists, realized that they would have to "get out of these offices and onto the street" to discover the truth. They have one car and one cell phone between the four of them. They have been given a task, but we are not told what it is.

The action of the film is tightly framed, in close up, placing the viewer within multiple time frames that do not yield sufficient evidence to discern which is which, who is who, when is now, before, or after. The film is not located in person or place but in the junction between them. "Seven young men died. I didn't know what they looked like," the journalist says. There are records from postmortems, inquests, and the court; it is finally apparent that this scene is occurring after the deaths and the journalist is taking the viewer to the various sites where they did their uncovering.

The film follows them re-enacting their search for evidence, cutting between this story, a thriller, about how these muckraking journalist/researchers break the big news of the involvement of *Vlakplaas* in the killings, the process of victim testimony and what the mothers go through, the courtroom drama of the Commission, its interviews of perpetrators (including two applying for amnesty), and the subpoenas of bigger and bigger thugs bringing more and more of the story to light.

The film hangs on the wire between three time periods: (1) 1986— the time of apartheid, township resistance, co-option and corruption, (2) 1996—the time of the Commission's inquiry into the deaths of the seven young men, and (3) 2000—the time of the film's production and distribution. Film is uniquely able do this because of its ability to make the past visible, giving it the immediacy of the present and putting the viewer in the position of the journalist uncovering the truth, but also in the position of the mothers whose traumas, when spoken, reveal and respond to the torment of this unburial. Like filmmaking itself, the film reveals the TRC to be a process: of evidence gathering, revelation through testimony and cross-examination, and also victim/family testimony with all the pain thereby associated and all the dignity accorded them by the Commission. In this sense, *The Gugulethu Seven* is truly documentary.

Khoisan tells us how, in order to crack the case, the team realized they had to find the occurrence book, which was locked up; how they located it, secreted away in an unused room; and how they took it away only to find it was encrypted. They deciphered the code and learned that "C1" stood for "C section," a unit in the South African police that worked with *Vlakplaas* operatives. We learn how they commandeered entrance into safe houses of the security apparatus in a way unthinkable a few years earlier; how they took risks, stood up to intimidation by police officials and became empowered as a result. "We needed to find Chris Bateman," says Khoisan. Bateman tells what the eyewitnesses in the hostel across the street saw and how their testimonies conflicted with the police report. We learn about a pattern of police interference, their trying to pressure families to bury the bodies immediately, their intimidation of undertakers, and their barring of journalists from the mortuary.

Only then does the film show the events of the Commission, the giving of testimony with translation, confirming that the tapes we heard at the beginning of the film are indeed the recordings of testimony on the Gugulethu Seven given before the Commission. Only now does the Commission become part of the proceedings. By limiting the spectatorial point of view, Wilson ensures that we are always caught in the intensity of the present tense. Next we see and hear an excerpt from the hearing's video in which Jabulani's mother describes to the commissioners how she saw her son's body on TV, how she found out about it that way. We hear her break into the present tense when she says "it's Jabulani." Then she breaks down. The film cuts back to the Khoisan showing us how he and his team went about improvising the search for evidence, and in the course of it, how they upset the order of power that had existed for years between colored people and police. In his recounting he is impish, ebullient, and still amazed.

Later, the policemen give testimony before the commissioners and are cross-examined. They testify in an expressionless tone
of voice, responding to claims that they are inconsistent with such
phrases as "I haven't looked into it." We are constantly shown photos
of the dead boys and other evidence, not only to be reminded that this
is evidence, but as a way of motivating in our gaze that everything is
being revealed and everything is traumatically there, in the mothers'
consciousnesses, in the proceedings. When the police video is shown
in the courtroom to the mothers who are present, we see them scream
and go wild with grief, and hear Dumisa Nsebisa, one of the commissioners, say, "Can we stop there. . . . stop the video. . . . we'll take
a break now, if you would just stop the video right at this moment."
What we do not see in the documentary, but which is present on the
unedited video footage of the hearings, is the shoe thrown by one of
the mothers at two of the policemen, an act that took place just before
the mothers broke down into screams and tears. In the remainder of
the film, the immensity of the connection to *Vlakplaas* comes to light
in the testimony of the *askari*, the former freedom fighter now working with the police. The film's closing shot is of the dead victims, forcing us as viewers to acknowledge their absence even as they are present in this moment of truth.

The Commission was not simply about truth in the sense of testimony, inquest, and the eruption of pain: the banner above the commissioners said in bold letters: TRUTH: THE ROAD TO RECONCILIATION.
Albie Sachs, writing in the first volume of the TRC report of 1998,
called this "restorative truth." And Cynthia Ngewu, mother of victim Christopher Piet, said, "This thing called reconciliation . . . if
I am understanding it correctly . . . if it means this perpetrator, this
man who has killed Christopher Piet, if it means he becomes human
again, this man, so that I, so that all of us, get our humanity back . . .
then I agree, then I support it all."[1] The penultimate moment of the
film has Thapelo Mbelo, the *askari* working for the security branch,
asking forgiveness of the seven mothers. They embrace, not without
repulsion, nor without regret. One says, "It will serve no purpose for
God not to do [not to forgive], even if it will not bring my son back."
These women embrace the man who helped to kill their children because they believe in "this thing called reconciliation." It was a thing

made possible by African religions, Christian faiths deeply invested in forgiveness and ultimate coming, religions fused with African traditions about marking the spot of the dead and letting them pass on to their realm of dwelling. Christopher Piet will live in this realm and on the windscreen of his mother's memory at the same time, a double life that is death.

This same spirit of forgiveness invested qualified amnesty, for which Thapelo Mbelo was applying, with the aura of reconciliation. Full disclosure that is the revelation of truth (insofar as this could be determined by the Commission) was central to the gift of this release (from prosecution). The possibility that torturers like Thapelo Mbelo were sufficiently psychopathic to act the perfect role of the penitent in a way that satisfied the Amnesty Committee raises doubts about the TRC's process and about the possibility of cinema's capacity to show us the truth. Perhaps we have been watching a show trial in which nothing is accomplished apart from letting murderers go free? The film deploys the metaphor of forgiveness and reconciliation as a way of mingling the present (the testimony in front of the Amnesty Commission) with the past (the TV news reports of the so-called attack on the police, the photos of weapons and grenades found on the "terrorists," and the discovery of *Vlakplaas*'s existence). Ultimately, the film recapitulates the doubts that have arisen in the viewer's mind as to the "truthfulness" of what they have been watching and reaffirms the success of the TRC as an act of healing and redemption. And so we have here an event—the TRC—whose very substance demands a race to the screen and for which the medium of cinema is uniquely satisfactory.

NOTES

1. Antjie Krog, *Country of My Skull* (New York: Three Rivers Press, 1998), 142.

THE TRC AS GENRE CINEMA

There were two types of TRC meetings: the Human Rights Violations Committee (HRV) hearings, which heard victims' testimonies on their experiences, and the Amnesty Committee hearings, where the perpetrators came forward and disclosed what they had done in the hope of getting amnesty. Each had their own kind of drama and protocol, although the HRV hearings were generally far more dramatic and poignant, with victims speaking in all 11 official languages (requiring simultaneous translation), uninterrupted for over an hour at a time. In contrast, the amnesty hearings were more legalistic, taking place in front of a panel of judges, with lawyers representing their "clients." The drama lay at the hearing's conclusion, when the applicant was either granted amnesty, which meant lifelong freedom from criminal or civil prosecution for acts committed under apartheid, or refused.

Red Dust, based on a novel by Gillian Slovo, tells the fictional story of ANC Member of Parliament Alex Mpondo. In his former life as a freedom fighter, he was arrested, tortured, and imprisoned by the Special Branch. Dirk Hendricks, the policeman who tortured Alex, has filed for amnesty with the TRC. Mpondo is appearing before the Commission to "find out what happened to Steve Sizela and to block the amnesty of a sadistic bastard."[18] Representing him in the Amnesty Committee meeting is Sarah Barcant, a former South African lawyer, now living in the USA.

The film was produced by Anant Singh's Videovision, with support from South Africa's Industrial Development Corporation (IDC). Hooper is a British television director, whose filmography includes John Adams (2008), Longford (2006), Prime Suspect 6 (2003), Daniel Deronda (2002), and Love in a Cold Climate (2001). The film follows the classical narrative format of the Hollywood movie, but nevertheless remains close to the moment of truth in all its haunted intensity. This is no doubt because Gillian Slovo is herself haunted, a South African daughter of Ruth First and Joe Slovo, two of South Africa's most famous anti-apartheid activists. Joe Slovo was the head of Umkhonto we Sizwe (MK), the armed wing of the ANC, and in the 1980s, the general secretary of the South African Communist Party. Ruth First, a labor journalist, academic, writer, and editor (she wrote and edited the first draft of Nelson Mandela's No Easy Walk to Freedom) was killed in 1982 by a letter bomb sent by the Security Branch to her university office in Maputo, Mozambique.

Red Dust uses a pattern common to genre film, where story events are reordered to alternate past and present in the plotline and manipulate causality. It is often used in detective or murder mysteries to create tension and build up to an all-revealing climax. The film intersperses scenes from the amnesty hearing with flashbacks of what would have been victims' testimony in front of the HRV committee. The flashbacks disturb the temporal order of the present and are themselves chronologically disordered. Thus, the film opens with close-up on a scene of gore: a pool of blood in the foreground, an indistinct head in the background. Blood smears across the floor, turning the dust red as a body is pulled along the ground. The viewer does not learn until the end of the film that the head and body belong to Steve Sizela, the friend who was arrested with Alex. No one had ever known what happened to Steve after his disappearance, and until the end of the film, the viewer is meant to assume that the opening shot is of Alex being tortured by Hendricks and dragged away. Only at the end does the viewer find out that Steve was brought into Alex's cell in this near-death state by Hendricks's superior, who has not applied for amnesty but is at the hearing to intimidate Hendricks from disclosing all the facts. Up until the end Alex, who has no clear memory of what happened during the torture, has blamed himself for identifying Steve under torture as a fellow fighter. Now he realizes that he is blameless. His identification did not cause Steve's death. Steve was already dying when Alex, half-dead himself, lifted one bloodied arm and pointed to him.

Red Dust structures the TRC's proceedings to conform to the generic conventions of the detective/political thriller. By starting in medias res with the shot of a bloody head, the viewer immediately speculates as to the possible causes of this event. The rest of the film explains how the event came to pass. Enter Alex's lawyer, Sarah Barcant. As in most thrillers, depth of information is limited to Sarah, whose cold, objective legal skills, tempered with empathy gained from the trauma (small in comparison to Alex's) she underwent at the hands of Sizela's murderer, make her the perfect lawyer turned detective. Most of the time, we learn about the case through her—as does Alex, who should know more about what happened than she does, except that he has amnesia. Thus narration is restricted to what Sarah discovers. This pattern of plot development builds excitement and curiosity, both necessary for political or suspense thrillers and mysteries. The narration only occasionally shifts toward the less-restricted end of the continuum, particularly in the scenes between Hendricks and his boss, Piet Muller. While these scenes give away some of the suspense/mystery, they increase spectatorial tension, also a necessary emotional state within the genre.

David Bordwell outlines three emotional states to which the political thriller genre gives rise: curiosity (who killed whom), suspense about upcoming events, and surprise at unexpected disclosures. All of these arise out of the giving and taking of knowledge, and in particular, its suppression and restriction. In Red Dust, we wonder who killed Steve and if Alex was indeed an informer (curiosity). We fear for Sarah's safety because we know how much is at stake for Muller (suspense), and we are surprised when we find out that Hendricks buried Steve's case book with his body, thus confirming Muller as the murderer.

An obvious departure in *Red Dust* from the classic narrative form is in its subversion of the "male gaze," Laura Mulvey's influential idea that the camera offers the spectator a subject position that is masculine, not feminine. Feminist film theory argues that "what the camera in fact grasps is the 'natural' world of the dominant ideology," which is patriarchal.[19] As a consequence, classic spectatorship was gendered as masculine and female viewers took on the masculine subject position by identifying with the gaze of the camera and the organization of looks within the film's diegesis. In her path-breaking article, "Visual Pleasure and Narrative Cinema," Mulvey outlined three looks that work to engender cinematic voyeurism as exclusively masculine: the look of the camera, the look of the characters at each other, and the look of the spectator.[20] In each case, the look works to objectify the female character and turn her into spectacle. Male characters do the looking while the female ones become the objects or 'bearers' of the look. A feminist cinema would, ideally, refuse this arrangement by denying the spectator the pleasure of any form of voyeurism at all. Later theorists proposed a female look, in which the male character becomes the object of the female character's desire.[21] This expansion has led to a variety of alternative gazes being suggested: black, gay, lesbian, queer. Each one offers the possibility for the existence of different modes of spectatorial identification, thus problematizing the idea of there being one "truth" in the diegetic world.

In *Red Dust*, there is a scene in which Sarah meets her client, Alex, at a public swimming pool that restructures the classic narrative convention of the male gaze. The scene begins with Sarah arriving at the gates of the pool only to find that they are locked. Sarah peeks over the wall and sees Alex swimming laps in the pool, a voyeuristic action that identifies her gaze as active and powerful, a position usually reserved for the male. She then takes off her shoes and climbs over the wall, which bears a faded "Whites Only" sign from the days of apartheid, when all public facilities were racially segregated. This image tells us that she has entered an illicit space. Under apartheid, it is Alex who would have been barred from the space because of his race. Those laws are now defunct. However, the laws of patriarchy are still very much in play, and by claiming the controlling power of the male character and taking Alex as the object of her gaze, she has broken the "law." She walks to the edge of the pool, squats down, and calls to him, but he ignores her and continues swimming. There is a shot of her sitting on a bench in the background watching him while he continues swimming in the foreground. Eventually, he climbs out of the pool and goes to shower off, wearing a small bathing suit, his body glistening in the sun. She moves toward him and the two are framed in medium close-up, then in shot/reverse shot, she wearing her black business dress and sling-back shoes, and he, all but naked, with water splashing off his chest and arms. The arrangement of looks that pass between them, as well as the camera's look articulated through the shot/reverse shot, clearly position him as an erotic object and as the object of her gaze.

Outside of the construction of the gaze as female, Alex, as the male hero of the film, offers a source of pleasure to the male viewer. Stephen Neale has argued, in his writing on the western, that the male hero, who is so dominant in the genre, is often produced as an object of male voyeuristic pleasure, thus "opening a space for . . . the male as privileged object of the look."[22] Further, one cannot ignore that Alex is black, which complicates the very idea of the male gaze. Black men have not been granted the same power of looking openly as have white men. As Pam Cook and Mieke Bernink put it, the male gaze is "not a universal given but is rather negotiated via whiteness: the black man's sexual gaze is socially prohibited."[23] This point is particularly important given South Africa's history of segregation and apartheid. So it is likely that Alex's positioning in the film as bearer of the look operates in a dual way: it is symptomatic of his historical position, even in the "new" (the film is set in 2000) South Africa, and it is an expression of female white empowerment. The reversal of the male gaze in *Red Dust* is further complicated by the way the hero's body is represented as both powerful and injured, scarred by the marks of his torturer. The moment in which Alex shows Sarah the scars on his back from when he was tortured by the Special Branch ("Do you think they can shoot this down?" he asks angrily in response to Sarah's concern that the evidence he gives at his torturer's amnesty hearing should be as complete and convincing as possible), which have up until then been concealed from the viewer, breaks through his objectification and holds out the possibility for spectatorial identification.

A pattern of flashbacks between past and present also structures another fiction film dealing with the TRC: Ramadan Suleman's *Zulu Love Letter*. Born in Durban and trained in theater in South Africa and then at the London International Film School, Suleman has also worked in Europe in documentary filmmaking and for Med Hondo and Souleymane Cissé, two well-known African auteurs. *Zulu Love Letter* was produced by his own production company, Natives at Large, and by Jacques Bidou, a French producer, with additional support from the National Film and Video Foundation.

The story begins *in medias res* with a shot of a woman unconscious in a car. She is taken to the hospital, where she regains consciousness and reassures her young daughter, who is deaf, that she will be okay for the girl's birthday party. This first story, which occurs in post-apartheid South Africa, is forestalled by a flashback to the second story, which takes place a decade earlier during the last years of apartheid rule. The film follows this pattern of development throughout as the woman, Thandeka Malatsi, a newspaper reporter, struggles to bring her past and present together, to bury the ghosts that are haunting and destroying her. Like many characters in European Art Cinema, Thandeka is constantly reflecting on her condition and the condition of those around her. In comparison to the goal-driven characters of the Hollywood movie, she appears irresolute, alienated from her surroundings. She seems incapable of having authentic relationships with her family and boyfriend. Suleman finds powerful imagery to indicate her alienated state of being, placing her in claustrophobic spaces and framing her behind objects that obstruct her passage through the diegetic space. The tight causality of the Hollywood narrational structure is loosened in this film, indicating the tenuous quality of life for black women in post-apartheid South Africa. We are not sure that Thandeka will survive in any positive way. She has a bad relationship with her daughter and her parents, writer's block at work, and a dysfunctional sex life. Initially the film is more of a melodrama, but when Thandeka testifies at the TRC on the death of a young woman who was shot in front of her and undertakes to find out where she has been buried, the film segues into a political thriller, which Charles Derry defines as a subgenre within the suspense thriller category.

Unlike the suspense thriller, which focuses on victims or criminals, political thrillers "are organized around a plot to assassinate a political figure or a revelation of the essential conspiratorial nature of governments and their crimes against the people."[24] Suleman skillfully exploits this generic convention to link Thandeka's personal story to the larger context of struggle. With the unearthing of the body, Thandeka is able to unearth her own demons and recover her sense of wholeness. The central scene, the murder of the girl, which acts as a catalyst for Thandeka's journey of self-discovery, is shown in the second story, and again, as in *Red Dust*, its meaning in the story only becomes clear over time, through a restricted range of information.

TWO COUNTRIES OF MY SKULL

The moment of truth pours into writing just as it does into film through poet/journalist Antjie Krog's words in her book, *Country of My Skull: Guilt, Sorrow and the Limits of Forgiveness in the New South Africa*.[25] Emerging from her work as an SABC radio reporter following the events of the TRC, the book is part journalism, part confessional, self-rumination, and poetry. Above all, it is concerned with Krog's search, as a poet and journalist, for a new kind of language capable of responding to the oral testimonies of both victim and perpetrator. As she puts it,

> In the beginning it was seeing. Seeing for ages, filling the head with ash. No air. No tendril. Now to seeing, speaking is added and the eye plunges into the mouth. Present at the birth of this country's language itself.[26]

With these words, Krog positions herself as a witness to the witnesses, struggling to find new modes of expression capable of conveying her experience to her readers. Her gaze at this birth is a critical one, deconstructive in its intention. She uses it as weapon of surveillance against herself; her people, by which she means the Afrikaners (indeed, the frontispiece of the book bears the following inscription: "For every victim who had an Afrikaner surname on her lips"); and the media's role in knowledge production.[27] Journalism becomes poetry at the moment when a testimony is that of the "eye plunging into the mouth" when the victim or witness is finally able to speak. The eye is also Krog's eye, the mouth her mouth, as she reports herself having witnessed the victim saying these words. This poetry places the writer and victim in the same space of seeing, speaking, and transmission. The result is an intentionally fragmented text that refuses to impose a traditional or classical narrative structure on the oral stories that formed the very substance of the TRC.

In charting the paths taken by post-apartheid South African autobiographical literature, especially those works dealing with traumatic events from the country's apartheid past, cultural critic Sarah Nuttall describes two emerging representational trends.[28] The first imposes a coherent narrative on the act of telling and remembering, or what Nuttall calls "speaking memory," presenting the author as a unified agent responding to the

exigencies of the time. The example for Nuttall is Nelson Mandela's autobiography, *Long Walk to Freedom*, which collapses the private self into the
public one and vice versa.[29] The memory of personal action is motivated
by the cause, in this case, the anti-apartheid struggle nullifying the possibility of a personal agency outside of the political arena. It is the collective
voice that is speaking. A more personal voice can also operate within this
mode, as Nuttall notes in her reading of Mamphela Ramphele's *A Life*.[30]
Characterized by Nuttall as more memoir than autobiography, Ramphele's
text serves the cause but in a different way. Instead of empowering the past
by speaking with the force of the collective, the reader is offered a mentor
or role model to follow. Success over adversity and healing over trauma are
achieved not solely through political activism, but through personal exploration and growth. Even though remembering the past is traumatic and
opens up contradictions and problems, ultimately these are resolved in the
service of redemption and reconciliation. The needs of the present are in a
dialogical relationship with these stories of past. As Nuttall puts it,

> In South Africa, the past, it sometimes seems, is being "remade" for the pur-
> poses of current reconciliation. The wounds of the past are being opened for
> scrutiny, perhaps most visibly in the public sphere through the Truth and Rec-
> onciliation Commission (TRC). But this is happening within the boundaries
> of a carefully balanced act of reconciliation.[31]

These boundaries are deliberately cracked open by the second mode of representation, which Nuttall describes as modernist in its rejection of wholeness and coherence in favor of disunity and dislocation. This stance is dis-
comforting and painful and does not accede to the historical push that
Nuttall feels is at play post-1994 for closure, mediation, and healing. This
mode self-consciously resists such ends, viewing them as a debasement of
the memory of trauma, and instead searches for new forms of representation capable of expressing, or at least preserving, the memory of loss. Nuttall
delineates a subgenre of confessional writing within this modernist mode
that is mainly produced by white South African writers. Here the self is presented as split: the present demanding that the past be acknowledged as un-
acceptable in order for the subject to progress into the future. Confessing
to complicity with the apartheid regime, even if one was not an active participant, motivates the writing. This willing assumption of collective guilt
at the individual level is the gel that binds together the fragments of Krog's
book, although in the final analysis, the text remains deliberately modernist and fragmented.

Krog's search for new formal devices to express the phenomenology of her mind (the country of her skull) finds no cinematic corollary in the filmic adaptation of her book, *In My Country*. Conforming to Nuttall's description of the first mode of telling, the film constructs a linear story chronology employing the Institutional Mode of Representation (IMR), Noël Burch's phrase for classical Hollywood narrative and narration.[32] In place since the 1930s and showing extraordinary staying power, the IMR uses continuity editing codes and *mise-en-scène* to create unity in space and time and to enable the construction of the classic cinema narrative. In this structure, the filmic events are organized in a cause-and-effect relationship proceeding in a linear fashion from the beginning of the film to the end, which offers resolution to the problem that propelled the events into action. Characters with particular, well-defined psychological traits motivate the action and move it along, foregrounding the importance of the individual agent in world events.

Of course, not all films in this mode offer complete resolution or closure, and not all characters have clearly defined motives. Genre conventions dictate different approaches to the narrative and its narration. Further, the classic narrative structure has been mediated by European art cinema codes, which loosen the bonds of causality through alterative editing codes, ambiguous characters, and auteurist stylistics. Classic Hollywood narrative has absorbed all of these features and more in its textuality, which may account for its global dominance. The Institutional Mode of Representation is the international mode of representation, which is why Ella Shohat and Robert Stam characterize Hollywood cinema as a term "not to convey a knee-jerk reaction of all commercial cinema, but rather as a kind of shorthand for a massively industrial, ideologically reactionary, and stylistically conservative form of 'dominant' cinema."[33]

In My Country, produced by Mike Medavoy and Robert Chartoff (David Wicht being the only South African producer on board) and released through Sony Pictures, is a Hollywood product as just defined. Krog's confessional autobiography becomes a vintage Hollywood romantic drama between Anna Malan, Antjie Krog's character, and Langston Whitfield, a journalist on assignment to cover the TRC from the *Washington Post*. Initially Anna and Langston are antagonists, separated by race and nationality. Anna is an example of the tormented, guilt-ridden Afrikaans intellectual that passionately believes in the TRC's work and "the power of traditional African justice (*ubuntu*) which is about reconciliation and not revenge."[34] Langston is the reverse figure, a street-smart African American whose own experiences of racism in the United States have convinced him that the TRC is yet another example of how "white people (be they American or South African) have a special capacity for getting away with murder." Both are outsiders because of their "race." "When are you going to stop taking their side against us?" Anna's father asks angrily when he hears that she will be reporting on the TRC for SABC and that she supports the commission unequivocally. Langston, like his namesake, the famous poet Langston Hughes who sought acceptance in Europe, tells Anna, "When you're black and American, every day of your life you're made to feel as if you don't belong."

The tensions between them play out against the background of the TRC. Through a series of events, most of them fictional, the narrative proceeds in a linear fashion toward a reconciliation of their differences. Their romantic desire for each other mediates their ideological differences so that each may enter the other's world without deformation and loss, thus representing at the individual level what the TRC is attempting to achieve at the national one. Their problems—Langston's cynicism, Anna's guilt—resolve when Langston discovers that he does, in fact, believe in redemption and has learned the meaning of *ubuntu*. He can take this moral lesson back to the United States, thus reinforcing the redemptive function that Africans and Africa have played in the western imaginary. He has no regrets about his experiences in post-apartheid South Africa, a point illustrated in the shots of him sitting on the plane back to the United States reading a poem by Langston Hughes. Through camera zoom and voice-over, we see and hear the words:

> *Out of love*
> *No regrets*
> *Though the goodness*
> *Be wasted forever.*
>
> *Out of love*
> *No regrets*
> *Though the return*
> *Be never.*[35]

For Anna, resolution is more painful and requires a significant amount of abjection on her part, a fact, one could argue, that ideologically undercuts the values of the TRC. She is put in the position of the perpetrators applying for amnesty when she confesses to her husband that she committed adultery with Langston and pleads with him for forgiveness. She is forced to reject her family and by extension, her "race," in order to move into the new interracial future. Her brother Boetie's implication in the sadistic tortures carried out by Colonel de Jager, an amnesty applicant, and his suicide after Anna confronts him at their family farm in the Orange Free State, is a direct result of the amateur detective work undertaken by her and Langston. The final scene of the movie is central to the issue of both her punishment and recuperation. As the camera pans over the lush, green beauty of a generic South African landscape, we see a close up of her worn and tortured face and hear in voiceover lines taken directly from Krog's text: "Forgive me, forgive, forgive me." We assume at the film's end that the "country," symbolized through nature and landscape, has indeed forgiven her and that her healing, and by extension the country's, has begun.

By pitting a white Afrikaner woman against an African American man and interweaving their stories with those of the TRC, the film has the potential for ideological subversion. The interracial love story could operate as a double that comments on the racist South African past, its bloodletting in voice and testimony, while perhaps also driving South African history forward by bringing American interracialism to the incipient South African stage. In this scenario, the United States could, however flawed and imperfect, become a role model for the new South Africa. However, none of this occurs, nor could it within the structure of classic Hollywood narration, which demands cohesion and consistency. Oppositional viewpoints are, under this constraint, downplayed or suppressed entirely. As Colin McCabe has pointed out, the classic realist text appears able to admit a plurality of contradictions and opposing subject positions, but in fact, reneges on this promise.[36] Instead, it endorses and valorizes one position above the others, creating a hierarchy or a dominant discourse that, as Pam Cook and Mieke Bernink put it, "acts as the voice of truth, overruling and interpreting all the others."[37]

The dominant discourse of *In My Country* is the unquestioning validation of the religious-redemptive discourse of the TRC and its enactment through public acts of remembering, from which can come healing and reconciliation. Langston and Anna enact the illusion of opposing viewpoints by appearing to take different positions, but in fact, both support the dominant discourse. They are the voice of truth for the audience, interlocutors for the audience, acting as mediators of the difficult legal questions of amnesty, proportionality, and restorative and transitional justice through their own personal identities. Importantly, Langston is not a character in Krog's text, but an invention by screenwriter Ann Peacock to act "as the window into the story from the outside world."[38] Played by Samuel L.

Jackson, Langston follows in a long line of Western/American male characters played by international stars that have dominated Hollywood's representations of Africa, with one exception. Unlike Robert Redford in *Out of Africa* (Sidney Pollack, 1985), Kevin Kline in *Cry Freedom* (Richard Attenborough, 1987), Donald Sutherland in *A Dry White Season* (Euzhan Palcy, 1989), Ralph Fiennes in *The Constant Gardner* (Fernando Meirelles, 2005), and James McAvoy in *The Last King of Scotland* (Kevin Macdonald, 2006), Langston is African American. Thus, while the invention of the character recycles the old colonial trope of using a non-African male as the voice of interpretive authority, the film updates the convention in a way that fits the historical moment of the film's diegesis, adjusting to the sociopolitical realities of the film's setting.

There is another dimension to the role played by Langston in the film. The politics of Hollywood's representations of race have generated much critical approbation in post-colonial circles. But that criticism has in the past two decades been mostly confined to the text and little else. The socioeconomic context in which the text is produced and disseminated around the world has largely been ignored since the demise of the Third World and the concept of cultural imperialism thesis. In its place has appeared globalization, described by Toby Miller et al as a "maddeningly euphemistic term" in which Hollywood appears "as a floating signifier, a kind of cultural smoke rising from the economic fires of a successful U.S.-led crusade to convert the world to capitalism."[39] But as Miller et al point out in their compelling analysis of Hollywood's hegemony, any discussion of culture must acknowledge polity and economy.

Screen texts are commodities whose key appeal lies in their meanings. Socioeconomic analysis is, therefore, a natural ally of representational analysis in seeking to explain global Hollywood.[40] *In My Country* is an example of global Hollywood both textually (through the IMR and the construction of the narrative) and economically. It cites South Africa as one of the production countries of origin (along with the UK and Ireland), but in fact, South Africa's involvement in the film's funding is miniscule (an investment of $20,000 from an NGO, the Industrial Corporation of South Africa). Both leading actors—Juliette Binoche and Samuel L. Jackson—are non-South Africans; the scriptwriter is an ex-South African and long-time resident of Marin County, California; and the main producers are Hollywood mainstays who have been in the business for over twenty-five years. In South Africa, only seven prints were distributed throughout the entire country and the film made around $20,000 at the box office.[41] It would appear then that the primary market for this film was the United States, and thus the casting of Samuel L. Jackson may be seen as a textually embedded marketing technique to help reinforce all those other marketing operations that accompany the distribution and exhibition of Hollywood films. By casting Jackson in the premier role, by inserting him into the story of the TRC, he takes center stage, and in doing so, America takes over the South African story, assimilating it to its own African American narratives of justice and freedom.

The moment of truth belongs to everybody, raising all manner of questions about authenticity: about which modes of representation, in cinema or otherwise, do violence to the dignity of the TRC and which do not. Film has not raised this self-critical question about its own representational intensities, nor has it to date seriously engaged in any criticism of the TRC. Rather, films like *The Gugulethu Seven* and *Between Joyce and Remembrance* are extensions of the dramatic moment, the moment when past and present are fused on screen in the manner of courtroom drama and TV news. Such a long arm (through documentary film) of the moment, such an extension of media from TV and newsprint to the resources of film, is historically and psychologically, socially and politically crucial. Through such work, the moment of transition is extended and captured for endless replay and for the archive. The race to representation is here a race to extend the terms of the political transition before they evaporate into the twenty-first century, where few talk about the TRC. That there is no film yet made which investigates critiques of the TRC seems to mean that the immediate role of the medium was to extrapolate the moment of truth in the way Lindy Wilson and Mark Kaplan so brilliantly managed to do.

Gugulethu Township, Cape Town. *Courtesy Iris Films.*

South Africa's National Film and Video Foundation logo.
Courtesy National Film and Video Foundation, South Africa.

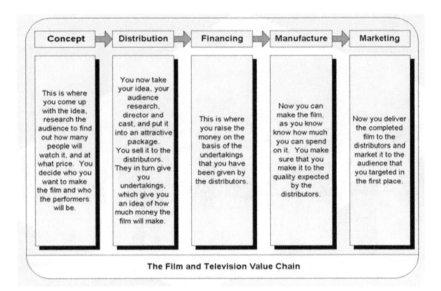

The Film and Television Value Chain. *Courtesy National Film and Video Foundation of South Africa.*

Castle Lager ad, New York.

Johannesburg, 2nd Greatest City After Paris (William Kentridge, 1989).

Illustration for National Film and Video Foundation.
Courtesy National Film and Video Foundation of South Africa.

Director Gavin Hood (*right*) and actors Presley Chweneyagae and Terry Pheto (*first and third from left*) celebrate *Tsotsi* winning the 2005 Oscar for Best Foreign Language Film with South Africa's president, Thabo Mbeki.

Zola Maseko wins the Golden Stallion for *Drum* at Fespaco, 2005.
Courtesy National Film and Video Foundation of South Africa.

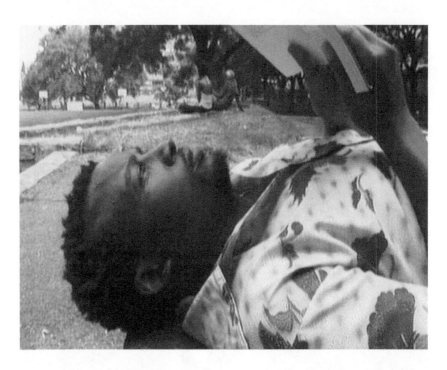

Conversations on a Sunday Afternoon (Khalo Matabane, 2005). Keneiloe (Tony Kgoroge) reads Nuruddin Farah's novel, *Links*, to overcome his writer's block.

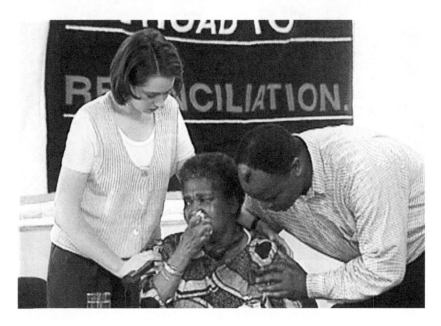

Eunice Miya (one of the Gugulethu Seven mothers) is comforted at the TRC hearings in *Long Night's Journey into Day* (Frances Reid and Deborah Hoffmann, 2000). *Courtesy Iris Films.*

Cynthia Ngewu (also a Gugulethu Seven mother) testifying at the TRC.
Long Night's Journey into Day. Courtesy Iris Films.

Mpondo (Chiwetal Ejiofor) and his lawyer, Sarah Barcant (Hilary Swank), attend
the funeral of Alex's murdered ANC comrade in *Red Dust* (Tom Hooper, 2005).
Courtesy Videovision.

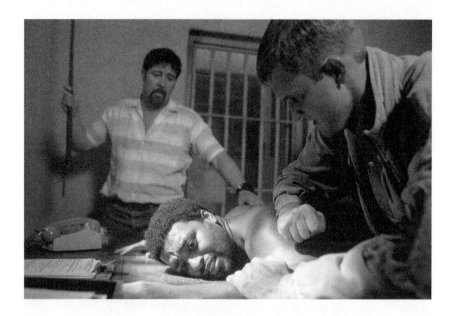

ANC activist Alex Mpondo (Chiwetel Ejiofor) is tortured by Dirk Hendricks (Jamie Bartlett) during apartheid in *Red Dust. Courtesy Videovision.*

Bev and Simon in *Simon and I* (Bev Ditsie and Nicky Newman, 2001).
Courtesy STEPS for the Future.

Joachim reunites with his wife, Rosita, in *A Miner's Tale* (Nic Hofmeyr and Gabriel Mondlane, 2001).
Courtesy STEPS for the Future.

STEPS for the Future series.

A *Luta Continua* (*The Struggle Continues*) (Jack Lewis, 2001).

Tselilo (John Kani) attacks Ashrat (Kurt Eglehof) in *The Native Who Caused All the Trouble* (Marnie van Rensburg, 1989).

Soho Eckstein in *Johannesburg, 2nd Greatest City After Paris.*

Johannesburg, 2nd Greatest City After Paris. Felix Teitlebaum as Kentridge's alter ego.

Prisoners breaking stones in the courtyard in *Proteus* (John Greyson, 2003).

Protea flowers in *Proteus*.

Claas Blank (Rouxnet Brown) and Rijkhart Jacobz (Neil Sandilands)
embrace in *Proteus*.

Relief statue of Piet Retief at Voortrekker Monument, Pretoria.
Photo by Georgio Candiotti, 1998. http://fr.wikipedia.org/wiki/
Fichier:Piet_Retief.JPG

Afrikaner Commandos during the Second Boer War.
http://en.wikipedia.org/wiki/Image:Afrikaner_Commandos.JPG

Plaque inscribed with the Vow of Blood River. The plaque is situated roughly in the middle of where the *Voortrekker laager* stood during the Battle of Blood River. *Photo by Renier Maritz, 2005. The wording of the vow is as follows:*

Afrikaans: Hier staan ons voor die Heilige God van hemel en aarde om 'n gelofte aan Hom te doen, dat, as Hy ons sal beskerm en ons vyand in ons hand sal gee, ons die dag en datum elke jaar as 'n dankdag soos 'n Sabbat sal deurbring; en dat ons 'n huis tot Sy eer sal oprig waar dit Hom behaag, en dat ons ook aan ons kinders sal sê dat hulle met ons daarin moet deel tot nagedagtenis ook vir die opkomende geslagte. Want die eer van Sy naam sal verheerlik word deur die roem en die eer van oorwinning aan Hom te gee.

English: Here we stand before the holy God of heaven and earth, to make a vow to Him, that, if He will protect us and give our enemy into our hand, we shall keep this day and date every year as a day of thanksgiving like a sabbath, and that we shall erect a house to His honor wherever it should please Him, and that we also will tell our children that they should share in that with us in memory for future generations. For the honor of His name will be glorified by giving Him the fame and honor for the victory.

There is no existing verbatim record of the vow. The version above is W. E. G. Louw's ca. 1962 translation into Afrikaans of G. B. A. Gerdener's reconstruction of the vow in his 1919 biography of Sarel Cilliers. *Courtesy http://en.wikipedia.org/wiki/Day_of_the_Vow#Wording*

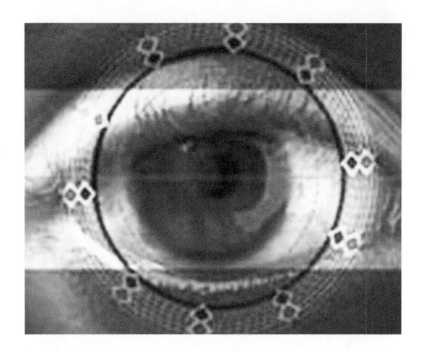

STEPS for the Future logo.

Delegation from the South African Native National Congress (forerunner of the ANC) sent to England in 1914 to object to the 1913 Natives Land Act. Back Row (*left to right*): Walter Rubusana, Saul Nsane. Front Row (*left to right*): Thomas Mapikela, John Dube, Solomon Plaatje. *Photo courtesy University of the Witwatersrand Library, Department of Historical Papers.*

4

Community and Pandemic: Cinematic Interventions in STEPS for the Future

On the one hand there are the masterpieces of transition: the power-sharing government of Mandela and de Klerk, which set a path for the writing of the Interim Constitution of 1994 and the first free and democratic elections in the history of South Africa (that same blessed year). The Interim Constitution in turn mandated the Truth and Reconciliation Commission, and in 1996, another equally blessed year, the TRC began its terrifying, astonishing journey into the history of darkness, in the name of reconciliation and light. Meanwhile, the final constitution appeared (the same year). But there was also something else: signs of danger, incipient disaster, hardly noticed or noticed by only a few, signs of illness, a gathering of storms, more illness. A mere two years later, in 1998, the scales fell from starstruck eyes, revealing disaster. It became clear that 20 percent of South Africans had been infected with HIV, 39 percent in KwaZulu-Natal province, the epicenter of the epidemic. The rate of infection showed no signs of diminishment, and the math showed that in twenty years' time, the majority of the South African population would be dead or dying if the rate of infection continued unabated. From a moment of glory emerged a pandemic. And the government of State President Thabo Mbeki began its disastrous campaign of active AIDS denialism.

AIDS was—it cannot be more tragically ironic—the first gift of South African freedom. It happened in two ways. First, the country's northern borders were opened to commerce, and truckers brought it down in the early 1990s from Mozambique, Zambia, Zimbabwe, and other areas. Second, and most devastating, it was brought by triumphant African National Congress cadres, returning from decades in their training camps outside of South Africa where, as men isolated from families and reared up with the energy of combat, they fell victim to the virus. And, of course, apartheid helped to create the perfect conditions for the spread of the epidemic in the single-sex hostels, where South African black men, living and working on the mines, separated from their families and unable to visit home except at Christmas, bought cheap commercial sex. This was the economy of segregation, where the Natives Land Act of 1913 disenfranchised Africans from owning 70 percent of the land and sent the men reeling to the cities and mines, where their labor was wanted, and of apartheid, where the single-sex hostel became a prison camp, given that the pass laws of the 1950s prevented these men from moving freely in the country and from returning home (had they the cash) at will.

In 1998, State President Thabo Mbeki took the bizarre stance that the human immunodeficiency virus (HIV) did not cause AIDS, but that AIDS was the result of poverty and its concomitant diseases, such as tuberculosis, malaria, and malnutrition.[1] This is not a surprising statement or even an inaccurate one. All diseases are made worse by poverty, a point made by Professor Malegapuru Makgoba, former president of South Africa's Medical Research Council. He then went on to say, "This is so obvious that you would not find a doctor who would say otherwise. However to conflate this factor with causation by clever wordplay is very dangerous."[2] Mbeki had consulted the "AIDS dissidents," academics and scientists who deny that AIDS has a viral cause, in the United States, including a professor of African history, Charles Geshekter, about the relationship between scientific practice, scientific truth, African history, and colonialism. The result was Mbeki's belief that since science had been deeply implicated in the history of colonial racism, that its practices and truths were nothing more than cultural constructions. Thus in 2000, he convened an AIDS panel, to which he invited both mainstream scientists, who believed that AIDS was caused by HIV, and the dissident ones for the purpose of re-examining the causes of AIDS, as if AIDS was a work of literature that one could argue about, and develop different interpretations regarding the motivation of this character or that one depending upon one's perspective. For Mbeki, the only perspective that mattered was the African one. Never trust the West when it comes to Africa and African lives: that was the message he felt he had learned from history, including and especially the violent history of his own country, South Africa. Africa, he came to think, would have to find its own scientific cures, since its diseases were different (distinctively African in symptomatic configuration) and its knowledge systems were unique. He made this clear in a letter he wrote to a number of heads of state, which included Bill Clinton, Tony Blair, and Kofi Annan.

> Whereas in the West HIV/AIDS is said to be largely homosexually transmitted, it is reported that in Africa, including in our own country, it is transmitted heterosexually. Accordingly as Africans, we have to deal with this uniquely African catastrophe. . . . (A) simple superimposition of Western experience on African reality would be absurd and illogical.[3]

Mbeki's attitude toward AIDS may have been a political move. By focusing debate on disease—whether HIV is the cause of AIDS—Mbeki focused it away from the practical question of whether the state should pay for the rollout of antiretroviral medications to pregnant mothers, rape victims, and the population as a whole. But that doesn't explain the depth of his purpose in proclaiming AIDS "denialism" as if it were a major moment in this history of postcolonialism.

For a possible answer, we must look to his development agenda. By discovering specific forms of African symptomatology, Mbeki believed he could show that HIV was caused by poverty-in-Africa, which in turn was the fault of neocolonialism and apartheid, thus assimilating science to development theory. His argument was given force by the fact that AIDS in Africa presented with the classic diseases associated with poverty—tuberculosis, sexually transmitted diseases, and malnutrition. Instead of relying on Western science, Mbeki seemed to be saying that he could cure the disease by curing the economic ills of the continent in the same way that tuberculosis, though a disease that has to be treated with antibiotics, can be prevented by social welfare: clean housing, well-treated sewage, a healthy diet. But even this explanation is difficult to believe given the Mbeki government's economic policy of cutting back on essential services such as water and electricity and reducing spending on health, education, and housing.

Endlessly it was asked: Why did Mbeki take this crazed position and, more importantly, cling implacably to it when every major scientist in South Africa, including black scientists like Malegapuru Makgoba, who had fought hard in the same anti-apartheid/anti-colonial struggle in which Mbeki had been engaged, completely opposed it? Why did he evacuate from his inner circle all those who were critical of the policy or even questioned it? Why, in the face of the scorn of the entire world and an overwhelming amount of scientific evidence about causal etiology (HIV causes AIDS), was he so adamant?

His stance was particularly baffling because Mbeki had never been against medical science per se, and had, throughout those years in which he stubbornly held to the position (1998–2003 and beyond), continued to fund the Medical Research Councils of South Africa in their quest for an AIDS vaccine. Had Western medical science arrived at a cure for HIV/AIDS, it is highly likely Mbeki would have accepted it—and gladly. That medical science had been stymied by the virus, achieving to date neither a vaccine nor a cure, allowed the issue to become a defining one for him.

A RATIONALE FOR THE IRRATIONAL

To many people, Mbeki's stance seemed completely irrational. But a number of rationales have been put forward—not to excuse it, but to explain it. First, at the time (1998–2000) Mbeki formulated his approach, the South Africa government faced exorbitant pharmaceutical costs, felt it could not afford antiretrovirals (remember, we are talking 20 percent of a population of fifty million), was uncertain about their true value in prolonging life, and was, in spite of its neoliberal position, furious at the international system of capital which was making mega-profits from drugs. The antiretroviral cocktail has serious side effects, which he and his cabinet exaggerated into a vision of death by cure.

Second, his postcolonial vision favored the indigenous in all things—this was part of his call for an African Renaissance. The goal was to seek African cures for African diseases in the rich botanic environment of the southern African region or in its long history of indigenous medicine. Had a plant been found in South Africa with the magic properties of curing or preventing transmission of this disease, suddenly he would have come around and said, "Yes, HIV does cause AIDS and look, we've found our own cure."

Third was the absolute fury, chagrin, and rage he felt at a state of nature, which had yet again formed an attack on the sexual prowess and freedom of the black African man who, as he saw it, had been systematically stereotyped as licentious and sexually depraved throughout the history of colonialism (which is largely true) and was yet again being branded as less than human by Western medicine. This profiling seemed to be a continuation of colonial violence by other means, a way of keeping the black African man

down just at the moment of his glorious emergence into postcolonial democratic freedom.

By 2002, the Treatment Action Campaign (TAC) had sued pharmaceutical companies for refusing affordable medications. It had also sued
Mbeki's government for its refusal to roll out antiretrovirals on the grounds
that the South African constitution states that its citizens shall have universal health care. The government continued to proclaim that a so-called indigenous diet of lemon, beetroot, garlic, and potato would do better in fighting HIV/AIDS than any medical cocktail.

This tells us that a response to state recalcitrance in a moment of national crisis in fact contributed to the formation of the new public sphere,
since for the first time former activists in the anti-apartheid struggle, for
whom party loyalty trumped all else, felt the need to stand up and voice
their dissent. A culture of non-violent but highly effective dissent emerged
from 1998–2003. Sadly, this did not stop the deaths. In 2008, a study by Harvard researchers concluded that 365,000 South Africans (35,000 of whom
were babies) had died premature deaths from HIV/AIDS as a result of not
receiving antiretroviral drugs during the years of the Mbeki presidency. The
researchers blamed the deaths on health policies that grew out of Mbeki's
denialism, stating, "We contend that the South African government acted
as a major obstacle in the provision of medications to patients with AIDS."[4]
It is now believed that one thousand people die of AIDS in South Africa
every day.[5] To place that figure in context, the total number of people who
died in the Northern Ireland conflagration with England over a thirty-
year period was around five thousand, or five days' worth of South African
deaths.

This discussion not only sets the historical context against which one
must read the cinema's engagement with AIDS, but also provides the subject
matter of many films. In *Ho Ea Rona* (*We Are Going Forward*) (Dumisane
Phakathi, 2002), the terror of finding out if one is HIV positive and the regrets that accompany such a disclosure emerge in the conversation of three
young men, Thabo (better known as Kwasa Kwasa), a local disc jockey;
Thabiso, a former boxer; and Bimbo, the intellectual of the group gather
together for a weekend *braai* (barbecue). Through anecdote and reminis-
cence of happier times, when they were free of the disease, when they were
young students at university, the sadness of their situation emerges in fits
and starts. There is no question of a polemic or sermon: Phakathi's camera
is too novelistic for such treatment. It roams, picking out the details that

suddenly emerge from the background—a dog sniffing around, meat being cut for the *braai*, a skateboarder, a friend passing by who is invited but
appears reluctant to join the group. Thabiso's mother walks into the frame,
perhaps returned from church or the town, as she is elegantly dressed. She
tells us he is naughty, but she's happy she can say this about him. It con-
firms his liveliness, his presence. Then she pauses, her voice dropping, her
head slightly moving from side to side as she is contemplating something
incredible, unbelievable. I have already lost two children to this disease,
she says. Tragedy suddenly intrudes into the convivial scene. And so it is
throughout the film, this alternation between sorrow and joy, humor and
sadness, braggadocio ("it's been a hell of a ride," says Thabo), and vulnera-
bility. *"Ho ea rona"* (We are going forward), the men sing, spontaneously
breaking into an old struggle song from their youth. Phakathi cannot show
us everything. That is impossible. But the things he does show us, although
they appear spontaneous, have a logic and tell a moral story that one cannot fail to grasp since it is lifted from reality. The last image completes the
story. It is of two little boys, each no older than three or four, who mug for
the camera, one tilting his head to the side and placing his arm akimbo in a
classic pose of cockiness. We complete the thought in our minds: If nothing
is done, if nothing changes and treatment is not made available to everyone
who needs it, these boys are doomed, and so is the future.

The documentary *Simon and I* (Beverly Palesa Ditsie and Nicky Newman, 2002) is a history lesson from below, not the kind of grand narrative
that speaks of the struggle against apartheid, but a narrative of the struggle
waged by two people—both black, both gay—in the fight for gay and lesbian
liberation. Ditsie, or Bev as she calls herself in the film, met Simon Nkoli,
one of the founders of the movement, when she was seventeen years old.
He became her mentor, opening her eyes to the fact that she was doubly op-
pressed, both as a black and as a lesbian. They take different paths in their
struggles. Bev agitates on the behalf of gay rights, while Simon, who is dying
of AIDS, becomes more involved in the AIDS movement. Many years have
passed between them, but in the face of Simon's impending death, they re-
unite and relive their experiences, the battles and defeats that form the material of a life in activism. We are witness to their personal stories, so personal at times that Bev confesses that there have been moments when she
has felt herself unable to continue with the process of filming. This admis-
sion makes us aware of the emotional cost of making this film, a point that
we cannot fail to grasp in one particular scene. Simon is in bed, ravaged by
AIDS, and Bev lies next to him, stroking his hands and his face. At this mo-

ment, we feel our presence to be an intrusion, precisely because it is a moment in which we share fully in their feelings, and also because we realize that the sadness that we, and they, feel does not come only from the fact that Simon is dying and Bev is losing a part of her life, but from the place this scene holds in the entire tragedy that is unfolding throughout South Africa.

Mother to Child (Jane Thandi Lipman, 2001) is a direct assault on the state's recalcitrance in rolling out a comprehensive mother-to-child antiretroviral program for HIV-positive mothers-to-be. One dose of Nevirapine, an inexpensive drug administered during the birth process, prevents transmission of the virus to the newborn baby 50 percent of the time. But the government will not listen, even to the doctors who urge them to provide the drug. In this documentary, we follow the lives of two HIV-positive pregnant women, Pinkie Nocwezo and Patience Mqoqi, who are among the fortunate few enrolled in a Nevirapine drug trial at the Chris Hani Baragwanath Hospital in Soweto. They are still consumed with terror at the thought of transmitting the virus to their newborns. They endure the terror of waiting to find out if the drug has worked (their infants test negative) as well as the trauma of disclosing their positive status to their families and partners. To be a witness to their traumas only makes one recoil with horror at the thought of what women in their position who are not on the trial must be suffering.

Night Stop (Licinio Azevedo, 2002), a documentary shot mainly at night, gives an eerie insight into the sex trade from the point of view of the gangs of prostitutes who service the male truckers traveling along what is called the Corridor of Death, a long-distance trucking route in central Mozambique where more than 30 percent of people are HIV positive. There is competition between the women as they vie for customers. They have been in AIDS prevention; they have condoms; but of what use is this knowledge, says one prostitute, when you have to compete for business and the men pay more for unprotected sex?

A Miner's Tale (Nic Hofmeyr and Gabriel Mondlane, 2001) is a searing indictment of the migrant labor system and the role it has played in the spread of AIDS. Joachim is from Mozambique, but he has lived and worked on the mines in South Africa for many years, far from his wife and family. Consequently, his life has been carved into two unconnected pieces, split between two countries, with a senior wife in Mozambique and a junior one in Johannesburg. He is HIV positive, and he intends to tell his Mozambican wife about his status when he returns to his village after a thirteen-year absence. But he knows that his status will cause great conflict in the village, for he is expected to impregnate his wife. In one scene, a traditional healer urges him to have unprotected sex with her so that she can conceive, assuring him that since his marriage is a good and truthful one, he will not infect her. How can he fulfill his duty to his wife and his community without exposing her and the unborn child to the virus? Joachim's dilemma is one facing many mine workers who are forced to leave their homes and their families for work on the mines. These dilemmas are not easily resolved.

STEPS: THE SOCIAL TRANSFORMATION
AND EMPOWERMENT PROJECT

All of these stories and more belong to STEPS for the Future, a media-advocacy project that has delivered thirty-six films of all lengths from six African countries using a variety of styles within the documentary genre about people living with HIV/AIDS. And the emphasis here is on the living. According to its manifesto,

> The STEPS collection portrays stories of people dealing positively with HIV, epitomized by a group of HIV+ people in the film, A Luta Continua (The Struggle Continues). They say, "HIV is not a death sentence!" By focusing on the lives of ordinary people living positively with the disease, by refusing to be pedagogic in approach, and by allowing people with HIV/AIDS to take control of their own representations, the films open up discussion about/on the existing prejudices and misinformation which contribute to its spread.[6]

The project was the brainchild of a South African filmmaker, Don Edkins, and a commissioning editor from Finnish public broadcasting, Iikka Vehkalahti. The Scandinavian countries, the Netherlands, and the Soros Foundation board—that triumvirate of European progressivity—provided the funds to get it underway in 2001. Local documentary filmmakers worked in tandem with people who had stories to tell about themselves or about others living with HIV/AIDS. The purpose was not to instruct, to scare, to terrify, or to preach. The scientific facts were there, but so were the feelings, the cultural complications, the local situation, and the individual personality—all necessary ingredients for building identification with the audience, which could then be used to initiate a dialogue or open up a conversation.[7] There were facilitators, often the very people who had been in the movie, accompanying the showing of the films. For example, when Mother to Child was shown at a maternity clinic in Alexandra Township, Pinkie and Patience appeared at the end of the film, urging the women to get tested and learn their status before giving birth. For without that knowledge, they cannot be provided with Nevirapine when labor begins. Their job is "to stand before the audience and say, here is my story and here I am to answer your questions."[8] That simple statement has been, according to Sister Peggy, who runs the Mother-to-Child Prevention Program at the clinic, amazingly effective in terms of getting women to take the test.[9]

Identification, action, activism, and empowerment are all part of the message. At the discussion following the showing of A Miner's Tale in Xai-Xai, Mozambique, a young woman described a similar happening in her village.

> There is a man in our village who worked in South Africa as a miner. He got his wife pregnant and then the wife gave birth and the child died. They all died, the husband then the wife. They left two orphans. The government took them.

And a married woman avowed, "If I find out that my husband is HIV positive I will not sleep with him unless we use a condom. That is what I have learned from this film."[10]

The films have been shown on television, but they have also used less-traditional exhibition sites such as university halls, church halls, police stations, clinics, private homes, and even shopping malls. (In A Luta Continua, we see people watching the film on a large screen in the mall.) Mobile cinema units screened the films outdoors in rural areas. These sites provided an opportunity unavailable to the television audience: they permitted two-way communication, which allowed the viewers, with the help of the facilitators, to personalize the stories, to make them relevant to their own lives and circumstances, a process that Hollywood has long understood and developed through camera angles, point-of-view shots, continuity editing techniques (shot/reverse shot), and character construction.

THE STRUGGLE CONTINUES

Out of the government's AIDS denialism has sprung a new generation of public activists, including those from the TAC and other related organizations. Many of these players have had to reformulate their relationships to the state, replacing vows of party loyalty forged when the African National Congress was an illegal, underground (Marxist) movement with a critical action-based consciousness that has, ironically (and thankfully), built a dynamic public sphere in post-apartheid South Africa. Civil society has grown in response to the pandemic. These are steps to the future of the new democracy, which, if it should survive this terrible plague, will emerge with stronger courts (which have sued the government over health policy) and critical voices. The STEPS project is a filmic experiment which has, in its own small way, contributed to building this public sphere.

A *Luta Continua* (Jack Lewis, 2001) is one such film in its fierce criticism of Mbeki's denialism. Triumphant, singing voices usher in the film. The camera swings upward on a crane shot of a shack in Khayelitsha Township outside of Cape Town. Then we are in the taxi with a group of young HIV-positive activists. It is their voices we heard in the opening and hear now. We follow them to Nyanga Junction, a local mall, where their own films are being screened in the concourse for everyone to see. These films are personal stories about their own experiences of living with the virus. "I never thought of using a condom," says Busisiwe Maqungo, a young woman with fashionably braided hair wearing an HIV POSITIVE t-shirt. "There were all these messages about AIDS, and condoms, everywhere, everywhere. But I never paid attention." We learn that she gave birth to a baby girl. We see a photo of her beautiful child. But then we are told that she was very sick and in and out of the hospital all the time. One day, Busisiwe went to the hospital and found her bed empty. Then we see the grave with Busisiwe sitting in front of it, on her knees, and in the background, the iconic outline of Table Mountain that appears on many of the tourist brochures advertising Cape Town as the new destination of choice for the adventurous traveler. The juxtaposition between the two images is startling and reminds us that HIV/AIDS is alive and well in paradise.

There is another story, this time of success. Nontsikelelo Zwedala is only twenty-five and she is dying. Her T-cell count is almost negligible. At home, her family, terrified of the disease, put aside a special bowl and utensils for her alone. She is a shadow of her former self, a stick figure. Then the miracle of antiretrovirals, made available through a special program, raises her cell count and restores her to human form. She is able not only to survive, but to take action, to become an actor in the struggle against the indifference of the state and the stigma of the disease.

At another point, the film circles back to the audience in the mall. The group—Busisiwe, Nontsikelelo, and Mathew Damane—are there, not on a podium or stage, but in the middle of the throng to answer their questions. Why don't the whites get sick with this disease, asks one man? Why is it only the blacks who are dying? The whites do get sick, explains Busisiwe. But they have money for drugs so they can survive. We are poor, so we die. Later, Busisiwe is in London to attend a conference on HIV/AIDS in

London as a representative for the Treatment Action Campaign, the activist organization started by Zackie Achmat, whose own story is told in *It's My Life*, another film in the series. At the end of the film, the group gathers to come up with a title for the film we have been watching. They decide to call it *A Luta Continua* because for them, this is the new struggle.

These films have vested the camera far and wide to a diverse population. Their populism has been an excellent example of the government's call for a radical democracy comprised of many voices on the radio, in the cinema, in the press, and in literature, all drawn from the South African population. There is a history of populism in the cinema in general and in South Africa in particular which dates from the struggle against apartheid and has proven relevant to the formulation of the STEPS enterprise. We can position the STEPS project within the tradition of experimentalism that developed in ethnographic documentary filmmaking in the late fifties and sixties. Prior to that period, indeed since the days of Robert Flaherty and *Nanouk of the North*, indigenous peoples had been in front of the camera as the objects of its gaze, not as part of the production process. Through the camera, the filmmaker spoke *for* them as opposed to *with* them. Things began to change in the late fifties and early sixties as the idea of an all-knowing filmmaker delivering the truth about his subjects was challenged. Ethnographic filmmakers in Peru and Bolivia collaborated with the indigenous people in recording their struggles against neocolonialism and exploitation.[11] In *Yawar Malku* (1969) and *Ukamau* (1966), Jorge Sanjines combined both fiction and documentary narrational modes, thus breaking away from the traditional method of presenting only factual information about the world.

Jean Rouch is the big name of this filmmaking style with his "ethnofictions," films that directly confront the question of the camera's relation to reality in documentary. Concealing the camera in an effort to be unobtrusive and impartial was, for Rouch, a deceitful act, an attempt to play down the subjectivity of the camera and enhance its objectivity, and of course in the process, empower the filmmaker as a producer of "truth." Rouch coined the phrase *cinéma vérité* to describe a style of documentary that acknowledged both the subjective and objective attributes of the camera, the fictional and the factual. The narrative space of the documentary could now open itself up to greater aesthetic experimentation without the fear that it was betraying reality.[12]

Rouch's radical intervention was inspirational and empowering. Since then, people, particularly those from marginalized groups, have claimed the right to create their own representations—a claim that involves access to technology. But without access to the means of distribution and exhibition, without access to the media (defined in its broadest sense), the films are fated to remain anthropological objects, which is not what they were intended to be. It is here that we can turn to the idea of community media, which seeks to use media technology as a tool for empowering and transforming the lives of individuals. Community media has had powerful theorizations. In a typology of normative media theories, Dennis McQuail describes the "democratic participant theory," a theory with origins in the Socialist democracies of Europe.[13] Like all normative theories, this one offers a view of how the media functions (what is) and how it ought to function (what should be). Democratic participant theorists are disillusioned with "what is." The overwhelming dominance of mass media monopolies (both private and public) have, they argue, subverted the concept of democracy. No longer is the media a forum for democratic participation at the grassroots level.

New competitors are absorbed through mergers and takeovers—the media industry's jargon for these practices is "synergy"—resulting in a closed economic system. There is no access point for those without capital in a business climate dominated by large media conglomerates operating as oligopolies. Adding the notion of social responsibility to that of freedom of expression, a concept that emerged out of the Hutchins Commission on the Freedom of the Press conducted in the United States in 1947, is also inadequate.[14] Calls for self-regulation by media institutions place too much trust and power in the hands of media professionals and watchdog organizations that have become institutionalized and distant from the people. Within this climate, diversity, choice, and self-regulation stand little chance of winning out against industrial convergence and institutional consolidation. On the other hand, "what is" also contains the new media technologies which democratic-participant theorists see as holding out tremendous potential for democratizing media provided that new structures of ownership and usage replace the current repressive ones in order to realize these potentialities.

Under the title of "Constituents for a New Media Theory," Hans Magnus Enzenberger, one of the chief proponents of this approach, provides a list of what a democratization of the media would entail. Decentralization would replace centralization. Each receiver would be a potential transmitter as opposed to the old mass-society program of one transmitter, many receivers. There would be a mobilization of the masses instead of the current immobilization of isolated individuals. Interaction and feedback would replace passive consumer behavior. Media would be engaged in a political learning process as opposed to one of depoliticization. Collective production would replace production by specialists. And finally, social control by self-organization would replace control by property owners or bureaucracy.[15] Many of these ideas influenced the shape of community media in post-apartheid South Africa.[16]

A brief history: In the 1990s, the terrain of community media in South Africa was shaped by a number of events. One of the most important was the Jabulani! Freedom of the Airwaves Conference held in the Netherlands in 1991. The conference sought to give a voice to a variety of groups who felt they had been marginalized and excluded from the official, government-appointed task group set up earlier that year to investigate the restructuring of the South African broadcasting industry in light of the coming democratic changes.[17] Composed solely of white men with no representation from the community media, advertising, or marketing sectors, the task force issued a document, the Viljoen report, that was considered inadequate to the task of restructuring media and society linkages in post-apartheid, democratic South Africa. Despite this, two major recommendations emerged from the conference and the report: The first was a proposal to establish an independent agency for regulating broadcasting in South Africa, which eventually led to the establishment of the Independent Broadcasting Act in 1993. This act created the Independent Broadcasting Authority (IBA) in 1994, which took over those broadcasting tasks previously under the control of the Minister of Home Affairs and the Post-Master General. These tasks included the licensing of broadcasters, the formulation of broadcast policy, the monitoring of license and program conditions, the planning of the frequency spectrum, and the adjudicating of complaints in the newly regulated environment.[18]

The second proposal was for a third tier of broadcasting, community broadcasting, to be added to the two existing tiers of public and private (commercial) broadcasting. The regulator defined community media as a form of media owned and controlled by community representatives drawn from a variety of institutions and organizations within a localized community: youth, civic, gender, religious, school, cultural, trade unions, and others. It was not profit driven, although the need to place the enterprise on a solid financial footing was acknowledged as a necessary goal for self-sustainability, one of the key problems facing all community media workers.

One of the major differences between community media and commercial media is the scale of the enterprise.[19] Community media are small-scale media with small-scale resources and small audiences. They concentrate on particular communication environments defined by such factors as culture, values, language, geographical location, common interests, or, in the case of STEPS, illness. They reflect the ideas of advocacy or special-interest groups in their specific locales. Based on the premise that people need to be able to represent themselves and their communities in the media; that access to media should not only be market driven but also serve as a channel for self-empowerment, community development, and grassroots democratization; and that not all media should follow a national, centralized, professionalized model, conceptually community media bears a family resemblance to access or developmental media, participatory filmmaking, shared filmmaking, dialogical anthropology, the Latin American idea of *comunicación popular*, and indigenous media (as exemplified by the Kayapo Indian Project).[20]

THE FACE OF HIV/AIDS

Brian Tilley's documentary, *It's My Life* (2001), produced for STEPS, is about the life of TAC founder Zackie Achmat. His organization successfully sued the South African government for failing to roll out an antiretroviral program to pregnant women by framing it as human rights issue, and then turned around and helped the government in its case against the pharmaceutical industry's claim to patent rights, which, with the TAC's help, the government won. When the government failed to take advantage of its victory, which permitted the purchase and distribution of generic antiretrovirals, the TAC launched a massive civil-disobedience campaign to push for universal access to antiretrovirals. Again, the group was successful. In 2003, the cabinet overruled Mbeki's embrace of denialism and voted to begin to roll out the necessary drugs. Since that time, it has been an ongoing struggle to force the government to live up to its promises, and to pressure companies into providing health care for their workers who contract the virus. Achmat has been central to all the struggle and conflict despite his own HIV-positive status.

It's My Life was filmed over a five-month period in 2001, during which time Achmat, in a gesture of solidarity with the thousands of HIV/AIDS sufferers who did not have access to treatment, refused to take antiretrovirals. The film gives us the facts on the ground: the number of people infected by the virus, the government's failure to provide them with antiretrovirals in the public hospitals, and Mbeki's denial of the link between HIV and AIDS. Despite this fact, when the TAC supports the government in its battle against the pharmaceutical companies' patent suit to stop the state from allowing people to buy generic AIDS drugs and files a brief with the court on the government's behalf. This is a delicate time for the TAC, politically and morally. It is coming to the aid of the enemy, fighting for the other side. We learn why through conversations between Achmat and his ex-partner and housemate, filmmaker Jack Lewis, and in interviews with the press, both national and international, who have gathered to see how this battle will turn out. If the government wins, says Achmat, they will have no excuses left for not providing antiretrovirals to all those who need them.

Achmat shuttles between the court and the crowds gathered outside, many of them wearing the TAC's red t-shirts with the words "HIV POSI-TIVE" on the front. Then, there is success. The PMA withdraws the suit; they look like monsters in the eyes of the world. The government can pass a law allowing South Africans to purchase inexpensive, generic antiretrovirals. But that is not good enough. Achmat and his organization are fighting for the impoverished majority who cannot afford even generics. They want a national rollout, free drugs for everyone in need, but particularly for HIV-positive pregnant women to prevent transmission of the virus to the newborns. When the decision comes down, Achmat is not there. He has been ill for a number of weeks, battling an infection. His friends gather at his house, upset by his condition and his continued refusal to take antiretrovirals. His sister comes to help Jack care for him. He explains his position to his worried compatriots, to his family, to news reporters, and to us:

> My decision not to take antiretrovirals is a very difficult decision for me to have made because I can tell you just from last week when I couldn't speak and my mouth was very sore I wanted to say, maybe I should take medication . . . but our politics have become generally empty of moral content. . . . In terms of the majority of people with HIV, they don't have a face, they don't have the political understanding; they are desperate, they are poor, they are alone and to advocate for their medicines is a very difficult task—for all of us, that's all our job. But me personally, with HIV, as someone who could access medication through friends and medical aid . . . I can't look them in the eye when I take medicines and I know they are going to die because they can't get medicines, and I cannot lead them if that is the case. I want the right to life for myself, but I want to live in a political community in which that right is extended to every person.[21]

The words are incredibly moving and a testament to his extraordinary integrity and courage. But what sends an even stronger message is his face. It is an appealing face, open to the world and therefore to us. Even if it were a closed, angry one, it would still be the "image fact" (to use the phrase coined by André Bazin) that allows us to understand what is happening, because it does not isolate the object, in this case, the face, from its surroundings, but associates it with the entire scene. It is his body and his face, his movements and expressions, that communicate something beyond what his words can convey. And because he is ill, and we know that it is potentially a deadly illness, we scan his face even more closely than we would otherwise, fascinated by its physiognomy. The power of the image in this film lies in Achmat's face, which is shown in close-up a great deal of the time. His face fills the space of the screen and becomes a canvas across which flit a variety of emotions: sadness, determination, anger, fear, and pleasure. And all of these emotions occur in a split second of time, yet we register and understand each one, both separately and together.

Béla Balázs, a theorist from the days of silent film, when the image was everything, believed that the cinema could recover the small world for us, revealing all its intricacies and secrets. We required this kind of visual redemption, for despite our own visual abilities, we had lost the art of seeing. Sunk into the abstraction of modernity, we no longer perceived life as having a materiality. Man had become "invisible," thus the title of his 1924 book, *Visible Man*. A number of theorists writing about film at the same time as Balázs, such as Sergei Eisenstein and Siegfried Kracauer, put forward similar ideas on the redemptive quality of the cinema, but Balázs's unique contribution to the debate was his emphasis on the close-up as a restorative tool. All close-ups provided naturalistic details, but only the good ones were revealing of what was hidden beneath the surface.

> In films with many good close-ups you often gain the impression that these shots are not so much the product of a good eye as of a good heart. They radiate warmth, a diffuse lyricism whose particular artistic significance is that it moves us without lapsing into sentimentality. It remains impersonal and objective. A tender feeling towards things is aroused without being made explicit (or described in the usual clichés).[22]

A "good close up" did not just happen. Expressiveness did not shine through the face in an unmediated way. On the contrary, the actor, the cameraman, or the director had to make the hidden visible through performance, framing, *mise-en-scène*, and editing—in short, through the art of the cinema.

How do these ideas apply to the film? Achmat is not a professional actor with a full range of expressive capacity. The film is a conventional documentary and limits experimentation in lighting, setting, and color to reality. We see Achmat preparing speeches and delivering them, flying to one meeting and another, entering and exiting airports, getting into cars. We also see him at home, in bed, eating soup prepared for him by his sister, talking on the phone. At one point, when he is feeling well, he dances by himself to the song, *It's Raining Men*. His past is dramatized in only one sequence as he recalls, in voice-over, his first sexual experience with an older white man. The challenge for the filmmaker then is to find a filmic way of bringing us closer to Achmat's substance and texture of this so that we fully comprehend the meaning of his sacrifice and his courage without resorting to clichés (such as the camera panning to birds flying over the sea when we hear that Achmat is sick, while Vivaldi's *Four Seasons* plays in the background).

It must be said that Balázs's theory belonged to the silent cinema and moreover to feature film, when gestures and body movements needed to be as explicit and detailed as possible in order to convey emotional meaning. *It's My Life* hardly fits this category, yet Balázs's emphasis on "the visible man," on the material body and face as the site for meaning and emotion, seems particularly relevant to this film, where Achmat is the event. The camera scrutinizes his face, allowing us to analyze each part of it as if it were a fact, and then put all the facts together. The result is a big picture, but not an abstracted one. His face becomes the face of HIV/AIDS, or put another way, the many close-ups of him put a human face to the pandemic.

WA N WINA; AIDS AND THE AESTHETIC OF REALITY

"I've been told that half of the people my age are going to be infected with the HIV virus by the time they are thirty. I went back to my neighborhood to see how people are negotiating with their lives in this time of the virus." So begins *Wa n Wina* (*Sincerely Yours*) (2001), Dumisane Phakathi's documentary of life and love and HIV/AIDS in his old Soweto neighborhood. The film follows a tripartite structure, each part linked to the other by the omnipresence of HIV/AIDS, lurking in this place where people are living their lives. In the first part, *Impilo* (*Life*), Phakathi's camera introduces us to the life of the street. Two young men, old school friends, joke with him (the camera). Don't forget to film the soccer field where we played when we were kids, they chide. He comes across an old woman, sorting through a heap of used coal for the pieces that still have some life in them. She washes them and reuses them. "We are poor my son, and it is cold," she explains. The street is bare of trees, unpaved, miserable. The light is the thin light of a Johannesburg winter sun. It casts a clear outline of Phakathi and his camera on the ground: the man with the movie camera, filming the life of Soweto, himself being filmed for us to see. The art of the film is on display for a moment. We are introduced to Timothy, a handsome young man. He's the one who always got the girls, says Phakathi. Then we meet Zonke, a cocky young man who always has a hard-on, or says he does. It's a sign of life for him. "I am surviving, I don't have AIDS yet." His brother Mwandile is HIV positive and councils people in the front of the house, while Zonke pumps iron in the back. In one shot, their father, an old man in overalls, stands between them. "My two cocks," he says almost proudly, "they like sex too much."

Phakathi uses a variety of point-of-view shots to present his characters' thoughts and feelings, yet the emphasis is not on the individual characters but on the neighborhood as a whole. The configuration of space in his framing is tight and claustrophobic, embodying what Hamid Naficy calls a "closed chronotope." Taking the concept of the chronotope from Mikhael Bakhtin, who proposed it as a way to analyze the representation of space and time in a text, Naficy uses it to analyze the stylistic components of what he calls the "accented cinema." By this he means those films and filmmakers who, since the 1950s, live and make films in the West, but whose historical trajectory is one of displacement and exile caused by colonialism, nationalism, Communism, or ethnic warfare. They are "the products of this dual postcolonial displacement and postmodern or modern scattering."[23]

According to Naficy, open and closed chronotopes appear in accented films in specific ways. The open chronotope is usually associated with nature, landscape. and external locations, while the closed one is encoded in interior settings that restrict movement and create a sense of phobic suffocation. Yet in all of its three acts, the film configures space and time as closed irrespective of whether the location is external or internal. Whether walking across an open piece of land, sauntering down the road, sitting in a dilapidated schoolroom, singing in the choir, or just hanging around on street corners, the people of Soweto that appear in his film are still imprisoned not only by their economic poverty, but also by the poverty of social relations, especially those at the gender level.

An absence of men in the lives of the women is a recurring theme. A woman cries for her father who has left home and hardly returns to see her. He exists for her as a photo in an album. Then there are the girls, with babies and no boyfriends. "My boyfriend told me that if I used a condom, I would be considered promiscuous," says one, her face heavy with resentment toward her foolishness and her long-gone boyfriend. The baby is sick, and the father is off with another woman, refusing to pay maintenance for his son, who "would be better off dead." The handsome Timothy loves his son, but not the mother. She loves Timothy and longs to be folded into the great family romance of Hollywood. It is not to be. Her face is a study in disappointment and depression as he visits her only to pick up the baby and leave, inflicting so much pain so easily. Phakathi's camera is extraordinarily sensitive to women, whom he often frames in awkward poses, occupying only a part of the frame, or behind some kind of barrier: a wrought iron fence with sharp spikes, a net curtain, a doorframe. In contrast the men crowd the frame, jockeying for position, pushing up close, like a pack of wolves filled with energy and nowhere to go. "It's funny how some things don't change," Phakathi muses. "The guys who were unemployed when I left are still unemployed."

The second part is about Phumla, another teenager with a child and no father. He shoots her from a low angle as she walks across some barren piece of land, looking like a princess in a school uniform, as beautiful as a supermodel, with jutting cheekbones, a full mouth, and an elegant nose. Her life, though, is anything but glamorous. She sings in a choir in a shabby hall, attends a school with teachers who preach about abstinence but don't turn up to teach the students they preach to, is in trouble with the police, relies on her parents to support her and the baby, and drowns her disappointments in a beer bottle. She is furious about the double standard that applies when it comes to what is acceptable behavior for boys and for girls. The boys are excused for behaving badly, while the girls pay the price. It's still the same old story, a fight for love and glory (as the song goes), but in this battle of the sexes, where the boys blame the girls and the girls blame the boys, and in their hearts know that they are both getting the raw end of the deal, life can turn tragic. Children are born sick and die, and beautiful girls with energy and intelligence, like Phumla, self-destruct.

In the third part, *Wa n Wina*, which gives the film its overall title, the oppressiveness of the setting increases, overtakes the characters, and a sense of hopelessness sets in. The camera becomes more frantic, responding to life in the street as it happens, right there, without plan or aesthetic design. It is as if the filmmaker has given up, or rather given in to the power of reality. The quotidian details take on a special meaning. An old woman with a tongue that flicks like a snake carefully takes the new garbage bin she has been given inside, so that it will not be ruined. It is the first new thing she has had from the state in thirty years. The most expressive image of entrenched poverty and deprivation, though, comes at the very end of the film. Another old woman, this time sitting in her kitchen shelling nuts, tells Phakathi that she does not know how old she is. She could not answer the questions that Busi, the census worker who has just departed, had asked her. Anyway, she does not like being counted, but can do nothing to stop it. "It is not our country," she tells Phakathi, and the camera moves from her face to her hands, black and gnarled, cracking the nuts. When he protests, she continues, "It's the white man's country. We left our way of life and came to his place." Her helplessness comes to encapsulate the helplessness of the millions of poor South Africans who have been abandoned by the state. The race to representation ends here, in this place where human beings are frozen, unable to stake their claims to freedom and independence. Phakhati's film shows that, for these people, the race to representation is not happening.

5

Quo Vadis? Counter-Cinema in South Africa Today

The virtual containment of film within capitalist industry and its journalistic and academic extensions has concealed the historical specificity of this one mode of film. As commodity production has become naturalized as the activity of the medium's essence, as its proper and inevitable usage, it has produced the kind of fetishism . . . "that transforms the social, economic character that things are stamped with in the process of social production into a natural character arising from the material nature of these things."

David James, quoting Karl Marx

In the last chapter, we saw cinema taking up a critical stance about a pandemic, engaging the most powerful, indelible, and private questions of sexuality and tradition and the most public questions of community, right to health, and state policy. The steps for the future are many, diverse, and made from multiple places and positions. Thus despite the condition so cogently outlined by David James in the quote above, the films that speak from the point of view of "the people," sharing their voices, their lives, and their problems in the name of radical democracy, are producing a colloquy of voices each entering, indeed comprising and creating, a critical public sphere. For the first time in South Africa, these films are, almost without knowing it, forming an alternative cinema. Earlier in this book, I suggested that the race to representation in the initial moments of a change of state of the kind South Africa has now seen three times demands films which will stabilize anxieties and generate imaginative forms of belonging in the wake of social disruption and the eruption of tremendous uncertainty, if not discontent, if not violence. Such films cannot be, I suggested, unduly critical: whatever criticisms they have must be matched and bested by a deeper sense of *participation*. The steps to the future are participative, but also critical, bespeaking a moment in the first decade of democratic change in which the state lost favor in virtue of its recalcitrant and inhuman policies. But these films were participative in another sense: by way of their populism, their individualities. In this, they stand as beacons for the anti-apartheid call to radical democracy and a public sphere. I suggested these films were in some small way part of the occasioning of a democratically public sphere, not only because of the critical values of some of them, but also because of the expressivist values of all of them.

Critique and individuality are the two signposts for the assumption of democratic freedom. On the one hand we have individuality, which may or may not add up to a larger solidarity; on the other there is critique, which may or may not emerge from the voice of that community. Both are related to formal experimentation, since the history of cinema has been one in which experimentalist shock (dialectical montage, jump cut, elision, narrative intransitivity, multi-vocality, lack of closure, and third stream) has been used to alienate audiences from their comfort zones and break through the illusion, signaling that all is not going well. Experimentalism was also a way of expressing idiom, the narrative inflection, the accented style, the auteurist signature of the camera.

The connection between individuality, critique, and innovation raises the issue of an alternative or counter-cinema in South Africa—one that is more critical, independent, and experimental, but still more organic to place, time, and people than the one envisaged by the state. This chapter is about the development of counter-cinema in a democratic South Africa. It is about the paths that alternative film has taken so far, and the ones that it might take in the future so as to claim the title of "progressive" or "counter. Is aims not to provide a set of theoretical prescriptions: such an attempt would not only be impossible, but also undesirable, a point that was made at the 1986 Third Cinema conference in Edinburgh, where Third Cinema theory and practices were scrutinized for their relevance to, for want of a better label, "oppositional film" and video makers today. What emerged there, a quarter of a century after the "fact" of Third Cinema, was the rejection of anything that smacked of a prescriptive universal third cinema aesthetic capable of embracing all the diverse critical and filmmaking activities under the banner of oppositional cinematic cultural production.[1] The topic of Third Cinema's critical productions is relevant to this discussion given its ideological importance to filmmaking in the third-world countries (including films produced both before and after the concept of a "third world" was in place).

The idea of a Third Cinema first emerged in the late sixties in Latin America, inspired by the Cuban Revolution and Brazilian Cinema Novo, and soon found theoretical expression with the publication of Fernando Solanas's and Octavio Getino's "Towards a Third Cinema," Glauber Rocha's "The Aesthetics of Violence," and Julio Garcia Espinosa's "For an Imperfect Cinema."[2] Continuing the lineage of ringing 1920s manifestos produced by the Russian Constructivists—Naum Gabo, El Lissitsky, and Vladimir Tatlin—the manifestos called for a revolution in filmmaking, both at the aesthetic and the narrative levels, to match the political revolution in politics that was underway in the former colonial states. But they also reveal the contradictory role of the theorist as one who both reflects on what has already been made and at the same time claims to theorize it into existence.[3] Third Cinema set about theorizing films that had already been made as part of the culture of opposition and resistance, films such as Nelson Pereira dos Santos's *Vidas Secas* (*Barren Lives*) (1963) and Getino and Solanas's *La Hora de los Hornos* (*The Hour of the Furnaces*) (1968). Yet also crucial to their position as avant-garde theorists was their attempt to theorize into existence a set of oppositional practices that would find articulation in the films created in the wake of their pronouncements.

In blurring the line between analysis and prescription, reflection and description, empiricism and prophecy, the idea of theory becomes expanded to the point that one becomes unsure of its meaning, an outcome that is difficult to avoid. In retrospect, one can see how the theoretical formulations of Third Cinema became overly prescriptive and hampered innovation. How, then, should we rethink the concept of the progressive, of those productions which might, in one way or another, count as radical or counter-cinema in the changed circumstances of a post-apartheid South Africa, a South Africa which is also that of the post-Communist world, a world dramatically different from the 1960s of the Cuban Revolution? The changes in the world, and particularly in South Africa, must transform the very idea of what it is to be progressive, oppositional, and cinematic. A South African counter-cinema must seek ways that make a difference, for this population group or that, for some or all, in a profoundly diverse society.

In South Africa there is a general failure of institutions to rethink such terms as "progressive" or "opposition" in the new dispensation. Universities, which in the past had clear and obvious terms of resistance to rely on, now find themselves having to invent such terms, while giving in neither to political correctness and the condition of being "in line" with the new power, nor to an old-style Marxism which is frankly unbelievable today. One might recall, with a certain sanguinity, that Marxism was also a theory and practice which diffused itself from north to south, causing Third Cinema to suffer, without knowing it, from global dependency on knowledge producers in the North, in Germany, in Russia, and in America, even while claiming the inheritance of the oppositional practices of such places. This failure of reinvention is, no doubt, also a global affair, an affair of Third Cinema, the "Post-Third World," and the first world. It is a failure, which also takes place in conditions of global dependency on the knowledge productions that give rise to vocabularies, such as the discourses of multiculturalism, post-colonialism, and postmodernism.

The post-colonial world (a phrase that has eclipsed "third world" since the 1980s) is often taken to exhibit the central aspiration to become a nation, and post-colonial culture (be it literature, visual art, film, or the media), not to mention cultural policy, is interpreted and legitimated in the light of the expression of that aspiration.[4] Read within this interpretative framework, the debates surrounding the idea of progressive or radical cinema and media become synonymous with the hotly debated issues of national liberation, cultural restitution, and nation building. The result is that both national and counter-cinemas appear as a single term and a unified field (like the nation) pointing to both a local and a global condition of postcoloniality—one that serves to unify the histories and cultures of countries as diverse as South Africa, Vietnam, India, Swaziland, and East Timor. This is clearly problematic and, in the minds of certain critics such as Ann McClintock, a repeat of the very binary categories that characterized colonial thought.[5] Different forms of colonization, McClintock points out, have given rise to different forms of decolonization. (Although, she continues, given the persistence of neocolonial practices, it is not even clear that postcolonialism is an established "fact" in the world.) "Can most of the world's countries be said, in any meaningful way or theoretical sense to share a single common past, or a single common condition called the 'post-colonial condition,'" she asks?[6] Her remedy for correcting this kind of generic, pan-optic view, out of which terms like "the post-colonial" and "the post-colonial subject" emerge, is to be specific at every level, to acknowledge the political and material facts at work in each case, and to develop theories of, say, gender relations (her specific interest area since she believes that the lack of shared experience is even more evident when one introduces gender into the post-colonial matrix), that are nuanced to the particular situations at hand.[7]

McClintock's critique is pointed at the global diffusion of the word, which obscures differences between nations and potentially continues the heritage of colonial thought. But it is relevant at the local level as well, par-

ticularly in the case of South Africa, where, given its progressive constitution, the nationalist aspiration is potentially always in danger of being
undercut by the goal of radical democracy. The cinema being called for in
the rhetoric of the National Film and Video Foundation's mission statement
and in the search for projects to encourage the development and consumption of South African cinema may result in films that are in opposition to
the ones envisaged by the manifestoes of the state. Radical democracy calls
for individuality through innovation, not simply the idea that one voice
seeks to stand for all others, creating communal solidarity (for the "national
cause").

Nations grow when individuals acquire the means, the confidence, the
wherewithal, and the freedom to speak in their own voices, to innovate so
that they may achieve individual visions. If this is a national goal, it is not
the usual one studied in film writings about a "national cinema." That goal
is, rather, that one size speak for all, that the state become the voice of the
people, that the people together never be defeated. National cinema in the
mode outlined earlier is ideological, about building voices into a choir of
one. In contrast, individuality through innovation is about building liber-
ties. Does this emphasis on the use of film as a form of personal expression,
what Cook and Bernink call "the development of cinematic forms equivalent to first-person discourse,"[8] ruin the possibilities for a collective identity
to emerge? In his discussion on new Caribbean cinema, Stuart Hall argues
that division and difference are, in fact, the materials for constructing post-
colonial identities.[9] The collective voice can speak in a way that openly acknowledges both the fault lines and rifts implicit in the critical and creative
process, and the complete necessity of these characteristics as conditions of
possibility. Filmmakers at the margins, like South African ones, can continue to negotiate a collective identity without imposition, repression, or appropriation.

South Africa has had its share of films aiming to bring about reconciliation by symbolic means, or to show it happening (in the TRC) by making
films that speak of the nation and to its throes. This chapter is about another
register of creation: that of pantheism, diversity, and multiplicity.

A MULTIPLICITY OF VOICES SIGNAL A BEGINNING

We begin by pursuing the importance of individual stories. This focus on individual liberty is central to democracy, whether it be critical of the regime
or not. Such stories are individual ones, but they are also about the big picture: for example, HIV/AIDS, its disastrous effects on individuals and com-

munities, and the (un)responsiveness of state government. Films have also been made in the past fifteen years in South Africa which do not address any big picture, only individual concerns. This is important for the new regime, and may be also seen as part of its race to representation, toward the assumption of individual rights and the filling of the public sphere with diverse films worthy of population, language, culture, ethnicity, idiom—in a word, place. Whether a letter from Soweto (Dumisani Phakathi's *Wa n Wina [Sincerely Yours]*, 2001), a fight in the silent-film world of rough-and-tumble Johannesburg (William Kentridge's *Soho Eckstein* series), a clothing worker's dream to be queen for a day (*Cinderella of the Cape Flats*, Jane Kennedy, 2004), or a story from the past of men being imprisoned and killed for homosexuality (Jack Lewis and John Greyson's *Proteus*, 2003), each is an individual story, a particular narrative of pain and prospect, of displacement and memory, wanting to be rushed into representation after such a long history of suppression, repression, an overwhelming focus on "the struggle," and a lack of means to make cinematic art.

For these filmmakers, the invention of new forms becomes necessary because their stories do not fit easily with the global language of Hollywood or with the avant-gardes that flourished in Europe in the twenties and then, post-war, in the United States of the fifties. These are stories which have alliances with "African cinema" as defined by Francophone scholars, but they do not speak in the name of the nation as is characteristic of the great Francophone auteurs. Some speak privately, choosing the epistle or memoir, others with the force of identities long refused. Like the makers of the STEPS for the Future films, these are people staking their right to free speech. They speak through changes in form, which carry the vividness of story and the force of critique. Some are political, others not—or less so. The constitution gives them the right to speak not on behalf of the nation, but as individuals, calling for greater access to the media, not just in terms of consumer choice (more of the same) but in terms of production. The issue of access is directly linked to the question of diversity—an essential ingredient in democracy. New voices should be encouraged as a corrective to "the skewed legacy of apartheid where public media were turned into instruments of National Party policy; where community media were repressed; where private media are concentrated in the hands of a few monopolies, and where a few individuals from the white community determine the content of media."[10]

One may consider these new voices to constitute "counter-cinema," to use Peter Wollen's term (coined to distinguish Jean-Luc Godard's work from modernism), but with a caveat. The cinematic productions are counter-cinema, but they are also part of the race to representation, the assumption of the right to speech for the first time in South African history as a right extended (in principle) to all and without censorship (apart from the constitutional refusal of "hate speech"). Counter-cinema, as Wollen defined it, was driven by antipathy to Hollywood's mode of illusionism and all the ills provoked by it (spectatorial passivity, unity of text, lack of contradiction, lack of access to the real world). Its features were in binary opposition to Hollywood's: narrative intransitivity instead of narrative transitivity, estrangement instead of identification, foregrounding instead of transparency, multiple diegesis instead of single diegesis, aperture instead of closure, displeasure instead of pleasure, and reality instead of fiction.[11] Wollen saw Godard's work as the continuation of the Soviet school of montage in the 1920s, which includes the conflict montage of Sergei Eisenstein, Vsevlod Pudovkin's additive montage, and the confrontational montage of Dziga Vertov. There is no such clear connection to the early Russian avant-garde in the work of the filmmakers discussed in this chapter. Nor is there a complete rejection by certain films of the institutional mode of representation that Wollen outlined in his analysis of counter-cinema. Both Hollywood and European art cinema practices are present in some films (*Proteus*, for example), while others have their stylistic roots in Third Cinema, neorealism, and what Hamid Naficy has called an accented cinema.[12]

There is an opposition to Hollywood's industrial practices, its colonization of South Africa's screens and minds, the fact that *it* determines and disseminates images of Africa, its history, its stories, and its people.[13] As in postcolonial cinema, these are individuals who gravitate toward the category of "independent filmmaker." Here, "independent" means "autonomous." This is not about South Africa as a nation being autonomous in cinema; it is about South African individuals in a particular global location vis-à-vis global Hollywood being autonomous to exercise individual liberty and so, act as free filmmakers in a South African state. It is not exactly, therefore, about national cinema, but about a nation's capacity to become a place for its own cinematic representations of the colliding worlds of its individuals.

ANTI-APARTHEID CINEMA

This position is not yet "oppositional" if one takes that word to mean an extreme or even revolutionary criticism of place. Indeed it is a race to fulfill the freedoms existent (in principle), and the (limited) opportunities found within that place. This is the sense of oppositional which is allied with individuality. Nothing could be further from the old anti-apartheid position of resistance than this. For anti-apartheid struggle was meant to root forms of representation in languages speaking for, understood by, and in the name of all the people. The aim was communalist, that of solidarity. A cultural worker was a person dedicated to making culture with a capital C. Individualism in film is a break with that past, which was so overwhelmed by its hatred of the system and its political need for vast solidarities across disparate domains that it suppressed individuality and difference, ignoring the ordinary and the everyday. This is sometimes called political correctness.

As it happened, the filmic expressions of this political ideal were those mostly of leftist, white, male, progressive filmmakers whose stylizations were fierce, assimilative of significant traditions of global political filmmaking, sometimes quite innovative, and also very good. Revolutionary culture has always been an unresolved battle between the avant-gardes and populist correctness. The former, at its best, was magnificent but elitist, out of touch with general populations, and inevitably intolerable to the revolutionary state (the Soviet Union's condemnation of Sergei Eisenstein's experimental montage is a perfect example). The latter, at its worst, was oppressive, as occurred in the imposition of Socialist realism by Stalin, which put an end to Eisenstein's formalism and in its place produced political, propagandistic documentaries.

A South African generation of severe and intense political filmmakers, that "fledging South African progressive film movement" in the words of Rob Nixon, appeared in the last two decades before the end of apartheid.[14] Films like My Country, My Hat (David Bensusan, 1981), A Chip of Glass Ruby (Ross Devenish, 1963), On the Wire (Elaine Proctor, 1990), The Schoolmaster (Jean Delbeke, 1991), The Stick (Darrell Roodt, 1987), Place of Weeping (Darrell Roodt, 1986), Freedom Square and Back of the Moon (Angus Gibson and William Kentridge, 1988), The Native Who Caused All the Trouble (Marnie van Rensburg, 1989), Any Child Is My Child (Barry Feinberg, 1989), Windprints (David Wicht, 1989), Mamza (Johan Blignaut, 1985), Jobman (Darrell Roodt, 1988), Saturday Night at the Palace (Robert Davies, 1987), Die Groen Faktor (Koos Roets, 1984), and Last Supper at Horstley Street (Lindy Wilson, 1983) took as their subject matter the horrors of apartheid and set out to counter "pro-apartheid" cinema produced by the then-state.[15] Dominated by young, white, mostly male directors who had studied film theory and production in the United States, Britain, and South Africa, and mostly financed informally or outside of the state's subsidy system by sociopolitical organizations such as the National Union of Students, The South African Council of Churches, European and British television stations, and the English-speaking universities of the Witwatersrand and Cape Town, these films must be seen as part of the mass opposition to the everyday structures of apartheid manifested in school, rental, and consumer boycotts, in strikes and stayaways, in new black trade unions that occurred in the decade following the Soweto uprising of 1976.[16]

Individuality was a luxury for these filmmakers, and would have seemed cheap as an ideal as they faced the 1976 Soweto uprising. This was no time for art for art's sake; it was a race to put into cinematic form the intensity of fire and conflagration. Such films were made as white South Africa began to seriously doubt the sustainability of its regime, and became intensely anxious about its own economic, political, and indeed physical survival. What was in effect a low-key civil war in the mid-eighties revealed to white South Africa that apartheid's social vision was ineradicably flawed and unworkable.[17] Since apartheid had presented itself as a coherent totality, a grand meta-narrative of governance, the unraveling of one part inevitably led to the questioning and eventual unraveling of the whole. These films attempted to contribute to that unraveling, but without a distribution strategy—the films were shown at non-traditional venues like school or university halls, community centers, or alternative film festivals—and without a grassroots movement to support their efforts, the filmmakers were isolated, mostly preaching to the converted. In addition, they faced a severe censorship system under which a number of films were banned. On the rare occasions when a film was exhibited at the multiplex in one of the upscale shopping centers in Johannesburg or Cape Town, it failed to attract an audience. Raised on a diet of European art films and American "indies," the upper-middle class (mostly English-speaking whites) that went to these venues were unprepared for South African films that did not easily fit into these categories, did not necessarily have high production values, and changed the act of going to the cinema from a social event into a political one. The films were well accepted, however, at overseas film festivals where they found an audience among anti-apartheid viewers hungry for validation.[18]

Read against this background, oppositional cinema meant the representation of censored images and the historical events that gave rise to them, and it meant speaking of that which was repressed in the sense of never being spoken of. It also meant projecting a stylistic montage whose force and immediacy realized the political and social chaos at hand, and reaching audiences both within and beyond South Africa in a way that neither sentimentalized the South African situation nor filtered it through an accepted American liberal ideology. Finally, it meant producing a visual document whose fierce political critique could not help but raise the question of utopian liberation.

COUNTER-NARRATIVES OF THE NATION

Many anti-apartheid films interrogated the dominant narrative of the nation through a variety of narrative strategies. Without homogenizing the films, it is striking how the classical tropes of postcolonial discourse are used: rape of the land and its subsequent pollution, human rights versus property rights, and the corruption of colonial law. In *The Native Who Caused All the Trouble*, the nation is revealed as a legal construction of the colonial power that works through property rights to disempower the human rights of the original inhabitants. The law of the land is put on trial, and found wanting. Set in 1937 in the era of segregation, the film tells the story of Tselilo, a black religious leader who takes over a shack in the Cape Flats owned by a South African Indian named Ashrat with the intention of building a church. Wielding an axe, Tselilo chases Ashrat and his family out of the shanty, claiming that the land is his since it is the site on which he and his followers have been worshipping for decades. Although Ashrat is the legal owner of the house and the land, he has no moral claim to it. According to Tselilo, that moral authority belongs to him, and armed with stick and axe, he is ready to take on the brute force of the colonial authorities, in the form of a bellicose policeman named Captain Barnes, to defend his property, which he sees "as much a gift from God as the air we breathe and the water we drink." Tselilo is finally arrested, and a court case ensues. In the trial, God's law, or rather Tselilo's belief in his God-given right to the land, is pitted against property law. Is the nation a creation of men (in this case, white British men), or is it a natural object, a piece of creation in which all God's other creations can participate? Clearly the latter view is the one taken by the film, which supports Tselilo's rights to pursue his dream in the land of his birth.

In *My Country, My Hat*, the nation under the apartheid laws is solidly the creation of men. Natural law has been subverted by apartheid law to the point where human beings need the right documents in order to exist. James Fingo, a homeless black man, does not have a "pass," a permit to work and live in Johannesburg. According to the law, this makes him a criminal, and if he is caught, he will be jailed, fined, and deported back to the homelands, where there is no work and where he does not belong anyway since he was born in Soweto to an "illegal" mother. Without a pass, James does not officially exist, or as he puts it, "When you lose your pass, you lose your life."

His lack of an official "life" makes him desirable to Piet, a working class Afrikaner whom he encounters. Piet is hiding a guilty secret. He has accidentally run over and killed a man whom he believes broke into his house, and if he can shift the blame for that death onto James, he will go unpunished for his crime. The fact that Piet is a garbage collector and that James has been thrown away like a piece of garbage, and the fact that Piet is let off the hook when James finds the body of the dead man and takes his passbook, thus assuming his identity and nullifying the murder in official terms—if James is the dead man, how could Piet have killed him?—are finely drawn pieces of ironic narration. But they are also indicators of a Foucauldian universe at work, in which both master (Piet) and slave (James) are metaphysical cogs in the system of relationships that makes them simultaneously possible within the epistemic regime of apartheid.

On the Wire is unusual for an anti-apartheid film because of its focus on gender and the effects of apartheid on women, both black and white. The historical context for the film is South Africa's ongoing border war with the front-lying states of Angola, Namibia, and Mozambique, which it tried to destabilize during apartheid. This was a hidden war carried out by covert forces and, like all secrets, it festers and becomes a source of infection for the Afrikaans community, represented metonymically by Wouter Fourie, his wife, Aletta, and their oppressive, patriarchal, Christian church. The film proffers a view of the nation as a farm, a piece of earth that has been wrested from the uncultivated land and that must be protected in order to survive, in much the same way as the ranch in the Hollywood western stood for the "garden" against the "wilderness" and also required protection by the cavalry.

The central issue of the film revolves around who is and who is not part of this protected unit. Hence the idea of the wire, and the border fence, which serve as the dividing line between what is acceptable behavior in defending one's land and what is not. Feminist scholars have shown how women have been figured in nationalist discourse in positions that are both contradictory and simultaneous such as guardians of traditional culture, victims of society's backwardness, or symbols of national modernity and progress.[19] In the film, the trope of women as cultural guardians is used as the excuse for enormous violence. Thus, while on border patrol with his group of "recces" (elite reconnaissance battalions recruited by the South African National Defense force in the seventies for the covert border operations), Wouter takes part in the gang rape and murder of a black woman (one of many, we later learn) accused of being a terrorist. Scenes from the rape and murder, shown on video during one of the group's reunions, and the resistance song which the victim sang before she was killed, recur analeptically throughout the movie. The images and the sound of the rape arouse in Wouter an enormous sense of guilt and self-loathing. At the same time, the memory provides a new erotic fantasy for him that is displaced onto Aletta. This dynamic is most explicit in the scene where he binds her wrists with wire so tightly that they bleed and "rapes" her only to find, to his horror, that she is both aroused and terrified by his sexual sadomasochism. The camera puts us in the position of the victim, but it is hard to identify with her because of the pleasure she finds in the act. What we see on the screen is a figuration of what Sumita Chakravarty has called "an erotics of history," which she defines as that force which is suppressed in history, but which requires articulation if there is any possibility of redemption.[20]

Indeed this is exactly what occurs. Wouter begins to lose his mind and sees himself as a polluting agent of his wife, his "tribe" (Afrikaners), and his land. Yet he can only find relief in increasingly violent acts of sex with Aletta, which make him feel he is back in control of his life. The camera dwells in close-up on Aletta's face during sex, indeed it is the only time that we feel we know her. During most of the film she is underexpressed, usually silent with eyes cast down. Outside of the bedroom, she is the traditional Afrikaans woman, strong in feature and body, silent in gesture, and submissive under the patriarchal order. Female sexual desire, repressed under patriarchy, finds alternative outlets. As Wouter grows weaker and more "feminized," losing interest in socializing with his military buddies, opting to stay home and start a family, Aletta grows stronger. She moves outside of the home, goes to the Dominee (a priest in the Dutch Reformed Church) to find help, and when she and Wouter are expelled for their sins with the words "you have learned the ways of demons," she does not crumble. Instead, she is appalled by the hypocrisy of a church that calls on Jesus Christ to give soldiers "the strength and the courage to carry out their duty" and return them safely to the fold. Wouter begins a descent into madness, which eventually ends in his suicide. Aletta's anger opens her to the possibility of redemption signified in the final scenes of the film, which show Aletta burning the grass, clearly an image of cleansing and rebirth. She rejects the Dominee's plea to return to the church. I am going to "take down the fences" and "make a garden here," she says. Lizzie, the black servant who had fled from the farm after learning about Wouter's activities on the border, returns. The final image of the two women, one black and one white, working the land together to cultivate a new home, reinforces the message of a gendered reconciliation.

TOO MUCH THEORY, TOO LITTLE REALISM

In terms of their subject matter, the anti-apartheid films and videos of this period voiced political aspirations resonant with Marxism and filtered through the ideology of third-world liberation movements. However, there was little embrace of the formal experimentation called for by Third Cinema theorists like Jean-Luc Comolli and Jean Narboni to accompany the political themes. Theoretical manifestos, such as theirs, that spoke of developing formal strategies to disempower the realist strength of dominant cinematic signs and codes were, according to film scholars, dismissed by most South African filmmakers as being too intellectual, too indulgent an approach in the face of the current social crisis.[21] And yet, that cannot be an adequate explanation for why formal reinscription, so important to Latin American film theorists and filmmakers, was so easily dismissed by South African ones.

There was no shortage of social crises in Latin America at the time of Third Cinema's conceptualization and diffusion, which although different from the social struggles taking place in South Africa, brought with them immense social dislocation. Yet, Third Cinema did not reject formalism in favor of realism, but took formal innovation to be the aesthetic and political response to these crises. Further, similar hegemonic practices by Hollywood had deformed the history of cinema in Latin America in much the same way as had happened in South Africa. Michael Chanan's description of Latin American cinematic evolution makes this clear.[22] As with South Africa, Hollywood had exercised the same monopoly over distribution since the silent era, offering films at prices that substantially undercut the efforts of local film producers. The bourgeois film audience expected to see Hollywood products and had little inclination to support local products that did not replicate Hollywood stylistics, themes, and production values; and given these market conditions, the banks, many of which were owned by American companies, were unwilling to fund local production. In this climate, local producers could do little but "imitate the Hollywood genres and invent a few of their own—musicals, comedies, and in Brazil nowadays, the pornographic combination of the two known as *pornochanchada.*

Therefore why one style is adopted as opposed to another is an immensely complicated question. One would have thought that in trying to determine how the camera, in the context of glaring social deprivation and repression, could best perform its liberatory task, both Latin American and South African cinema would have embraced a realist aesthetic, perhaps the type of realism espoused by Siegfried Kracauer, when he talked of film's capacity to redeem reality, to inoculate the spectator against spectacle and show the microscopic and the immense. It also seems intuitively appropriate to expect that South African cinema might have embraced, on the other hand, Bazin's aesthetic of reality exemplified by Italian neorealism, which also emerged after a period of enormous political and social crisis. By that same logic, so too would the cinema in the Russia of 1916 and 1922—a land mired in civil war, and then gripped by reconstruction—have turned to realism. And yet the Russian cinematic response, articulated in terms of concepts of social transformation through the heightening of sensation leading to cognition in the form of montage, seems as powerful today as a representation of suffering as anything Kracauer or Bazin would have championed.

So at stake here is not only the question of a choice of styles in the name of a disenfranchised population, but also the question of what realism and its representation of reality is. There are two further points to add to this picture. First, we may recall that when Luis Buñuel, the great Spanish filmmaker, made his shattering documentary on the struggle to survive of an isolated, rural people in the southwest of Spain, *Las Hurdes: Terra Sin Pan* (*Land Without Bread*) (1933), he blurred the distinction entirely between realism and surrealism. Even Bazin, the guardian of cinematic realism, noted that what Buñuel's film revealed is how a surreal world emerges when the camera shows a situation of massive suffering in ways that refuse both sentimentality and explanation by relating what is shown to some grand realist narrative. Second, we may understand the choice of a formalist position by the Latin American theorists not only in the context of their deep links to European avant-gardist thought (despite their rejection of the avant-garde as too bourgeois) and cultural Marxist theory, but also in terms of longstanding Latin American affinities for the baroque. These, combined with a specific sense of the colonial moment as a moment of social rupture and the clash of cultures—"Cortez versus Montezuma"—gave rise to Third Cinema theory.

In contrast, the cinema of Spain, while even more deeply imbricated in the culture of the baroque turns, as Marsha Kinder subtly charts in her analysis of specific Spanish film texts during the Franco era, embraced the stylistics of neorealism.[23] The relationship between cinematic choice and cultural background is conceptually complex and not easily fathomed, as is the more metaphysical question of what the very terms of realism are when the camera confronts the dizzying texture of reality, a reality whose structure is both that of continuity and montage. In terms of trying to explain South African oppositional cinema's lack of textual experimentation, a number of factors seem to be relevant. One can point to an ongoing conservative colonial English sensibility deeply rooted in the texture of the South African colony, which tends to eschew the European diasporic experiments in modernism in favor of a more nuts-and-bolts empirical approach. It is a sensibility that has found general purchase in Anglophone Africa, which has been a filmic desert, both theoretically and in terms of production, when compared to Francophone or Lusophone Africa. There have been many historical reasons put forward by African film theorists and scholars to explain this lack, such as the absence of assimilationist policies in British colonial holdings which led to a dearth of cultural activities, a narrow view of economic colonialism as being strictly a "business affair," and the general poverty of cinema in Britain itself at the time.[24] Within this climate, a climate that has continued to prevail in post-independent Anglophone African countries, the kinds of intellectual thought and cinematic experimentation that one finds in Latin American cinema could not have taken root except in small ways. The lack of film culture in South Africa is an ongoing problem and a constant topic of discussion at film festivals and *indabas*.

One can find explanatory pointers in the critical debates around literature, which has a longer and far more illustrious history in South Africa than does the cinema. Anti-apartheid literature, like cinema, shows a retreat from formal experimentation, so much so that South African writer and scholar Lewis Nkosi, writing in 1960, accused it of being nothing more than "journalistic fact parading outrageously as imaginative literature."[25] Njabulo Ndebele said much the same thing in the 1980s when he claimed that the documentation of oppression did little more than produce "an art of anticipated surfaces rather than one of processes." According to Ndebele, the kind of polemical exposition found in South African fiction engaged the reader's faculty of recognition but did little more. For David Attwell, the structural conditions of apartheid were the cause of literature's commitment to documentation and witnessing through codes and conventions of realism.

> Life under apartheid seems to demand a realistic documentation of oppres-
> sion. Both the White liberal tradition since Olive Schreiner, continuing down
> to the radicalism of Nadine Gordimer today, and contemporary Black prose
> narrative since the era of *Drum* magazine in the 1950s have adopted various
> forms of realism as the unquestioned means of bearing witness to, and telling
> the truth about, South Africa.[26]

According to Attwell, writers who attempted to push politics into the background or recast it in more cosmopolitan terms (here Attwell is talking of
the work of J. M. Coetzee) were viewed with suspicion.[27] As late as 1992, the
ANC Conference on Culture and Resistance in Gaborone deemed art to be
a "cultural weapon," which sounds very much like Third Cinema's call for
the camera to perform like a gun firing at twenty-four frames per second. I
do not, however, interpret this as a call for aesthetic experimentation to accompany the politics of representation. More likely, the imperative behind
the idea of art was driven by a narrow political agenda such as the need
for the ANC to remain "Marxist" in orientation during "the transitional
phase"; that period from the late 1980s to 1994 in which the country moved
toward constructing, in theory and on paper, a new democratic order.

INDEPENDENT BUT NOT RADICAL

There is a contrast between the anti-apartheid formulation of a revolu-
tionary/critical cinema and the new dispensation, in which the critical goal
is to be independent, and so, individual, a citizen exercising his or her right
to freedom of expression. The exercise of freedom of expression is a race
toward the assumption of human civil and political rights, rights also dependent on opportunities (funding, cash, education, mobility) and hence
not available to the majority. This vast limitation on availability and its relation to entrenched poverty and related social ills has not become thema-
tized as yet by these or any films. Rather, it is the telling of individual stories which matters.

With William Kentridge's films, individuality is carried through formal
innovation. Kentridge's first works from the late 1970s were charcoal drawings and prints, but since the late 1980s his art has flourished in the theater,
opera, and the cinema. Continuing in the tradition of the French avant-
gardists from the 1920s—artists like Louis Delluc, Man Ray, Marcel Du-
champ, and Georges Méliès, who sought to extend their formal experiments in painting and photography through the use of film—Kentridge has
combined stop-motion photography and drawing with charcoal on paper

to redefine animation as a visual art. The animation of the drawing is, for Kentridge, an extension of the process of drawing, not a fundamentally different form:

> What does it mean to say that something is a drawing—as opposed to a fundamentally different form, such as a photograph? First of all, arriving at the image is a process, not a frozen instant. Drawing for me is about fluidity.[28]

His animation technique matches his philosophical stance. It is artisanal, unusual in our age of complex computer-generated imagery. Think of the number of artists credited in a Disney or Pixar movie, and the contrast is overwhelming. The formal simplicity ("it is more about making a drawing—albeit a grey, battered and rubbed-about drawing—than making a film") permits Kentridge to exercise complete authorial control over what is traditionally a highly segmented team process.[29] He draws in charcoal on paper, photographs the drawing, erases parts of it, redraws, and records. This process of drawing, recording, and erasing is painstakingly repeated numerous times to produce the films. By rubbing out and redrawing on the same surface with charcoal, Kentridge builds up a record of the changes he has made, producing an aftereffect that acts as a counterpoint to the conventional animation process, which seeks to efface the act of transformation.

Kentridge's technique slows down image change like an anchor, reminding the viewer of where the movement came from in the very moment that it is occurring. Each frame carries the traces of what has come before. Imperfection and chance are an intended part of the effect. Charcoal is not a precise medium. It is not easy to erase and always leaves a trace on the paper. Also, the camera is shaky. Kentridge celebrates these "contingent" facts and their contribution to "a film with a very specific nature, for which I have to take responsibility, but which was not consciously, deliberately or rationally planned."[30] Importantly, editing takes place in the camera, each drawing being the equivalent of a sequence, not a shot. The shots are not preserved as they are in the conventional cinematic process; instead, Kentridge explains, "a film of the drawing holds each moment," as that actual stage of the drawing no longer exists.[31] A complete film can require up to twenty-five drawings, each one altered numerous times.

The artisanal quality of the animation, delight in object transformation, and richness of Kentridge's imagery return the viewer to an earlier stage of cinema, to the cinema of the French avant-gardists—in particular, to the cinema of Georges Méliès, whom Kentridge has explicitly acknowledged in his suite of films, 7 *Fragments for Georges Méliès* (2003). In theorizing the potential of the cinema as an art, Méliès privileged what he called "transformation views" or, to use his preferred phrase, "fantastic views," in which he included "trick shots" (a phrase he did not like for its cheap connotation). It was in the construction of "fantastic views," which required all the techniques of the other arts, that the art of the cinema, the seventh art, was to be found.[32] For Méliès, the art of the cinema lay in its formalism, which in turn lay in the construction of the *mise-en-scène*. And nowhere is the *mise-en-scène* more central than in animation, with its ability to escape from the bounds of representation into fantasy and abstraction and to articulate the personal vision of the artist.

Early cinema—in particular, Méliès's love of "fantastic views"—is marked in Kentridge's work in the way he presents each sequence of altered drawings as a series of scenes. The camera is static, offering a unified spectatorial viewpoint. From that position, the action occurs as it does in the theater in a unified, homogenous space. Yet, due to Kentridge's inventive formalism of animation, charcoal drawing, and erasure, the viewer can see the history of the image's change in the traces that remain. There is a delight in this act of visual comparison which is not dissimilar to that offered by *trompe l'oeil* paintings such as the painted backdrops found in early cinema and, in general, to use Tom Gunning's term, the "aesthetics of astonishment" that characterized cinema's first decade. Gunning held that early cinema was less concerned with narrative than with "exhibition." Unwilling to suppress discontinuity in the service of narrative coherence, it sought to engage the viewer's curiosity by displaying the inventiveness of the technology itself, which was able to produce an endless variety of activity and transformation. Gunning has drawn a connection between the cinema of attractions and early avant-garde cinema, and one can extend that connection to Kentridge's formalism.[33]

Cinematically, Kentridge's most sustained works belong to the *Soho Eckstein* series: nine animated films of varying lengths made between 1989 and 2003.[34] The films have simple plots that highlight the twentieth-century history of Johannesburg's rise to a modern metropolis fueled by mining capital. In 1875, the city was a cow path on the way to Pretoria. Then, the discovery of the Witwatersrand, the ring of gold-bearing reef stretching for sixty-two miles around Johannesburg, put the city on the map. Mines were dug, and the city's white population rapidly increased. The Boer War was launched as an excuse for the British to colonize the Transvaal—thus gaining control over the gold—and the city rapidly rose from nothing to

Johannesburg, 2nd Greatest City after Paris, as the title of one of Kentridge's films put it. The speed of Johannesburg's growth, simultaneously eight thousand feet down into the earth and twenty stories above it, was like a Hollywood epic adventure, a Jules Verne journey downward toward the burning core of the world and upward toward a Gothic rise to the sky. In Kentridge, this journey becomes gifted representation that races into existence with the speed of drawing. Kentridge has taken the characters and plots of early cinema—dark-haired villains with thick moustaches fighting heroes who want to bring law and order to the land; farm girls being tied to railroad tracks, falling into prostitution, being kidnapped into the white slave trade; the crowds of the new metropoles—and transposed them to Johannesburg, to South African white history, and to his personal history, which has its roots in the small but influential South African white Jewish community. In this setting, they have transformed into Soho Eckstein, a heavy, middle- European capitalist, replete with striped suit and fat cigar, who devours food and burns through money, and his alter ego, Felix Teitlebaum, a dreamy poet, usually shown naked, who is the lover of Soho's wife. In the background are the black masses, the silent crowd of the South African metropolis.

Kentridge's Soho Eckstein films recapitulate the city's history in the form of animated tableaux. In the first film, *Johannesburg, 2nd Greatest City After Paris*, Soho and Felix end up trying to club each other to death in a primitive expression of rage worthy of this brutal city of mines, miners, black poverty, and white money. While the two white men battle over Mrs. Eckstein in their white, privileged world, a tableau of black miners walk in a slow, dehumanized line to and from the mines, pitching historical moments together like the harmony and counterpoint of musical composition.

Mine (1991), the third film in the series, juxtaposes Soho's comfortable life with the misery endured by his miners. From the scene of consumption—Soho having breakfast in bed, replete with cigar and pin-striped suit—the viewer travels to the scene of production, to the black miners sleeping in their single-sex hostels, packed together like rows of sardines in a can. A French press coffee maker sitting on Soho's breakfast tray transports the viewer from one scene to the other. Down the plunger goes, through the sheets, the bed, the foundation of the house, deep down into the mine compound and then into the mine itself, as if traveling down a mine shaft. En route are close-ups of black miners' faces deep in sleep and the shabbiness of their surroundings. They shower and work at the rock face, sweating as they drill to extract the ore from the rock (one ounce from one ton) and send it back up to the surface, to Soho's bedroom where the breakfast tray has become a ticker-tape machine belching stock prices. Suddenly, the machine belches out a series of carved African heads that look like the carvings tourists buy in African countries as souvenirs, and then a small rhinoceros appears, roams around the bed sheets for a while, and finally eats out of Soho's hands. The message is clear: Soho turns everything, from people to wild animals, into property, into traded commodities. Empires rise and fall with the rapidity of ticker tape yielding the day's stock prices, and entire buildings implode under the force of capital and consciousness. Meanwhile, the black miners toil beneath the earth, hidden from view, producing gold, a product that is the perfect expression of Marx's commodity fetish since it is a noble metal, untarnished by its roots, that never decays. In contrast, those who dig it up out of the rock-hard ore on which Johannesburg sits live and die in degradation, unrewarded and unseen.

Kentridge's technique is not only remarkable in its capacity to visualize the processes of memory and recall, but also in its ability to constantly bring history back into the present. The drawings create a haunted, melancholy, profound, and amusing mood. That which dwells beneath the surface of Johannesburg's development is constantly there, like a watermark that appears on a piece of paper when one holds it up to the light. The compression of history into a dream-work places the film in the hall of memory and remembrance, where the past haunts the present. The evocative nature of this haunting is at once national and totally personal, a point that Kentridge made in an interview on the topic of the fifth film of the series, *Felix in Exile* (1994):

> Felix has been a character in the films from the beginning. His name came from a dream. It was a dream phrase, as was the name Soho Eckstein. At that point I was keeping a dream diary and I would write down odd phrases. There were not images, there were just phrases. When I did the first film, I needed a name for my two characters and I remembered my dream diary and went through it and found these two names. But I had never understood, who or why the name Felix. And just a few months ago, and it seems so obvious, someone pointed out that my mother's name is Felicia. And I suddenly think [about a famous scene in *Felix in Exile* where Felix looks into a mirror], "is that me looking back at my mother in the mirror? Who is the Felix in it? Where does Felix fit into the dream?"[35]

Kentridge's *Soho Eckstein* films are a dreamlike intersection of national history and personal story, of memory and recitation. They are precisely the expression of that transitional genius which begins at the end of a moment of terrible politics and opens the moment out in the form of individual liberty. The films are about the race of a city to rise and plunge its way into existence, to dominate and then to collapse, leaving Johannesburg, Kentridge's "second greatest city after Paris," a seething, vital financial center in which fourteen million South Africans vie for existence, too often beating each other with clubs in the process.

Sometimes present history can be best illustrated by stories from the past, which is the case and the motivation, according to Jack Lewis, for the making of *Proteus*, a gay love story. The film is based on the true story of two Robben Island prisoners—Rijkhaart Jacobz, a white man from Holland, and Claas Blank, a "native" of the Cape (whose last name ironically means "white" in Afrikaans)—who were executed for sodomy in 1735. Lewis is an activist, prominent in the South African struggle for gay and lesbian rights (which are now enshrined in the constitution, although there remains widespread condemnation of these sexualities in South African society). We may consider the film to be a sign of the Lewis's story of success, since his dreams have been actualized through the laws of the society, which allow gay marriage and prohibit all forms of sexual discrimination. And we may consider it his critical response to ongoing social conditions which castigate, scold, beat up, marginalize, and refuse gays and lesbians. There is still a great deal of homophobia in South Africa, let alone in the rest of Africa. Just cast an ear to the north and listen to the hate speech of Robert Mugabe, who claims that homosexuality is not natural to Africa, but is colonial detritus. Gays and lesbians are, he has said, "worse than pigs or dogs."[36] *Proteus* offers Lewis a filmic way to celebrate his new freedom and all the others that followed with the demise of apartheid, and at the same time, a way to issue a warning. Directorially, the film is collaboration between Lewis and John Greyson from Canada, a fellow gay activist and filmmaker (he embraces the title of "queer filmmaker") who made a landmark film in South Africa during apartheid, *A Moffie Called Simon* (1986), on behalf of the movement (*moffie* is a semi-derogatory word for gays).[37]

Proteus is based on a court record from that period, which tells of the trial and execution of Jacobz and Blank. The report is comprehensive, detailed, written in beautiful copperplate script and perfectly preserved. Every plot point in the film comes out of the report. An image of the report fills the screen at many different points in the film, and we also see a reenactment of it being produced by the court clerks. These clerks, however, are women dressed in the fashions of the 1960s, sporting beehives, smoking cigarettes, and using the technology of the day. In another scene, a pair of bounty hunters, in historical dress and speaking eighteenth-century Dutch, drive up in a Land Rover, and some of the police, especially the sadistic ones at the Castle, wear South African police issue, circa 1960s. These startling historical anomalies are stylistic strategies by the filmmakers to break through the illusionism of the classic film text, forcing the viewer to question mainstream codes of representation. These codes usually pass unnoticed, imaging the events portrayed in the film as "the way things are in the real world." As Colin McCabe puts it in his discussion of the characteristics of the classic realist text, "the camera shows us what happens—it tells the truth against which we can measure the other discourses."[38] But the fact that these 'objects' (the fashion, the technology, verbal expressions) do not belong to the time and period being shown in the diegetic world destabilizes the camera's claim to capture the real world and present it to us as a unified, understandable entity. The world is ambiguous and complex: there is no one overarching explanation, no clear system of order that will encompass the endless varieties of plants and human behavior in it.

The mixing and matching of the 1960s with the 1730s is also a deliberate reference to the importance of the 1960s to the struggle for gay liberation and the struggle against apartheid. In the United States, Illinois became the first state to repeal its anti-sodomy laws in 1962. Shortly thereafter, the first gay student organization was established at Columbia University, and at the end of the decade, a major turning point came when gays, lesbians, and transsexuals fought the police officers who were harassing them at the Stonewall Inn, a gay bar in Greenwich Village, in an event known as the Stonewall Riots. In South Africa, gay rights fared less well in the 1960s. South Africa's own Stonewall incident, when police raided a house in Forest Town, Johannesburg, where 300 gay men were partying, resulted in the laws against homosexuality being tightened. *Proteus* revisits South Africa events such as the Forest Town one obliquely, through the lens of the eighteenth century, recruiting unto itself languages of political struggle central to, and indeed iconic of, South Africa. In doing so, Lewis and Greyson redefine gay struggle as a central political item rather than a marginal aspect of anti-apartheid history.

We all know that in 1964, at the conclusion of the Rivonia Trials, Nelson Mandela was convicted of treason and sent to Robben Island, along with others, to begin serving a twenty-five-year sentence. There is a famous picture (one of the few from that period) of him sitting in a row with other prisoners in a courtyard breaking stones with hammers. The film copies that image at the moment when Blank is sent to work after arriving on the island. At the end of the court case in which they are found guilty of sodomy and sentenced to be roped together and drowned in Table Bay, both men repeat the words spoken by Mandela during his 1964 trial for treason: "Some of the things so far told to this court are true, and some are not true."[39] Lewis and Greyson's intention is to convert a marginal history into a central one, and to do so in the name of the new dispensation in which constitutional rights place sexual freedom at the same level as other civil and political rights.

The 1960s is indeed an important period for the film, but so is 1735, the real date of the events. This is the publication date of the first edition of *Systema Naturae* by Carl Linnaeus, in which the great botanist classified and named all living things including the protea plant, which is indigenous to the Cape. 1735 is a moment of naming in which the world is classified and ordered hierarchically into kingdoms—animal, plants, minerals—and within each kingdom there are phyla, classes, orders, families, genera, and species. Linnaeus was interested in plants in particular, and he imposed on that vast kingdom a systematic and orderly taxonomy in the belief that he was revealing God's divine order of creation. Prior to this point, plants had been given a name followed by a description of their special features. Many of these features, however, were not unique to one plant, resulting in a disorderly mess of classification. Linnaeus's binomial nomenclature brought order to the chaos. He gave each plant a class or genus and an order or species based on the morphology of its sexual organs. The genus was determined by its male organs (the stamens) and the order by its female ones (the pistils). His strict obsession with plant sexuality as the defining marker of difference was artificial and led to a number of groupings that did not find expression in the natural world. For example, the class Monoecia, order Monadelphia that included pines, firs, cypresses, and a few flowering plants, like the castor bean, contained plants with separate male and female "flowers" on the same plant (Monoecia) and with multiple male organs joined onto one common base (Monadelphia). "Plants" that had no visible sexual organs (algae, moss, lichens, fungi, and ferns) were considered to have hidden ones and were grouped together under the class Cryptogamia.[40]

Linnaeus was aware that his binomial system could not encompass all the varieties of plant species that he and his students encountered in their travels. Nonetheless, he considered an artificial classification to be better than the messy system that had preceded it. His vision was reformist in character, spurred on by his Lutheran beliefs in order and clarity. He would make the divine order of creation understandable to the European scientific mind; indeed, with the publication of *Systema Naturae,* a document only eleven pages long, the living organisms of the world would become the objects of scientific study. It did not matter that Linnaeus's system was faulty or inadequate to the task. As Michel Foucault has pointed out, what is important in understanding the historical production of knowledge is not whether documents are true or false, but how they are organized, defined, unified, made relevant, or ignored:

> The document is not the fortunate tool of a history that is primarily and fundamentally memory. . . . In our time, history is that which transforms documents into monuments. In that area where, in the past, history deciphered the traces left by men, it now deploys a mass of elements that have to be grouped, made relevant, placed in relation to one another to form totalities; it might be said, to play on words a little, that in our time history aspires to the condition of archaeology, to the intrinsic description of the monument.[41]

In *Proteus,* we see Linnaeus's document transformed into an oppressive monument dedicated to upholding the system of incarceration and punishment. There are many scenes of plants being collected, preserved, and categorized. One cannot help but imagine the specimens making their way across the seas from the Cape to Scandinavia and thence to Linnaeus's laboratory. The protea plant is of particular interest to the botanists in the film. It is native to this part of the world, and there are over two hundred species, from the miniature to the king, each gorgeous in its desert stem and exotic flower. This diversity of species is also reflected in the diverse peoples of the Cape, but as in Linnaeus's system of classification, it is a diversity that cannot be acknowledged. Order must be imposed on racial and sexual difference and those who violate it, who are misfits of the epistemic system, must be punished.

The film's opening montage is one of Protea flowers opening their petals so that we can see their stamens and pistils, an immensely sexual image which is substantiated by intercutting to shots of Jacobz and Blank embracing, entwining their naked bodies together, one brown, one white. The pair is part of a group of prisoners chosen to work for Virgil Niven, a Scottish botanist who is cultivating a garden on the island. Niven lusts after Blank, who is seductive, hoping to get something out of him—which he manages to do. He agrees to tell Niven the Hottentots' names for the plants in exchange for money, which he will give to his mother when he gets out. Since he does not know anything about botany, he makes the names up using Nama slang words for human genitals. This is a prod to the audience that what passes as scientific knowledge is not always accurate.

Systema Naturae classified people into different groups. While man was classified with primates and other mammals, he was differentiated from them too on the basis of reason. All men could reason (women, it was commonly believed, could not reason), but some less well than others due to cultural factors, so there were four categories of the species *Homo sapiens:* Americanus (Native Americans), Asiaticus, Africanus, and Europaeus (which were the most civilized). The Hottentots were at the bottom of the heap, a sort of unclassifiable subspecies along with cave dwellers, wild men, dwarfs, and others. Before Linnaeus and the great biologicization of the races that followed, race was equivalent in concept to nationality, but now there was a larger category offered, Europaeus, who happened mostly to be white.[42]

The film tells us that Blank was a Hottentot, or at least partially one (we don't know about his father, but his mother was Khoi). Given Linnaeus's system of classification in social practice as the schema for ordering human beings into classes, one can imagine how offensive was the relationship between Jacobz and Blank in the eyes of the court: an act of sodomy that not only crossed racial lines, but was almost bestiality given Blank's racial classification (or lack thereof). The film's eighteenth-century focus is on the biologicization of human difference as normal and degraded, higher and lower, superior and inferior.

Homosexuality is seen as a glitch in the system, since the system produces multiple stereotypes, multiple well-known superior/inferior codifications: European/native, white/black, civilized/savage. Where homosexuality enters the scene there is a screwup, because here white becomes corrupted, and liable to bond (therefore) with black. Homosexuality might be considered the bugaboo of classification: since it reveals degradation at the top, it allows people to jump boundaries between racial or colonial types.

At the core of the film is the illicit power of illicit love. Indeed, the film explores the illicit as a generator of erotic power, and carves out a space within the prison where the Protea may ironically blossom. This space is, of necessity, outside of normal society. In the film, the prison has become a temporary asylum.

In fact, Blank and Jacobz had a love affair that lasted seventeen years. In the film, the number of years is condensed into ten. Still, it is a long time to keep a relationship like theirs a secret, under the constant surveillance of guards, in this Foucauldian, panoptic world of prison on Robben Island. And here the structure of surveillance is subverted because it turns out that everyone knew what was going on and turned a blind eye to it, until a cer-

tain key moment when things changed. But what changed? None of this information is in the court trial document. Like all good critical filmmakers,
Lewis and Greyson did their research and discovered that in those years,
a homophobic panic (like the Salem witch trials in Massachusetts a century earlier) had swept through the Netherlands, resulting in the execution
of over seventy "sodomites."[43] The film shows a frightening reenactment of
street violence in a Dutch city, where buildings are on fire and people are
screaming. Virgil Nevin is there, walking down the street; he appears to be
with a group of gay men, and then, suddenly, he is grabbed and garroted—
the European punishment for sodomy.

Proteus is about the search for individuality in a system of classification, of regulation, of colonial demarcation, of prisons and hideaways and
also blind, even sympathetic eyes. It is, in its own way, a recitation of everything terrible about the history of South Africa and the long, painful, devastating, and profound march toward individual freedoms, a march toward
emancipation—in film and in fact—that is hardly over. That the march is
so painfully slow is finally what makes the race to representation so furious,
and so fast.

6

The Dialectic of Reconciliation in **De Voortrekkers** and **Come See the Bioscope**

[M]y knowledge of movies, pictures, or the idea of movie making, was strongly linked to the identity of a nation. That's why there is no French television, or Italian, or British, or American television. There can be only one television because it's not related to nation. It's related to finance or commerce. Movie making at the beginning was related to the identity of the nation and there have been very few "national" cinemas. In my opinion there is no Swedish cinema but there are Swedish moviemakers—some very good ones, such as Stiller and Bergman. There have only been a handful of cinemas: Italian, German, American and Russian. This is because when countries were inventing and using motion pictures, they needed an image of themselves. The Russian cinema arrived at a time they needed a new image.

Jean-Luc Godard in conversation with Colin McCabe

In this chapter I turn to two films made at two very distinct and traumatic historical moments, when, in the words of Godard, the nation desperately "needed a new image." The first is *De Voortrekkers* (Harold Shaw, 1916), an extraordinarily ambitious epic of Griffith-like proportion produced in Afrikaans just six years after the creation of the Union of South Africa.[1] It was, in the words of film historian Thelma Gutsche, "a national film documenting a climactic point in South African history." And, as Gutsche notes, it was "totally out of proportion to the reputation of the nascent film industry . . . evidence of the courage, confidence and optimism which attended its launching."[2] The second film is *Come See the Bioscope* (Lance

Gewer, 1997), a short film produced by M-Net's New Directions initiative three years after the first democratic elections in South Africa's history, which brought an end to legislative apartheid. While the film may be less ambitious in length, it is far more ambitious in its conception of cinema as a powerful tool in creating conditions for modern political organization, especially among a conquered people. To examine these two films made at different ends of the twentieth century is to consider the terms of reconciliation each invokes in its conceptualization of nation, citizen, and cinema. These terms tell a great deal about the historical events being represented, but they speak even more loudly to the historical moment of their production, illustrating that there is no one role for cinema to play in the national project. The production date of *De Voortrekkers* shows that the race to a cinematic representation that would produce national reconciliation goes back to the very formation of the South African nation-state in 1910.[3]

The film takes as its broad subject what is known in South African history as the Great Trek—the self-imposed 1838 exodus into the hinterland of groups of Afrikaans farming communities from the Cape in search of self-rule. This period of Afrikaner expansionism was a long and drawn-out process lasting almost twenty years (1836–1854). *De Voortrekkers* concentrates on the first few years of that period, which contains events that have become iconic in the pantheon of Afrikaans ethnonationalism. In the film, they are broadened to provide a national fable: the uprooting and departure of the farming communities, the betrayal and murder of *trekboer* leader Piet Retief and his party by the Zulu under King Dingane, and the "Battle of Blood River," which forms the great epic "moment" of the narrative.[4] All that history is the subject of the film, but in 1916 when it was made, its objective was to satisfy or at least address the two most pressing present needs of the South African colony from the point of view of the settler groups: reconciliation and nation building between the English (which included the broader linguistic category of English speakers) and the Afrikaners. Here, then, is one evident role for the cinema to play in the new nation: to endorse the newly formed state that had emerged six years earlier from the Union of South Africa in 1910. The state was a white minority-rule state created out of the political union between two former enemies, the Boers and the British, in the interests of white power. The homogeneously conceived racism, which would be imported with modifications into the later thinking of the apartheid state, is already there in this film.

Come See the Bioscope fictionalizes the life of Solomon Tshekisho Plaatje and his traveling bioscope. Born on a farm in the Orange Free State in 1876, Plaatje was part of the educated African elite that founded the African National Congress, sub-Saharan Africa's first liberation movement, in 1912.[5] He was also one of the early pioneers in South African film exhibition, known for his traveling bioscope, as well as being a linguist, politician, journalist, translator, interpreter, newspaper editor, and Secretary General of the newly formed ANC. The early black nationalists believed in English liberalism and its doctrine of universality. They believed that Africans were part of a universal human family and should be included in the new state as citizens. Writing about the founders of African nationalism, ANC politician and historian Pallo Jordan elaborates on their belief in the values, traditions, and principles of modern liberal thought:

> Though racially excluded from its institutions, they sought the legitimacy of the white state. Their political tactics sought to affirm that blacks too were British subjects, entitled to the same rights as other British subjects, the whites. Their deeply held liberal convictions led them to believe that moral persuasion was a sound strategy. . . . Thus in 1925, when the ANC adopted the African Bill of Rights, it demanded "the franchise for all civilized men."[6]

Plaatje was one of those "civilized men" who saw the cinema as a technology for transformation, a way into modernity, and thus a way out of poverty and exclusion. Tracing Plaatje's role in the development of film culture in South Africa, Ntongela Masilela reveals how Plaatje's pedagogic approach to film exhibition emerged out of his involvement in the New African Movement, which emerged after the end of the Boer War at the turn of the century. For Masilela, the Movement heralded the beginnings of an African modernity that would later find further expression in the Sophiatown Renaissance of the 1950s. Yet, as he notes, this earlier moment of modern thought and practice has been eclipsed by the 1950s, which has assumed an iconic status in South African cultural history. Masilela's historical work on the period is invaluable, not only because it re-invigorates the archive, but because it complicates the story of modernity and cinema in South Africa, a story that is often focused through the lens of postcolonial cultural theory. Thus Ella Shohat and Robert Stam have argued that the beginnings of cinema coincided with the height of imperialism and that the leading film-producing countries were also the leading imperialists. As a result,

> European cinema, in its infancy, inherited the racist and colonialist discourse whose historical contours we have outlined here. Cinema, itself the product of "Western scientific discoveries," made palpable to audiences the master-narrative of the "progress of Western civilization," often through biographical narratives about explorers, inventors, and scientists. . . . Cinema thus be-

came the epistemological mediator between the cultural space of the Western
spectator and that of the cultures represented on the screen, linking separate
spaces and figurally separate temporalities in a single moment of exposure.[7]

I do not seek to dispute their argument. *De Voortrekkers* is evidence of its
rightness. But Plaatje's view and use of the cinema in the rural areas of
South Africa complicates the stories told of cinema's complicity in colonial
thought and practice. In a manner that reminds us of Ousmane Sembène's
view of African cinema as "night school," Plaatje, as Masilela puts it, "introduced film form to the New Africans as a pedagogical instrument com-
patible with a Christian civilizational interpretation of modernity."[8] Plaatje's
view of the cinema as a tool for uplift and education may now appear to us
as typical of progressive Victorianism, which would fit his historical period.
But that is not the way cinema is positioned in *Come See the Bioscope*. Instead, the film articulates his vision as a past moment or promise retrospec-
tively imagined for contemporary South Africa, a non-racial South Africa in
which a new kind of cinema and a new kind of spectator can develop. Both
films are, in the words of Siegfried Kracauer, "surface level expressions" that
"provide unmediated access to the fundamental substance of the state of
things," that substance being the ideological role of cinema in history, two
words that have been bound up with each other since the beginning of the
cinema.[9] *Cabiria* (Giovanni Pastrone, 1914), *Potemkin* (Sergei Eisenstein,
1925), *Napoleon* (Abel Gance, 1927), and *The Birth of a Nation* (D. W. Griffith, 1915) are all examples of films that take a fundamental national "moment" as the subject of their representational force, thus enhancing the status of the cinema as an artistic form.

The development of classical codes that foregrounded transparency
and narrative linearity encouraged the viewer to interpret such films as historical documents that showed events as they had "actually occurred," producing what Miriam Hansen calls a cinema of "referential realism."[10] These
exploited the medium's capacity to reproduce the real without the heavy
hand of the artist intervening in the process, thus satisfying that which
Andre Bazin intuited as our compulsion or need to represent the world
as it is. Since this need was a psychological rather than an aesthetic one,
Bazin argued that the camera satisfied it better than any other visual art
form, such as painting, precisely because it *was* a machine and not an artist that made the transference of the image possible. "Only a photographic
lens can give us the kind of image of the object that is capable of satisfying
the deep need man has to substitute for it something more than a mere ap-
proximation, a kind of decal or transfer. The photographic image is the ob-

ject itself, the object freed from the conditions of time and space that govern it."[11] This gives it the appearance of truth: the truth of how things were
independent of anyone's perspective, turning historical myth into the stuff
of natural history and turning human aspirations toward a reconfiguration
of how things should be into the stuff of historical inevitability. What Eric
Hobsbawm called the "invention of tradition" is here an invention of past
prescience. Past prescience proves that the aspirations of the historical present are transhistorical, shared by the past as by the present, and hence the
stuff of absolute destiny. The Hollywood western, conceived at the very moment the American Wild West ceased to exist, recapitulated its raucous and
violent past in the form of a six-gun will toward civility. Indian and outlaw
had to be vanquished so that with their brave bones in the ground, America
could be as we, the viewers of the present, know it. The Wild West, presented as the route to statehood and national power, became the symphonic
symbol of both. The unstated message was, "we continue the drive to claim
terrain in the America of the twentieth century; the world and the West are
the same." This message takes the past and through it, motivates the future
as the next place in the same river of destiny. Historical films motivate the
future by casting the present in their inevitable flow.

Historical films may also seek a bridge between present and past that
allows the present to complete a mission aborted by a side turn in history
which is now, finally, able to be overcome. The goal is to reach into the past
and retrieve the kernel of its spirit, showing that new times are the fulfillment of that spirit in spite of the sidetracking of intervening history. In this
instance, the goal is caught up with an act of mourning: mourning for the
abortion of spirit which kept the prescient actor in his place. And the goal
is to return the flow of history to his name, causing him to live a second life
in our imaginations. Retrieving one's spiritual paternity or maternity sets
the nation on its course, confirming the dignity of that course and demon-
strating that it carries the imprimatur of the mother or father. The historical
film is hardly confined to these two modalities, but they prove central at
moments of disruption, since both aim for the restoration of continuity, a
continuity in which the concerns of the present are clarified and shown to
carry the inevitability of power or spirit.

The two films whose discussion serves as the substance of this chapter
illustrate these two modes. Both are ways in which home or homeland are
shown to be *always already* in place as Louis Althusser would put it (or as
destiny would have it), and both help to explain the deep attachment people
have to their nation, and why nations often exist in people's affections and

identifications long before they become realized as nation-states.[12] Homeland is people, the origin of self, and origin can only be grasped through the image of this place, not another. Hence the other way in which film is called upon to present homeland as destiny. In it, the narrative of history gives pride to place, the film being a medium that naturalizes location, seeks its physiognomy, and renders it expressive.

As has been shown in the case of the Basques, the Palestinians, and countless others, a group's idea of themselves as a nation rests more on the idea of themselves as a people with a common ancestry than it does on the instantiation of a nation-state. As Tony Judt remarked, the standard Marxist account of national sentiment as an illusion induced by manipulation resulting in a nation of duped citizens lost ground in the nationalist debate to the more constructionist view of the nation as the modern creation of intellectuals and teachers supported by invented traditions and customs, symbols, and spectacles expressive of nationalist sentiment.[13] These identificatory mechanisms, it is argued, work to obscure the role of chance and opportunity in nation making. They continue to promote the myth that a nation's origin is not the work of nationalist intellectuals seizing a historical opportunity (Judt points to the chaos and disruption that follow the breakup of empires as the most common kind of such an opportunity) but resides, as Eric Hobsbawm has phrased it, in the mists of antiquity. In this sense nations have no beginnings or endings, unlike individuals—"I am born," reads the first chapter heading of Dickens' masterpiece, David Copperfield—but "travel up" as opposed to descending down through time,[14] all of which sounds like the perfect storm for cinematic representation.

Cinema has the capacity to take historical reality and turn it into myth. Certain genre are particularly apt in this respect. Andre Bazin noted how the western was the quintessential example of a genre that in its most classic avatars was able to find an "ideal balance between social myth, historical reconstruction, psychological truth, and the traditional theme of the western mise-en-scène."[15] But many genres outside of the western can use its codes and conventions to turn the raw facts of history into myth, producing its own forms of knowledge, which then enter into the language of the nation. The oppositions between black and white, savage and civilized, courage and indolence, hero and villain, honesty and deceit that structure the narrative of De Voortrekkers were all already in social circulation. It remained for Gustav Preller, the scriptwriter and historian, to produce the story from the mythic material. Preller was exceptionally talented in his ability to popularize history. In her exploration of his work as a historian, Isabel Hofmeyr

writes, "In this area Preller was quite breathtaking and spectacularly successful, since it is largely his interpretation of the great trek and more importantly, his *visual* version of that social movement which has been widely
received as the dominant one for the last seven decades or so."[16]

FACTS AND FICTION

The bare historical facts of *De Voortrekkers* are these: Seeking to escape the
constraints of British colonial rule of the Cape in general, and motivated in
particular by the end of slavery and the introduction of more liberal labor
laws by the colonial authorities (acts which deeply offended many Afrikaans
farmers' notions of self-determination and the "natural order" of white racial superiority), small bands known as *trekboers* began to leave the Eastern
Cape in 1836. According to Piet Retief, one of the prominent *trekboer* leaders who wished to expand the great Afrikaner trek into the interior of what
is now KwaZulu-Natal and was then the Zulu Kingdom, the *trekkers* were
resolved to form permanent settlements wherein they could govern themselves without British interference. While rejecting slavery, they sought to
"maintain such regulations as may suppress crime, and preserve proper relations between master and servant."[17] Later, in recalling the emancipation
of the Cape slaves, Retief's niece, Anna Steenkamp, would write the following in her memoirs:

> It is not so much their freedom that drove us to such lengths, as their being
> placed on an equal footing with Christians, contrary to the laws of God and
> the natural distinction of race and religion, so that it was intolerable for any
> decent Christian to bow down beneath such a yoke: wherefore we rather with-
> drew in order thus to preserve our doctrines in purity.[18]

Both statements are important today, for they precisely describe the con-
stellations of relationships about self and other, purity and contamination,
master and slave, cultural preservation and desecration that would later find
codification in apartheid ideology. These binary oppositions would also become the primary target of anti-apartheid films (especially those that appeared in the eighties), thus showing how indelible—and, as many have
argued, deforming—their influence has been on both the apartheid imagination and its counterpart.[19] This is not to say that behind *trekker* writing
lies the whole shape of what South Africa would become in the next century, a century that begins with the Anglo-Boer War and ends with the
Truth and Reconciliation Commission. Nevertheless, it is fair to say that

such attitudes prepared the ground for the successive waves of attacks on all those "others" who would break the "natural" law, challenge the master/ slave relationship in the century to come, and finally, require reconciliation (not to mention reparation).

In ox wagons with their families, servants, livestock, former slaves, and all other possessions, the *Voortrekkers* (literally, in Afrikaans, those who came "before" [*voor*]—in this case, before the nation) journeyed into territories already ravaged by internecine wars and ruled by independent African societies. Natal's abundant rainfall and the presence of a harbor made it the most attractive destination for the majority of *trekkers*. Retief was sent to ask for a land treaty from the Zulu regnant of the region, King Dingane, which he first secured and then lost, along with his life, when the King reneged on the contract in a particularly brutal fashion. Retief and his party were clubbed to death at the Royal Kraal while attending a beer festival to celebrate the compact, while the rest of the settlers were murdered in their encampment by Dingane's *impis* (warriors). Within the diegesis of the film, which runs for over two hours, these events occupy roughly the first half. The second part of the film is an allegory of revenge and resurrection. The murder of Retief and his party is avenged at the Battle of Blood River, where, on the banks of the Ncome River deep in the heart of Zululand, a commando of approximately five hundred men led by Andries Pretorius turns to face down an army of almost ten thousand men and wins against overwhelming manpower with overwhelming gunpowder.[20] At the end of the battle, the bloodiest in South African history even today, the river ran red with the blood of three thousand dead Zulu, with no loss of life on the part of the Afrikaners. This devastating defeat split the Zulu kingdom in half. Dingane's brother Mpande subsequently joined forces with the *Boers* and chased Dingane to the north where he was killed by the Swazis, leaving Mpande in control of the former kingdom.

In the following years, the *trekkers* spread out over the area around the Tugela River, in the mountainous interior of the region, appointed a *volks-raad* (people's council) as a governing body, and declared what was, in effect, a mini republic. Needless to say, citizenship was limited to Afrikaners who had trekked from the Cape and did not include the Zulu. Indeed, other whites were mistrusted and had to prove their loyalty to the community. Here, then, are the beginnings of what would become the apartheid blueprint—a white minority trying to exclude, through the mechanisms of statehood (be it a full-blown nation-state or a people's republic), a black majority in the name of autonomy, self-determination, manifest destiny, language, religion, and race—while marginalizing other white "tribes" in the process.[21] Significantly, the film does not include these events, but ends with the *Boers'* celebration of their victory in church as evidence of a covenant that existed between God (defined in Christian terms) and their people. In 1910, victory day, which was the 16th of December, was declared a national public holiday. First named Dingane's Day and later the Day of the Covenant, it was celebrated as a sabbath by the Dutch Reformed Church until it was renamed, in 1994, the Day of Goodwill or Day of Reconciliation. In the naming and renaming of the day lies the structure of the century.[22]

RECONCILING THE WHITE "RACES"

The Treaty of Vereeniging in 1902 marked the official end of the Anglo-Boer War, the most traumatic war in South Africa's history. In its wake were the remains of what used to be four self-governing colonies, two of which had been British, and the two now-defeated *Boer* republics, each operating with a greater or lesser degree of autonomy. Something had to be done to bring political stability to the fractured region, and the idea of a South African federation was seen as the answer.[23] While the idea fit with British ambitions of empire building, ironically it also appealed to Afrikaner nationalists, who hoped that unification would resolve divisions among Afrikaans anti-imperialists, ultimately weakening imperial interference. In describing the events leading up to the inauguration of the union, Leonard Thompson observed that

> [h]aving completed their work in South Africa, the four colonial governments sent delegates to London, since only the imperial parliament had the legal authority to give effect to their decisions. Members of the Western educated Black elite in southern Africa—clergy, journalists, teachers—and a handful of White sympathizers had also sent a deputation to London to agitate for the removal of color bars (limitations and restrictions on employment and voting based on one's race) from the constitution. They were supported by the *Manchester Guardian* and several prominent individuals. However, though most members of Parliament preferred that the constitution should not contain a color bar, nearly all realized that it was politically impractical to attempt to alter the wishes of the four self-governing colonies. Indeed the crucial decision had been made in 1902. The political color bars in the Transvaal and Orange River Colony constitutions, and the color bars in the draft South African constitution, were natural consequences of Milner's decision to appease the fighting men of the republics at the expense of the Black population.
>
> ... [O]n May 31, 1910, eight years to the day since he had lain down his arms as leader of the military forces of the Afrikaner republics, Louis Botha became Prime Minister of a British dominion with a population of 4 million

Africans, 500,000 coloureds, 150,000 Indians, and 1.275 million whites. That outcome was not what Lord Milner (British High Commissioner of South Africa at the time) had encouraged British South Africans to expect; nor was it what had been expected by the many Black South Africans who had supported the British cause in the war.[24]

Mapped against this historical background, the Anglo-Boer War (1899–1902)—or, as the Afrikaners pointedly called it, the Second War of Freedom—was too divisive and painful a topic to attempt filmic narrativization in the name of a fragile national collective, despite being the pivotal event in the move toward unionization.[25] On a broader level, the subject of the Anglo-Boer war raised the specter of white-on-white conquest and domination at a time when the notion of South African citizenry, of who was and who was not part of the new nation, had been constitutionally redefined in racial terms. Anxious to rid itself of all traces of British imperialism, the government sought to downplay the history of white-on-white conflict and give white South Africans a new national identity and geo-political future. This they did by defining a new enemy in racial terms.

Politically and historically, the new enemy was very much the same as the old one, for the history of the area from the beginnings of colonization by Europe in the 1600s was one of conflicts and battles over land fought against various black societies by both settler communities and the imperial power.[26] The idea of warring with black social units or "tribes," as the colonial power and settlers had called them, was not a new one. But the idea of a homogenized "native" population, contained within the borders of the nation and united, despite cultural and "tribal" differences, under the essentialist banner of "blackness" (or "nativeness," to use the term of the day), was, as was its counterpart, a white South Africanism that transcended intra-white cultural and linguistic divisions.[27] In short, the film participated in the construction of modern South African racism by participating in the definition of two homogeneous groups: whites and natives to a national collective which had rather thought of itself in more fluid, amorphous terms, situating itself within more tribalized and localized categories of English, Dutch, Cape Coloured, and the like. The film was in this sense a clear product of English racism, which consistently mapped the world in terms of East and West, white and black, European and native, upper and lower.

De Voortrekkers has general implications for the symbolic functioning of all self-consciously national narratives, filmic or otherwise. All such narratives attempt to "naturalize" the nation and present its realization as an inevitability, the assertion of a right long overdue and legitimated by fate,

God, or history. In *De Voortrekkers*, the celebration of the covenant between God and the Afrikaner is founded on an allegory of fulfillment as well as one of collective bravery and courage, or better, on the connection between these. The *trekkers'* victory at the Battle of Blood River merely realizes the covenant as a primordial given, a point that is made evident in the intertitle (the title card inserted between shots in a film) anchoring this section of the film which reads: "And in keeping our covenant we shall, on every Sixteenth Day of December, render thanks to Thee, Almighty God, for our safe return and the preservation of our Race and Country." This covenant required a brave people as well as a religious one, one whose religiosity required bravery and whose singularity is predicated on both.

There is little evidence to suggest that the *trekkers* themselves viewed the events that happened to them as fulfilling some divine ordination. As David Bunn puts it in his essay on monuments in South Africa,

> These historical events (the Great Trek) in the life of the *volk* (people) were seen in allegorical terms by later generations. Recent historians have argued that the Great Trek was not a consolidated, self-conscious process, and have shown that *Voortrekker* parties were riven by dissent. While it is clear that the early *trekkers* did identify with biblical narratives such as the exodus from Egypt, at the time there was little overall sense of religious predestination or a defined mission. In the work of later interpreters, however, events were given a strong Calvinistic coloring so that the *trekkers* became a chosen people, through the imagined descent of the word to chosen leaders. . . .[28]

However, national history is not told in multiple voices, which could reveal the contradictions, dissension, and differences in how the "original events" were perceived and reconstructed by the various parties concerned. To do so would reveal the contingent, self-fabricated nature of history, and by extension the contingent and self-fabricated fantasy at the basis of national identity. The *trekkers* really did beat the Zulu: that is not fantasy but fact. What exists in the realm of fantasy is the sense of destiny supposedly at the basis of it all, a sense which later history will unpack as "in the cards" like the ace of spades. It is here, with the final trick, that justification of the nation through appeal to destiny and character takes place. The trick can, befitting its card, turn deadly: it is always one which treats historical subjects unequally by "proving," that is, by narratively establishing, that some people are more equal than others, more central to national destiny than others.

To translate such "new thinking" for South Africa into cinematic terms required sketching a linear narrative out of the *trekkers'* ordeals, their fortitude in the face of the unknown and hence the uncivilized, their presence as bearers of Christian, European civilization, their betrayal by the savage forces of Dingane, their vow to keep a covenant with God should they be victorious against his *impis,* their victory at the Battle of Blood River, and its memorialization with the building of a church. This story had long achieved the status of a foundational narrative for Afrikaans ethnonationalism. Now it required deracinating the bible from its Afrikaans accent and turning those thought of as Afrikaners into a more amorphous category called "The White Settler." With this shift in narration, a space of spectatorial identification opened not only for Afrikaners, but also for English-speaking viewers—a deliberate move, as Edwin Hees has argued on the part of historian-turned-screenwriter Gustav Preller. Preller was, as Hees states, a supporter of the government's policy of reconciliation and thus "any hints of anticolonialism or anti-British sentiment in the book are suppressed in the film" although they were evident in Preller's 1917 historical biography of Piet Retief.[29] Hees continues:

> The virtual elimination of the British from *De Voortrekkers* is a carefully adapted version of Preller's story of Piet Retief—adapted in order to bring the film more into line not only with the British Imperialist ideology of its financial backers, but also with the accommodating stance of General Louis Botha, whose South African Party was eager to promote reconciliation between the English-speaking and the Afrikaans-speaking sections of the population after Union.[30]

Preller's true political colors can be seen later in his endorsement of National Socialism in the 1930s along with his support for those Afrikaners who agreed with him.[31] At this stage, however, faced with the difficulties of creating white unity, it is clear that he suppressed his ethnic nationalism, and in this, he was not alone. We may see his response—a rejection of the particular in favor of the general, a willing of the nation into existence—as exemplary of the times, an act which brings us back to Goddard's epigraph that a cinema becomes national when its process of self-invention conjoins with that of the nation. The arranged marriage between the two white "races" in the name of South Africa, however, was an unstable union from its inception. Ten thousand feet of celluloid could not manage to obliterate the divisions of dislike that existed between Boer and British throughout the twentieth century and even post-1994. The film is, in fact, antagonistic in its view of the nation to the later Afrikaner nationalist narrative of the *trek* and poses itself in opposition to the exclusivist rituals that characterized much of its retelling in many Afrikaans communities. It does this in order to reinterpret that moment of history (the birth of the South African union) as a moment for the white colony rather than one that is exclusively Afrikaans in destiny. And yet, paradoxically, the film will have a later life as precisely the latter, being translated in the Afrikaner nationalist's imagination as important only in its representation of the role of Afrikaners' suffering, deprivation, and courage in conquering the Zulu nation and establishing the "true" South African one.

Its next great moment of glory occurs during its exhibition at the 1938 *Voortrekker* centenary celebrations, a carefully orchestrated spectacle of ethnic Afrikaans mobilization which involved an actual reenactment of the original trek with ox wagons and *trekkers* in full historical costume. This second trek aroused an enormous emotional outpouring among Afrikaners, and it is easy to see why. Due to the worldwide depression, the great drought, and the increasing capitalization of agriculture by mostly South African, English-owned corporations, many *plattelanders* (rural Afrikaners) had been forced into the cities where they rapidly found themselves reduced to the status of "poor whites." Read against the events of the 1930s, the film's evocation of an idealized heroic pastoral order, a time of both courage and an ensuing rustic peace in a God-given land of plenty, offered a powerful message of hope to an increasingly desperate people. Certainly, the parallels between the past disenfranchisement of the *volk* due to greedy English colonialism and their current feeling of being dispossessed strangers in their own land overwhelmed the film's message of reconciliation between white and white. There is no doubt that the emphasis of the Fusion government (the 1933 coalition between J. B. M. Herzog's National Party and the South African Party led by Jan Smuts) on white unity and the presumed equality between the two white groups predisposed them to interpret the problems of the country only in black and white or "native" and "European" terms.[32] In short, the government underestimated or failed to see the immense dissatisfactions that existed among the Afrikaners, particularly among newly urbanized communities. The homogenizing discourse of "white unity" failed to take hold in these dislocated communities, a fact that Afrikaans nationalist intellectuals successfully exploited in their articulation of apartheid.[33] There can be little doubt that ten years later, these communities contributed a great deal to Jan Smuts's defeat and the victory of the National Party at the general election, which ushered in South Africa's apartheid era.

NARRATIVE STRATEGIES OF RECONCILIATION

There are two self-conscious narrative strategies that *De Voortrekkers* takes up to try to achieve its original project of reconciliation.[34] In view of the new union, the new enemy, the funding from England, and the producers' desire to market the film in England for profit as well as engender a reconciliation between English and *Boer* in South Africa, no longer could the story of the Great Trek be told in terms of a colonial encounter between a settler society (the *Boers*) and a colonial bully (the English).[35] Nor, of course, could it be told as a story of Afrikaans settler invasion and conquest. Therefore, the film had to displace the sources of conflict onto other parties, outsiders (even if inside) who could be assigned hatred and blame, thus rewriting history in a way that could allow English and *Boer* to believe that they were never really that far apart.

As a remark about theory, it has often been said that the enunciation of unity within a group or nation typically requires the remaking of lines of division and conflict in ways that bring together those who require unification at the expense of specific others. Rene Girard calls this the "reconstruction of sacrifice." Ernesto Laclau and Chantal Mouffe speak in a more structuralist vein, arguing that both differences (the syntagmatic) and similarities (the paradigmatic) are used in creating a vision (that is, revision) of social reality.[36] Michel Foucault makes the point that the games of rejection, division, and negation that society plays and the way it institutes systems of inclusion and exclusion in its drive to unify people are internal to its reconstruction of the relationships of power (or practices that attempt to do this).

Given the need to displace hatred, blame, and guilt onto some sacrificial people or groups, the film in questions chooses two: King Dingane and the Zulu on the one hand, and two fictional characters—a pair of scheming Portuguese traders—on the other. Each of these displacements is required. The first functions to displace onto the Zulu the blame for the Afrikaner killings in the Boer War and the taking of their land. One conflict (the murder of Piet Retief and his settlement by Dingane) is substituted for another (the English assaults on the two Afrikaner republics in order to gain control of their newly discovered gold and diamond deposits). This is a natural substitution, since both the Afrikaners and the English had fought the Zulu nation as enemies, and this experience would have been fresh in the minds of the contemporary settlers on both sides of the English/Afrikaans divide. Moreover, displacement of perpetration and blame onto blackness was a natural extension of the racist/colonizing act of power, which the larger colonial and settler picture demanded: a picture of white colonization in fact impeded by English/Afrikaans divisions. Thus, the film begins with the Great Trek without any investigation of the events leading up to it. The trek is presented as a foreordained act of national righteousness, a way of establishing a New Jerusalem in the African *veld* (grasslands) of which the Union of South Africa will be the logical outcome.

The second displacement, onto two fictional Portuguese traders, functions to remove the Afrikaans *trekkers* as the usurpers of Zulu land and goods, replacing them with the Portuguese. In the film, there is no hint of intended exploitation of the "natives" by the *trekkers*. The intertitle simply states, "Being a God-fearing people, we shall trade fairly with the natives, and thereby gain their assistance in establishing a Model Republic for our posterity." This message is delivered to a group of *trekkers* including women and children, who are about to join Retief in the "national movement" to the north. The setting is biblical: the chosen grouped around a patriarch with a long white beard, an Afrikaans Moses who may not, given his age, make it to the promised land. The poignancy of the scene is deepened by the audience's knowledge that these people are unwittingly going to their deaths. They are not invaders and usurpers of other people's land, but sacrificial lambs for the coming republic.

It is the Portuguese traders who, on hearing the news of the intended trek northward, fear that the honesty of the *Boers*' dealings will, as the title puts it, "teach the natives trade valuations and ruin our business." As a counterstrategy, they decide to poison the Zulu king against the *trekkers* by telling him that they intend to steal his lands and cattle. (Ironically, this is exactly what did happen.) They are, in effect, positioned as the figure of the Jew or the Levantine in the European imagination: crafty, duplicitous, cosmopolitan, and corrupted to the point of caring about nothing beyond usury and self-interest. Their Semitic coding is overt in their lush, orientalist city garments which make them immediately suspect as cosmopolites; their hook noses; their dark features; their oily hair; and their creepy, unctuous behavior. They spy from behind bushes and make overt sexual advances to the blonde daughter of the *Voortrekker* patriarch. Making a fortune from their trading on Zulu goods, it is they who decide to sell arms to the Zulu, who, in a related fit of stereotyping, are chaotic, savage, violent, and gullible: too simple minded to get the real picture. Only because the Portuguese have poisoned the Zulu against the Afrikaner does, in the causal terms of this film, the Afrikaner/English conflict take place. It is a mere effect, as it were, of the poison injected into South Africa by the true agents of harm: the Zulu and the Portuguese/Orientalist.

These two agents of harm allow the film to reconstruct the English/Afrikaans battle (the Boer War) as an effect of race. The Portuguese traders are coded as borderline whites, marginal European subjects whose signs of hybridity are mulatto and whose characters are appropriately degenerate. Since the cause of white/white (English/Afrikaans) conflict is now coded as racial in origin—the effect of an alliance between degenerate racial types— the English and Afrikaans, who are the true European whites, are now free to revise their views of each other. They were each the dupes of degeneracy rather than blameworthy, self-interested, and prejudiced parties to the conflict. What they share are the trappings of civility, which derive from their true Europeanness: their white skin. They can now know themselves and each other in these terms: "We are the ones whom those of inferior races have brought harm to. We are alike in this. We are one." Thus are the terms of reconciliation rewritten in the cultural imagination as those dependent on racialist (read: racist) ways of knowing.

REWRITING *THE BIRTH OF A NATION*

It is hardly fortuitous that the most popular silent film in South Africa when *De Voortrekkers* was being made was D. W. Griffith's *The Birth of a Nation*,[37] a film that rewrites history in a similar way. *The Birth of a Nation* opens with the statement that the seeds of conflict in America began with the bringing of the Negro there. This theme becomes the central explanatory determinant of the civil war, which is portrayed as a hopeless and terrible waste in which white people are fighting white people (brother fighting brother). The film's two main families, one from the north, the other from the south, play out a series of embroilments "caused" by a cast of mulattos, blacks, and degenerate carpetbaggers. Reducing its plot to the extreme, what the film shows is that once these bad seeds are removed (valiantly by the Ku Klux Klan, whose actions are shown with the excitement of cowboy films), these two white families are free to become one. The final moment is a double marriage between them (brother marrying sister, sister marrying brother), in which the foursome, ecstatically filmed as part of glorious American nature, meditate on their foundational role in the creation of a better, purer, American subject: clearly a racist one, a white one. The reconciliation between north and south therefore requires the recognition that the shared property of whiteness is the unifying link. Substitute English and Afrikaans for north and south and you have the connection between the birth of the American nation and the birth of the South African one.

The reconstruction of South African history and identity in terms of a reconciliation that follows from the recognition of unity through whiteness is of course Christianized, as also happened in America. And a series of racial subtypes follow from its Christianization. Thus, there is in both cases the black with a soul of gold, the good black or Christian black. That the good black is always portrayed as white in spirit allows humanity to be coded as paradigmatically white in character; hence the character of Sobuza, one of Dingane's chiefs who converts to Christianity under the influence of the missionary Reverend Owen. Through being blessed by the Reverend, he becomes, in essence, white. He is first shown accepting communion in the *veld* from the Reverend while the intertitle reads, "Honour thy father and thy mother that thy days may be long in the land which the Lord thy God giveth thee." Clearly the land is only God's to give, and one's acceptance in it is predicated upon one's acceptance of the gospel. This is the Reverend's point of view and it becomes ours too, just as it narratively becomes Sobuza's through his conversion. Then, there is an immediate cut from the missionary preaching love and nonviolence to a scene in which Dingane is sentencing a child and his nurse to death. It turns out that the child is Dingane's son and must die in order to prevent him from conspiring in later life against his father. With this juxtaposition, the two discourses of Christian civilization and tribal barbarity are once again re-evoked, which the accompanying intertitle emphasizes is "Dingane's Way," in contrast to the way of the missionary.

The film's rhetorical schema relies heavily on the intertitles to anchor the visual images as representations of historical accuracy and truth (what really happened), and to limit, as far as it is possible to do so, the polysemy of the text. Like Lacanian *points de capiton* (meaning "quilting points," like buttons that serve to anchor the stuffing down), they work to wrest meaning from the film's unstable field of signifiers. As Slavoj Zizek explains Lacan's concept, "the multitude of floating signifiers is structured into a unified field through the intervention of a certain nodal point . . . which quilts them, stops their sliding and fixes their meaning."[38] Later, when Sobuza, having become a Christian, refuses to obey Dingane's orders to kill the child, he is accused of having a "White heart within the body of a Zulu warrior." Sobuza's conversion to Christianity opens up a new ordering principle in the construction of the nation: the idea of acceptable natives and "others" versus those aliens and people who cannot be assimilated. Later, this list will come to include Roman Catholics, Communists, "Coloureds," Indians, Chinese, and Jews, all of whom must be excluded.[39]

Christianity does not resolve the racist problematic in South Africa, but it does secure a zone of acceptance for Christian blacks within the nation's frontiers. The importance of the Christian element in the reconstruction of South African history is as crucial here as it is in *The Birth of a*

Nation, where woman is given a cinematic innocence and grace worthy of the Christian miracles. In Griffith's camera the process is miraculous, but always white, blonde, quiet, and soft. Softness, the alternative to barbarity, is a property of the good black, who is in effect raised from barbarity through a natural womanliness. Thus, the gendered character of the good Christian—hard, male, uncompromising, and just on the one hand, and soft, feminine, and capable of grace on the other. In the final frame of the film, Sobuza sits outside the church, newly built to commemorate the victory at Blood River, while the *Boer* community goes inside to pray. Inside the church, the daughter of the old patriarch holds her new baby, symbolizing the (re)birth of the Afrikaans nation in a state of reconciliation with the English and, outside, the Christianized black.

And the Portuguese? They are Griffith's colored people, unnatural in birth, less than white and more than black, morally depraved and intellectually conniving, motivated by the desire to possess whiteness, and through envy, to destroy it. If there is a Satan in this story it is this group. Ironically, the Portuguese were restored to whiteness by the apartheid state, a whiteness they had in the beginning, when on the ships of Bernal Diaz and Magellan, they first made contact with the Khoi and the San. Races are historically remade each and every time the state formation changes: the race for representation is also a race to rewrite the terms of race.

ALTERNATIVE CONSTRUCTIONS OF RACE

The fact that a white heart can beat in a black body—the body of Sobuza—means that there are alternative constructions of race at work in this film, as there are in the history of nineteenth century European racism in general. Biology will be used to assign inferiority as a direct concomitant of skin color, which, if one follows through on this line of reasoning, would make it well nigh impossible for a black body to possess a Christian soul. Taken to extremes, biological racism leads to the Nazi vision of the Jew: a virus which must be eliminated without exception. That Sobuza is not only imaginatively possible, but central to the final ending of the film as the one who is outside but also inside, shows that colonialism could not exclude the idea that there is a place for the good native subject in its social constructions.

The natives are here to stay, a majority, crucial for capitalism, the mines, commerce, and the enrichment of the European. English liberalism will depend on this, in the mines for example, where it will be crucial for the "Randlords" (mining magnates) to believe that the black worker is capable of consensual agreement with work and policy, while also requiring the greatest possible monitoring and control. Only when apartheid enters the scene in 1948 will the Christian ideal give way to a legalized concept of racial otherness: then the black will not be outside the church, nodding and smiling his acceptance of his outsider/insider status, but in his appointed Bantustan where his own identity can be given free rein to express its own terms of existence.

TRACING MEANINGS

In 1916, *De Voortrekkers* translated the dispersed events of the Great Trek in terms of white unity and the state-institutionalized discourse of segregation. In the thirties, the failure of the Fusion government to provide satisfactory modes of identification for the Afrikaners who remained at the bottom of the white economic scale resulted in a rejection of that particular translation. This meant a rejection of the project of reconciliation for one that engaged the historical narrative of the Great Trek and the great battle as a moment of glory solely for the Afrikaner people.[40] In 1998, another act of transmission reinvented the battle in response to post-apartheid South Africa. On the Day of Reconciliation (formerly the Day of the Covenant), busloads of Zulu people in full traditional attire and singing *amahubo* (traditional songs) journeyed to the banks of the Ncome River (the Zulu name for Blood River) to remember the proud and brave warriors who died in their thousands defending their homeland against colonial invaders. Led by King Zwelithini ka Cyprian ka Bhekuzulu, the crowd paid tribute to their dead and mourned the moment as one which preceded their long period of suffering and humiliation at the hands of the whites. "The Zulu nation fought for its inalienable right to this God-given land, and for freedom and liberty," said Mangosuthu Gatsha Buthelezi, the Minister of Home Affairs at the inauguration of the Ncomal Blood River Monument, adding that in the whites' appropriation of the historical events, not only the bodies but the very soul of Zulu culture had been debased.[41] But, as in *De Voortrekkers*, reconciliation was in the air. Speaker after speaker called for a coming together of the new South African nation through a joint commemoration of the battle. The mingling of the blood of both sides became the symbolic trope of the day, as did the waters of the river which washed the blood away. Again in biblical rhetoric, Buthelezi intoned, "One could not distinguish then, as one cannot distinguish now, the blood of the Afrikaner from the blood of the Zulu. . . ."[42]

Yet not everyone, particularly on the Afrikaner side, seemed to be in accord with this mingling. Two signposts, one saying "Ncome Monument" and the other "Blood River Monument," marked out the two very different commemorative spaces, ironically each on different sides of the river. At the Afrikaans site, seventy ox wagons were drawn up into a *laager*, or circle, to encase the *volk*, but somehow, a number of Zulu had made their way into the *laager* and were interestedly looking around. Perhaps the two most telling moments were the comment by the Zulu king who asked, "What happened to the so-called reconciliation?" and a photo flashed across the television that night of a young Zulu girl in the *laager* bending down to smell the flowers placed at the steel plaque engraved with the vow the Afrikaners had made to their god 170 years ago. Reconciliation alone is not enough. What is required is a politics of recognition, the recognition by others of one's own particular history and its meaning for one's own group identity. It is around images of particular histories—histories that occurred in the same place but under different terms of reference—that the stakes of reconciliation are formed.

SOLOMON TSHESIKO PLAATJE AND COME SEE THE BIOSCOPE, THEN AND NOW

In discussing the relationship between nation and history, Prasenjit Duara notes that far from being a site of unity and cohesiveness, nationalism "marks the site where different representations of the nation contest and negotiate with each other." Most of these representations are chronically subdued by the ascendant power, which claims the power, the glory, and the terms of distribution and citizenship as its own. But this means that these representations are always on the scene of history, always present to disturb the cards. Everyone is special and everyone is not, everyone adds something to history and everyone does not, and to single out a specific segment of the population on the grounds of character and role as essential to national destiny (to the exclusion of all others) and make it stick, there must be a continual telling and retelling of the story, the myth, and the invention of tradition which justifies this specialness—hence the special place of the story of Piet Retief and King Dingane and the importance of such films as *De Voortrekkers*.

From *De Voortrekkers* in 1916 we arrive at the prehistory of Afrikaner nationalism in the 1930s, which culminates in the apartheid state a decade later. This story never succeeds in erasing liberal, Marxist, Pan-Africanist, and other competing narratives of the nation, not to mention stories which deal with other groups' different roles, such as the role of English capitalism or the work of the early black nationalists, the forerunners of the current ruling party. It is the African nationalist vision, a vision that was crushed and ground into the red dust of South Africa first, during the era of segregation, and second, by the apartheid state, that finds representation in *Come See the Bioscope*. This countervision to the one in *De Voortrekkers* was the vision and hope of Solomon Plaatje, who is the subject of the film, and his party, the ANC, and it had its genesis at almost precisely the same time as the production of *De Voortrekkers*. Just two years separate the 1914 trip Plaatje made to England as one of the ANC delegates sent to argue for the repeal of the Natives Land Act in the name of British justice and fair play from the 1916 production of *De Voortrekkers*. *De Voortrekkers* may be considered an early example of South African film production, while the story of *Come See the Bioscope* is one story of early South African film culture. It is the story of Solomon Plaatje's efforts to build a film culture among rural black people who had been dispossessed, forced off the land into servitude, and driven into the cities to live in single-sex mining compounds, leaving broken families behind. Tragically, Plaatje's attempt to build an inclusive South African modernity was repressed, untold until over eighty years later when, under a new dispensation and a new directive, it was told in the cinema.

CINEMA MOVES FROM CITY TO COUNTRY

> Awakening on Friday morning, June 20, 1913, the South African native found himself not actually a slave but a pariah in the land of his birth.

Plaatje wrote these words to describe the drastic effects of the 1913 Natives Land Act on the native populations of South Africa—an act which dispossessed black farmers of their property, forcing them and their families into overcrowded "native" reserves that comprised a mere 13 percent of South African territory, or into the cities to work as cheap laborers for the mining companies. In Gewer's film, we see Plaatje writing these words in his notebook by the first light of day. The film begins with the shimmering image of a car driving through the dust and intense sun of the western Transvaal toward a small village of black tenant farmers and white landowners. The landscape is dry, filled with rock and stunted bush, grey and khaki in color. The year is 1923. The car stops and a well-tailored black man in a three-piece suit and hat, his eyes as intense as the sun, gets out and stretches. Bare-foot children in rags giggle at the sight of the automobile, a rarity in that dusty patch of *veld*, and at the even more unusual sight of a black man get-ting out of a car.

A single child approaches him, timidly. The man greets the child and asks what his name is. "I am Musi, and what is your name?" is the reply. "My name is Solomon Plaatje. Can you tell me if there is a church in this town?" The pair climbs into the car and proceeds to the white, gabled, Cape Dutch church where Plaatje approaches the minister, asking if he can use a white wall for a bioscope show that night. Clearly nervous, although im-pressed by his visitor, whom he knows by reputation, the minister prevari-cates, telling Plaatje that he will have to ask the authorities for permission.

In the next scene, the image of the cleric is replaced by that of Mr. Ma-hommed, an Indian man in Muslim dress sitting on the stoop of his country store filled with the minimal necessities needed to sustain rural black life—bags of cornmeal and beans, needles, bales of material, tin cups and plates, and drums of paraffin used for cooking and heating. In contrast to the cleric, the storekeeper immediately agrees to let Plaatje use the white wall behind his store for the show with the words, "a bioscope show, how de-lightful." The film cuts to Plaatje having supper in the simple hut of Musi's grandmother, who tells him that Musi's father is in Johannesburg working on the mines and can only come home to visit once a year, while his mother has left to find work in the city. Only she and Musi, the old and the young, are the remnants of what used to be a family unit. And they, too, have been displaced many times after having been evicted from their original land. Plaatje takes notes as she talks, transforming her story into the graphic, emotive vignettes that form the substance of his book *Native Life in South Africa*.[43]

The next morning, the children, with Musi as leader, hand out adver-tisements for the bioscope show, and mismatched furniture is arranged fac-ing the wall behind Mr. Mohammed's store for the evening's show. Plaatje sets up the equipment, explaining to the children what a bioscope is, how it works, and how it speeds up movement, and then demonstrates the ac-tion they will see by waddling like Charlie Chaplin toward the wall where the film will be broadcast and back. By now, a small crowd of villagers has gathered. Plaatje begins by explaining that he has recently been to Europe and America and wants to show them something of his travels, of what he saw there. "Let the show begin," he announces, placing a recording of *Nkosi Sikelele Africa* (the theme song of the ANC, which will become part of post-apartheid South Africa's official anthem seventy years later), sung by its composer, Enoch Sithole, on the wind-up gramophone.

The first reel of "film" is a travelogue of the most famous sites and events in Britain: the Houses of Parliament, opening day at Ascot, The king and queen driving in carriages through London, and the like. Other short "actualities" of events, places, and things are screened, each little visual slices of life in England, for which Plaatje serves as commentator and guide. The group is surprised to see white miners and asks, "Is such a thing possible?" The banality of the images is offset by Plaatje's commentary on his trip to the English parliament to present the case the South African Native National Congress (now the ANC) had marshaled against the Land Act. "Lloyd George, the British Prime Minister, said he would look into it," says Plaatje, "but we are still waiting." The crowd members nod their heads understandingly, indicating that they are well acquainted with the condition of waiting. Plaatje then shows a short film he received from the Tuskegee Normal and Industrial Institute on the activities of students there, who were training to become teachers and learning skills in construction, agriculture, and other practical trades. The audience receives this with immense enthusiasm, an enthusiasm that is suddenly cut short as the flickering light stops and the images disappear.

The police have arrived and stopped the show. In belligerent tones, they demand to know what Plaatje is doing. "Having a bioscope show," is Plaatje's simple response, adding that no law has been broken in the process. But that is of no matter, for the police here are the law, and Plaatje is, to use his own words, "a pariah in his own land," as vulnerable a subject as the people he has been researching, who have been disenfranchised by the Native Lands Act and thrown off the land to become beggars and vagrants. Musi asks him if he will go. "I have to," he replies, tensely and sadly. The bioscope is packed up and put away, but not before he has cut a small piece from the film stock in the projector and placed it in his pocket. Before leaving for the next village and the next bioscope show, he gives Musi the piece of film stock to keep, to help him remember his first contact with the bioscope.

We may think of that piece of film as *Come See the Bioscope* itself. The intervening years of history, evoked without being mentioned by the brutality of the white police, will keep that piece of film from becoming something whole. Only now, with the ANC in power, is Plaatje's political goal of black enfranchisement capable of being completed, and with it, his cinematic goal of making a rural people part of things, giving them access to the wider world and its riches. They are, the film suggests, already moral, already dignified. What they need are information and equity. The film is Plaatje's return to live among us.

A MAN FOR NEW TIMES

In June 2000, a special ceremony was held in Pretoria to celebrate the re-naming of the Department of Education building as the Solomon Plaatje building. With this act, Plaatje's legacy as a novelist (*Mhudi* was the first South African novel published in English by a black man), a political leader, a journalist, and a man at the forefront of South African black public affairs was resurrected and memorialized.[44] This is not to say that he was unrecognized in his own time. The memorial tombstone unveiled in 1935, three years after his death, by G. A. Simpson, fellow journalist and editor of the *Diamond Fields Advertiser*, reads, "No mere words of mine can adequately pay tribute to his memory—the memory of one who was an outstanding figure in the life of the people of South Africa." But in the fifty years since his death, the years which saw the beginning and entrenchment of apartheid in South Africa, the story of a man like Solomon Plaatje was deliberately obscured and buried, as deep as the victims unearthed by the Truth and Reconciliation Commission. Only now can it be recovered, not only so that it might enter South African historical memory, but also so that it might become part of the present and help shape a future vision for the nation. For despite being born on a farm in the Orange Free State in 1876, Plaatje was a man of immense cosmopolitanism, a modern man at the time when South African black people were not meant to be the subjects of modernity but merely its objects, its raw material to be used in much the same way as the gold and diamonds buried in the South African soil were used to build a modern state for whites only. Plaatje was hardly a drawer of water and a hewer of wood. He spoke eight African languages. He loved Shakespeare, and saw no reason why his plays should not be accessible to literate black South Africans as it was to whites. He translated *A Comedy of Errors* into Setswana as part of his efforts to preserve the language, history, and cultural traditions of the Tswana people by feeding it with new material from other cultures. He was the publisher and editor of two bilingual newspapers, in English and Setswana, which contained a wide variety of stories of both local and international interest since he had negotiated exchange agreements with sixty-one international newspapers. He was the founder of the South African Native Press Association in 1934, and secretary-general of the African National Congress formed in 1912 to combat the increasing oppression of the South African black population, an oppression which ran counter to the belief held by many black intellectuals that the unionization of South Africa would mean a greater degree of freedom for its black people. In sketching African responses in the years immediately following the union, Tom Lodge comments,

> [a]mong many members of the African elite hopes raised initially by the defeat of the republics in the Anglo-Boer war had been swiftly disappointed. Despite African expressions of imperial loyalty intermingled with politely phrased reproach at the prevalent discrimination against Black men of "training, character and ability," the British government made it clear that its paramount concern was the question of White unity in South Africa.[45]

Along with his colleagues, John Dube and Pixley Seme, Plaatje saw the Union of South Africa as a system of racial estates which would finally lift up black people, bringing them into citizenship and into the domain of formal and substantive rights and making their rural lives and urban existences more bearable and fruitful. After all, they had played a large role in the war in support of the British. And Plaatje, a court interpreter for the British during the siege of Mafeking and the product of English missionary education, believed firmly in the fairness of British liberalism.

It seemed almost unbelievable to Plaatje that after the Boer War, the British would turn against their black allies in favor of their white enemies. "The Gods are cruel," he wrote in his journals, "and one of their cruelest acts of omission was that of giving us no hint." There was no hint that the Land Act would not be rescinded, but instead would be followed by a further series of disempowering laws against the black population enacted under the union's segregationist policy, like the Native Affairs Act of 1920 and the Urban Areas Act of 1923, which organized and institutionalized influx control and the segregation of urban residential areas. There was no hint that under the Industrial Conciliation Act of 1924, "natives" would be excluded from the title of "employee," thus refusing them the right to strike. There was no hint that job reservation for whites would be ensured under the Mines and Works Act of 1911, and then deepened under the Native Taxation and Development Act of 1925.[46] And, of course, there was no hint of the apartheid state which would be brought into power after his death in the 1948 elections. Hence, Musi without his father and mother. Hence, these villagers as tenant farmers. Hence, the refusal of the church to let him put on his bioscope show. Hence, the power of the village police to close down the show and expel Plaatje from the village. Hence, Plaatje's pessimistic question in his 1923 journal: "How are we going to build a future?" Hence, his deep commitment to the bioscope's ability to "educate" these throwaway people, to pass onto them what he had been exposed to overseas and give hope where there was only despair.

GETTING A BIGGER PICTURE

It is not insignificant that the portable movie projector used by Plaatje was a gift from the Reverend J. A. Johnston, head of the African Methodist Episcopal (AME) church in Philadelphia, or that some of the films came from Booker T. Washington's Tuskegee Institute. These facts are evidence of the cultural connections between Africa and America, connections that are often lost in cinema theory by the creation of typologies such as mainstream/Hollywood cinema, oppositional/alternative cinema, or even national cinemas. While useful pedagogically and historically in film scholarship, as, for example, the typology offered in Teshome Gabriel's critical theory of third-world films, they have also tended to become dogmatic and frozen, obscuring the deep connections that exist in the history of the cinematic institution and the global connections which cinema history, as part of broader history per se, must seek to acknowledge even as it also acknowledges the differences at work. The connection between American popular culture, especially American black culture, will be so central to the story of South African black culture that the rise of its black urban spaces like Sophiatown or District 6 will be predicated on the importation, transposition, imitation, translation, and remaking of American culture there. In the thirties, the films of Fred Astaire will influence African dance performance. In the fifties, jazz bands like The Manhattan Brothers, the Woody Woodpeckers, and the Harlem Swingsters were integral to the creation of Sophiatown's urban black culture, while *Drum Magazine* featured a Philip Marlowe character and a style of presentation almost indistinguishable from *Life* and *Look* magazines. The Pan-Africanist discourses of South Africa's Black Consciousness Movement, formed in the 1960s by Steve Biko and other activists, were predicated on the writings of W. E. B. Du Bois about Africa as the site of a racialistic unity defined by lines of cultural descent, a legacy to the present which made black consciousness and the consciousness of nationalism the same. Indeed, it is because of the complex forms of dependency and identification, of cultural circulation and communication between South Africa and the United States, that cinema history, as well as history in general, must be written as taking place betwixt and between these sites.

Charles Taylor's idea of "alternative modernities" is useful in understanding how modernity gets both decomposed and recomposed in its journey between places. The very term highlights the fact that modernity is not a singular, finished process but a plural, fungible one embedded over years in the exchanges, practices, arrangements, and encounters that mark its diffusion throughout the world. While the effects of its presence are much the same worldwide—that is, industrialization, bureaucratization, secularization of thought and belief, forms of popular government—they take on different shapes which reflect the particularities of place and culture, especially when those structures of meaning are still strong and extant. The process is more active than reactive, a point Taylor makes when he says, "a successful transition involves a people finding resources in their traditional culture, which modified and transposed, will enable them to take on the new practices."[47] Neither is it an either/or case: blind imitation engulfing more indigenous ways or complete innovation in the name of authenticity. The changes wrought by modernity are profound and inevitably bring about a repertory of new institutions, social relations, value systems, cultural forms, and subjectivities that contain both convergences with and divergences from Western modernity.

For Dilip Gaonkar, alternative modernities are best understood as an attitude or way of questioning the dilemmas of the present:

> The questioning of the present, whether in the vernacular or in cosmopolitan idioms, which is taking place at every national and cultural site today cannot escape the legacy of Western discourse on modernity. Whoever elects to think in terms of alternative modernities (irrespective of one's location) must think with and also think against the tradition of reflection that stretches from Marx and Weber through Baudelaire and Benjamin to Habermas, Foucault, and many other Western (born or trained) thinkers.[48]

This exposure to other traditions of thought and life is exactly Plaatje's mission in *Come See the Bioscope*. Plaatje had been deeply impressed during his travels in the United States and Canada by the achievements of the African American middle class in those countries, and largely attributed its success to education, a process in which the bioscope had its place. He was not traveling from village to village to foment resistance or violence, but to show his bioscope to those whose horizons were restricted in the hope of broadening them. In this sense, his mission was didactic and educational, about the politics of citizenship, about readying a class of rural subjects for a role he staked himself on believing would eventually open up for them: that of citizens in a modern state. The language of "improvement" and "cultivation" may seem archaic to us today, a remnant of Victorianism that smacks of a colonial subjectivity. But in the South Africa of 1923, it was still possible, indeed reasonable and noble, to stake oneself on this mission of the cultivation of modernity in people who have been systematically denied access to its possibilities.[49] Of course, the widening of horizons is not distinguishable from the pointing out of problems, "the questioning of the present," as Gaonkar puts it, but both were meant to bring rural black people into modernity, a modernity of which urban blacks in the cities had far more awareness, the city being the site of proximity to capital, consumerism, mobility, the system of power, and the way things are in the bigger picture. The connections between the cultural history of modernity and the city have, since the time of Baudelaire, been tightly entwined. The city has been figured as the source of modernity, the experiential site for all those vast changes in social and economic life that are grouped under the label of the modern.

"Modernity cannot be conceived outside the context of the city," state Leo Charney and Vanessa Schwartz in their introduction to a recent anthology on the subject.[50] And neither, it would appear, can the cinema, which along with other technological innovations of the nineteenth century such as photography, the telegraph, the railways, and architecture, is seen as one of the modes by which modern culture can best be grasped and understood. But with his traveling show, known as "Plaatje's Bioscope," Plaatje challenged the site of modernity by taking one its favored talismans, the cinema, to the country, to rural people who had never seen a city and were unfamiliar with its representations, its forms of entertainment and leisure activity, its distractions and sensations. He was not alone in this transposition of cinema from city to country, but he was the first to address his mobile bioscope to African audiences. White country audiences had been exposed to the cinema since its beginning by traveling exhibitors working the country routes. Small-time entrepreneurs would take to the road with a projector and material obtained from large distribution companies, which they would show in a variety of settings ranging from storefronts to churches. This practice did not diminish with the establishment of permanent cinemas from 1910 onward, but continued and was aided by the improvement in roads and access to motorcars. According to Thelma Gutsche, there was an unquenchable desire for these mobile or traveling cinemas despite the fact that parts of the program, like the newsreels, were often out of date.[51] Talkies, of course, required greater technological investment, but that too appeared after a hiatus, during which silent films continued to be shown, with the use of vans equipped with sound technology.

These practices were applicable only to the white, mostly Afrikaans rural population. In the urban areas, the cinemas were segregated and Africans could attend if they sat in specifically designated areas. In examining the role of the American Mission Board in early cinema in South Africa, Bhekizizwe Peterson details how, in the early 1920s,[52] the Reverend Ray Phillips initiated a project for exhibiting films to African miners in the mine compounds—rural Africans serving out their contracts under the rules of the Chamber of Mines. Nevertheless, they were now within the ambit of the city, and so this cannot be considered as a diffusion of cinema into the rural. Nor, in fact, was the motivation behind the project in any way similar to that of Plaatje's bioscope. As Peterson reveals, Reverend Phillips used the cinema as an anodyne, a healthful diversion or what he called "an antidote to the degrading influences of the slumyards and liquor dens" of the city.[53] Playing on the ever-present fear of strikes and violence by the hundreds of thousands of mineworkers in the compounds, Phillips argued that the cinema could even suppress such "criminal behavior." In contrast, Plaatje believed that for all Africans, irrespective of their location, to assume their rightful place in any new dispensation of rights, they would have to become modern subjects, more knowledgeable about the ways of modernity, more questioning about its effects, more urbane and able to sustain them within a modern state system. He staked his faith in the young, in the next generation, writing to Robert Moton at Tuskegee, "[w]ith the poverty of the natives it is a profitless job: but when I see the joy, especially of the native kiddies . . . it turns the whole thing into a labour of love."[54]

A thousand questions open up around this act of cultural transposition, as these films move through space from one set of cultures to another, from one pair of eyes (the eyes of a Londoner, or a New Yorker) to another pair of eyes (the eyes of Musi, and the villagers) accompanied by different music (the music of South Africa's national anthem, *Nkosi Sikelele*) and a different commentary (Plaatje's). It is impossible to know how the audience, adults and children alike, received them. In view of the worsening economic climate for rural blacks, Plaatje's message of educational self-liberation (although I think he would have seen it more in the old-fashioned terms of self-help or moral improvement) may have been difficult to comprehend, irrelevant even, in a state which controlled almost every aspect of black life. But it is clear what the act of transposition meant for Plaatje. For if Plaatje's parting gift to Musi is a little piece of film stock so that Musi might remember this man, this film, this night, and what happened to the wall on which the images were projected, then Plaatje's presentation of the bioscope in the film is also that of a gift, the gift of the modern. It underlines his belief in the link between the cinema and modernity (a link which is only now being examined in contemporary cultural theory) and in the emancipatory potential of mass culture to bring about a better understanding of the world and help develop critical capacities.

ENDINGS AND BEGINNINGS

The plot of *Come See the Bioscope,* made in 1997, is also more or less what really happened to black people from the time of union in 1910 to the passing of the Land Act in 1923. In between these dates, in 1916, *De Voortrekkers* was produced. There is a special *correspondence,* as the French would say, between these moments: 1916 and 1997. Each is a cinematic moment early in one version of "the new South Africa," each version a system of racial estates and a new nation, each called, by a certain irony of history, "South Africa," one following the other. These representations begin and end our story, a story of the cinema in South Africa, a story of the cinema *and* South Africa. 1916 is a moment fairly close to the beginning of film history itself, while 1997 is close to where we are now, in the first decade beyond the millennium. This pair of national dispensations, in which the cinema has lived, limped, died, and been slowly resuscitated, one in the past, the other in the present, although radically different, are inevitably linked. The first is the union established after the Boer War in which Plaatje, one of the ANC's founders, believed that black people would be blessed with citizenship by their new British colonial masters. The second is the post-apartheid dispensation in which a film like *Come See the Bioscope* could be made and seen, a dispensation in which cinema has now potentially become the property of everyone. It is only in this second nation, the post-apartheid one, that we can celebrate Plaatje's dream for the first one, and mourn its failure. It is only in the second one that we can come and see the "bioscope," and try to understand what role it might play in this new nation. Which is what part of this book aims to do: to read cinema since the end of apartheid all the way through to the present, with leaps and bounds, gaps and additions, fragments and continuities, but in the image of this newly forming nation of which the bioscope of the past is still a part.

Post-apartheid South Africa is now ready to return to its past in a way that is inclusive rather than disenfranchising, to do so in the name of a new dispensation of rights which is equally inclusive and to do so in order to unlearn the illusions of the past, in the name of redress and reconciliation. Since the project of national reconciliation is that of inclusion, *Come See the Bioscope* can now be made. In 1923, Plaatje's project of enfranchising black people as citizens through cinematic means, that is, experimentally, was desiccated first by the terms of the union, and then, after his death, by those of the apartheid state which produced further waves of disenfranchisement and raced to represent reconciliation in racist terms. But now his party, the ANC, is in power, and his ideal of inclusive citizenship is at least constitutionalized. His desire to uplift people through cultural expansion may require reconsideration today: given global postmodernism, what Ella Shohat and Robert Stam call the transnational imaginary, the relationship between globalization and substantive rights is hardly straightforward. But at least South Africa can now use cinematic means as part of the attempt to recover its past, to return to what Plaatje did and include it in the national archive. That this act of making a film about a man who brought cinema to black South Africans in the name of citizenship can *only* now be performed is a historical scandal. That it *can* now be made is a historical blessing, a fulfillment of his legacy. One might say that *Come See the Bioscope* was almost made by Plaatje himself, for its intention is his intention, and he would have recognized himself in it. Thus, history strives toward the impossible, to reconcile with the dead and bring their spirits to life again. As Plaatje lives on screen, so he lives in the very intention and substance of this film. Those who watch become modern subjects, traveling back in time to reclaim what they can now call their roots. The South African experiment in the consolidation of citizenship that is happening now, an experiment in which cinema is seeking to play its part, is an experiment in time travel. Finally, as South Africans we can come see, that is, return to, the "bioscope."

Notes

Introduction

The first epigraph is from Jeremy Cronin, "Running Towards Us," in *New Writing from South Africa*, ed. Isabel Balseiro (New Haven, Conn.: Heinemann, 2000), 5. Jeremy Cronin is the Deputy General Secretary of the South African Communist Party and serves on the National Executive Committee of the African National Congress.

The second epigraph is from Frantz Fanon, *The Wretched of the Earth* (New York: Grove Weidenfeld, 1963), 36.

1. In a move totally out of character with its rhetoric of transparency in state affairs and reconciliation, the ANC unsuccessfully attempted to obtain a court interdict to prevent the release of the report in which prominent ANC officials were cited for human rights abuses, including the killing of civilians in its military operations, torture in its military camps, and the deaths of civilians in its landmine campaign in the former eastern Transvaal. Also cited were the Inkatha Freedom Party and its leader, Chief Mangosuthu Buthelezi, who came in for heavy criticism in the section of the report devoted to the black-on-black killings in KwaZulu-Natal during the early nineties. The ANC's action against the TRC included a twenty-five-page affidavit viciously attacking the commission. See the *Mail and Guardian*, October 30 to November 5, 1998, for a full discussion of the ANC interdict against the TRC's final report.

2. Fanon, *The Wretched of the Earth*, 35.

3. Benedict Anderson, *Imagined Communities: Reflections on the Origin and Spread of Nationalism* (London: Verso, 1991). Anderson's approach is problematic. One of the criticisms leveled against him is that he overstated the speed with which this unified time and space was created (see Steven Kemper). Another is that there is a limit to the insights one can get from this approach. Whether nations are imagined or "invented" (to use Trevor Ranger's phrase), they are "facts" and have profound material consequences. More importantly, talk of an "imagined community" or "invented traditions" suggests once again that nationalism is, as the Marxists have proposed, an illusory affect, a historical mistake that can be righted through rational analysis. See Tony Judt, "The Old New Nationalisms," *New York Review of Books* 41 (May 26, 1994).

4. Stuart Hall, "The Local and the Global: Globalization and Ethnicity," in Anthony D. King, *Culture, Globalization and the World System* (London: Macmillan, 1991), 36.

5. Since eugenicists saw human life solely in universal biological terms, the idea of manipulating human reproduction in much the same way as one did in animals through husbandry practices did not seem farfetched. Thus Francis Galton, a major figure in the field, wrote in 1869, "as it is easy . . . to obtain by careful selection a permanent breed of dogs or horses . . . so it would be quite practicable to produce a highly gifted race of men by judicious marriages." Nancy Leys Stepan, *The Hour of Eugenics: Race, Gender and Nation in Latin America* (Ithaca, N.Y.: Cornell University Press, 1963), 23.

6. Mark Schoofs, "Aid: The Agony of Africa: Building a Movement on the Ruins of Apartheid," *The Village Voice*, December 22–28, 1999.

7. Abebe Zegeye and Richard L. Harris note that while the subgroup identities encouraged by the apartheid regime continue to exist, they are now shared with a strong overarching national identity. Abebe Zegeye and Richard L. Harris, eds., *Media, Identity and the Public Sphere in Post-Apartheid South Africa* (Leiden: Brill Academic Publishers, 2002), 251. This observation was confirmed by a Human Science Research Council survey of public opinion in 1999, where 84% of respondents indicated that "being South African is an important part of how I see myself." The only other major source of identity was religion. This research also indicates that subgroup identities are interlinked and provide a basis for building societal cohesion, and it further indicates that class or socioeconomic status is related to South Africans' sense of national identity. In 1997, national identity was weakest among people at the lower end of the socioeconomic scale and strongest among those at the higher end. By 1999, however, South Africans in the middle of the socioeconomic scale exhibited the strongest sense of national identity. Human Sciences Research Council (HSRC), *Public Attitudes in Contemporary SA: Insights from an HSRC Survey* (Johannesburg: HSRC Press, 2002).

8. Marsha Kinder, *Blood Cinema: The Reconstruction of National Identity in Spain* (Los Angeles: University of California Press, 1993), 7.

9. Keyan Tomaselli, *The Cinema of Apartheid: Race and Class in South African Film* (New York: Smyrna/Lake View Press Books, 1988), 54.

10. John Tomlinson, *Globalization and Culture* (Chicago: University of Chicago Press, 1999): 2.

11. Ian Angell, "Winners and Losers in the Information Age," in *Production of Culture/Culture of Production*, ed. Paul du Gay (London: Sage, 1998).

12. Sarah Nuttall and Achille Mbembe, "Writing the World from an African Metropolis," *Public Culture* 16, no. 3 (2004).

13. Ibid.

14. Department of Arts, Culture, Science and Technology (DACST), *White Paper on Film*, DACST, 1996, http://www.info.gov.za.

15. See Thomas Elsaesser's discussion of the construction and development of New German Cinema in *New German Cinema: A History* (New Brunswick: Rutgers University Press, 1989).

16. These positions are themselves contradictory. Auteurism, for example, emerges from the art cinema of the West and reifies individual, not collective, expression, yet it has been the paradigm for West African filmmakers since the 1950s.

17. Gutsche completed her study in 1946, just one year after the war and two years before the advent of the Apartheid State in 1948. There has been no cinema study of this magnitude since. My book is far less ambitious and less historically sweeping, but it could not have been written without Gutsche's work.

18. Gutsche, *The History and Social Significance of Motion Pictures in South Africa: 1895–1940* (Cape Town: Howard Timmins, 1972), 112.

19. Ibid., 311.

20. I discuss *De Voortrekkers* in detail in chapter 6. Other feature films produced at this time by African Film Productions were *The Story of the Rand*, *The Illicit Liquor Seller*, *The Water Cure*, *The Splendid Waster*, *Gloria*, *A Tragedy of the Veld*, *The Dop Doctor*, *Symbol of Sacrifice*, *Bond and Word*, *The Voice of the Waters*, and *The Blue Lagoon*.

21. Between 1956 and 1962, sixty films were made. Forty-three were in Afrikaans, thirteen were in English, and the remaining four were bilingual. See Martin Botha, "The Song Remains the Same: The Struggle for a South African Audience," *Kinema*, Spring 2004.

22. Gibson Kent's feature film, *How Long?* (1976), was the first feature film directed by a black South African. Due to its critical stance against apartheid, it was never distributed within South Africa.

23. See Tomaselli's *The Cinema of Apartheid*, chapter 3, for greater detail on the subsidy schemes for black films.

24. The Constitution of the Republic of South Africa, 1996. Chapter 2, Bill of Rights, section 9, "Equality," point 3, http://www.gov.za/constitution/1996/96cons2.htm.

25. The market has taken up this idea with a vengeance. Just to give one example, post-1994, South African Airways launched an advertising campaign that painted the tails of its Boeing jets with the national flag and used the slogan, "We speak many languages, but we fly one flag."

26. For more information on these ideas, see Grant Farred's article, "The African Renaissance at the Crossroads of Postcoloniality and Postmodernity," *Contours: A Journal of the African Diaspora* 1, no. 1 (2003).

27. See Jeremy Cronin, "Post Apartheid South Africa: A Reply to John Saul," *Monthly Review* 54.7 (December 2002): 28–42.

28. Ben Dowell, "BBC will screen Minghella's final drama," Guardian.co.uk, March 23, 2008, http://www.guardian.co.uk/media/2008/mar/18/bbc.television.

29. Toby Miller, Nitin Govil, John McMurria, Richard Maxwell, and Ting Wang, *Global Hollywood* 2 (London: British Film Institute Publishing, 2005), 51.

30. Ibid.

31. See Elsaesser, *New German Cinema*.

32. Pallo Jordan, keynote address, *National Film and Video Foundation Indaba*, August 18, 2005, polity.org.za/article/jordan-national-film-and-video-foundation-indaba-18082005-2005-08-18.

33. "Multiplier Cinemas for Soweto," http://www.bizcommunity.com/article/196/97/17784.html.

34. Jordan, keynote address.

35. Pieterson was the first person killed by the police in the 1976 Soweto Uprising. The Hector Pieterson memorial in Soweto is a favorite tourist stop on the Soweto Tour.

1. The Burdens of Representation

The epigraph is from Ms. B. Mabandla, *White Paper on Arts, Culture and Heritage*, June 4, 1996, p. 5, http://www.dac.gov.za/white_paper.htm.

1. Homi Bhabha, ed., *Nation and Narration* (London: Routledge, 1990).

2. Anderson, *Imagined Communities*.

3. Bhabha, ed., "Introduction: Narrating the Nation," in *Nation and Narration*, 3.

4. See "The Law Report: Customary Law and Human Rights in South Africa," December 6, 2005, http://www.abc.net.au/rn/lawreport/stories/2005/1525543.htm.

5. The Constitution of the Republic of South Africa, chapter 2, section 16, http://www.info.gov.za/documents/constitution/index.htm.

6. Rex A. Hudson, ed., *Brazil: A Country Study* (Washington, D.C.: Government Printing Office, http://countrystudies.us/brazil/.htm.

7. Martin Botha, L. Mare, Z. Langa, R. Netshitomboni, K. Ngoasheng, J. Potgieter, and M. Greyling, *Proposals for the Restructuring of the South African Film Industry* (Pretoria: Human Sciences Research Council, 1994).

8. Report of the Arts and Culture Task Group (Pretoria: Government Printer, 1995).

9. Independent Broadcasting Authority Act: Review of Local Content Quotas: Discussion Paper, http://www.info.gov.za/view/downloadfileaction?id=70333.

10. Ibid.

11. Ibid., 286.

12. National Film and Video Foundation Act, Government Gazette of the Republic of South Africa, Act No. 18489, Pretoria, 1997.

13. Independent Broadcasting Authority Act: Review of Local Content Quotas.

14. "TM Mbeki: Adoption of RSA Constitution Bill," South African Government Information, http://www.info.gov.za/aboutgovt/orders/new2002_mbeki.htm.

15. The idea of the African Renaissance could easily slide into reverse racism. In this regard, it is worth recalling some of the points Anthony Appiah has made in his analysis of negritude and Pan-Africanism. While acknowledging its crucial rhetorical force, he claims that it is essentially an inversion of racism or counter-identification. This is false: when one considers the disunity of Africa, one cannot find a common sociocultural meaning that can be derived from the word "race." "Time and time again," he states, "cultural nationalism has followed the route of alternate genealogizing. We end up always in the same place. The achievement is to have invented a different past for it." See Anthony Appiah, *In My Father's House* (Cambridge: Oxford University Press, 1992), 170.

16. See Dale T. McKinley, *The ANC and the Liberation Struggle: A Critical Political Biography* (London: Pluto Press, 2000); Hein Marais, *South Africa: Limits to Change* (London: Zed Press, 1988); and Ashwin Desai, *South Africa: Still Revolting* (Johannesburg: Impact Africa Pub., 1999).

17. Patrick Bond, *Elite Transition: From Apartheid to Neoliberalism in South Africa* (London: Pluto Press, 2000).

18. Ibid.

19. Harvey Ibrahim, "Defender of the ANC and the Presidency," *Mail and Guardian*, July 21–27, 2000, 31.

20. Mathatha Tsedu, "African intellectuals struggle to pave their road ahead," *The Sunday Independent*, December 20, 1998.

21. Soyinka delivered these remarks in 1999 in his lecture "Arms and the Arts—A Continent's Unequal Dialogue" as part of the T. B. Davies Lecture series established in the late fifties by University of Cape Town students to commemorate the former vice chancellor's crusade for freedom of speech and human rights.

22. Ice Media is a film production and distribution company that started in Harare, Zimbabwe, and moved to Johannesburg in 2000. It is headed by Joel Phiri,

a force in the new South African filmscape. Working intermedially (film and television) and across types (documentary and feature), Phiri has now moved into transnational co-production. He is currently producing *Wah Wah*, a feature film directed by Richard Grant.

23. Joel Phiri, "Company Director 8 Executive Producer," http://www.africaine.org/?menu=fiche&no.=11346.

24. "Africa at the Pictures Celebrating African Cinema," July 3, 2005, http://www.africaine.org/?menu=evt8no=5039#top.

25. Ibid.

26. "South Africa's Film and TV Foundation Launched," *Africa Film and TV Edition*, February–April 2000, 3.

27. Ibid.

28. National Film and Video Foundation (NFVF), *Value Charter*, 2002, p. 1, http://www.nfvf.co.za.

29. The Department of Arts, Culture, Science and Technology was established in 1994 after national elections in April of the same year. The Department is responsible for promoting and preserving South Africa's arts, culture, and heritage and for enhancing the country's scientific research and technological capacities in line with the government's Reconstruction and Development Programme. After the science and technology sectors split off to form their own department, the name was changed to the Department of Arts and Culture (DAC). The remainder of the chapter refers to the department by its current name.

30. *White Paper on Arts, Culture and Heritage.*

31. *White Paper on Film.*

32. *White Paper on Arts, Culture and Heritage.*

33. *White Paper on Film.*

34. Ibid.

35. Elsaesser, *New German Cinema.*

36. The "B" scheme collapsed in 1989, almost at the same time as the main scheme fell into crisis.

37. Johan Blignaut, "Lights, Camera, Shelve It!" in *Movies, Moguls, Mavericks: South African Cinema 1979–1991*, ed. Johan Blignaut and Martin Botha (Johannesburg: Showdata, 1992), 111–118.

38. Ibid., 113.

39. Andrew Worsdale, "From Silence to Subterfuge," *Mail and Guardian*, December 23, 1999.

40. Gus Silber, "Tax, Lies and Videotape," in *Movies, Moguls, Mavericks*, eds. Blignaut and Botha, 119–129.

41. Ibid., 128.

42. W. Nel, *Profile 2000: Towards a Viable South African Film Industry* (Johannesburg: Pricewaterhouse Coopers, 2000), 4.

43. Ibid., 21.

44. NFVF, Indaba 2001, *Consolidated and Final Summary* (Johannesburg: NVFV, 2001), 1.

45. *Mr. Bones* (Darrell Roodt, 2001) is the most successful local film to date.

46. Cape Film Commission, Film Stats, 2002, http://www.capefilmcommission.co.za.

47. NFVF, Indaba 2001, *Consolidated and Final Summary.*

48. In 2001, the budget was around $1.8 million. By 2003, it had risen to around $3.15 million. In 2005, the NFVF spent around $3.6 million on production and $550,000 on research and development. Currently it has a budget of $764,000 for features. Figures are approximate and are based on the exchange rate of the rand to the dollar in June 2008.

49. National Film and Video Foundation Act.

50. *RDP White Paper*, 1994, 22, http://www.anc.org.za/ancdocs/policy/white.html.

51. Ibid., 8.

52. Growth, Employment & Redistribution: A Microeconomic Strategy, http://www.finance.gov.za/publication/other/gear/chapters.pdf.

53. NFVF, "What is the National Film and Video Foundation?," http://www.nfvf.co.za/about-nfvf.

54. NFVF, *A Report on the NFVF Film Indaba 2005. 18–19 August 2005, Midrand, Johannesburg*, p. 3, http://www.nfvf.co.za.

55. Ibid.

56. Interview with Associate Professor Martin Botha, Centre for Film and Media Studies, University of Cape Town, March 2005.

57. "Sustainable SA film industry depends on funding," *Filmmaker South Africa*, October 19, 2007, http://www.filmmaker.co.za/readarticle.php?article_id=1432.

58. Lauren Beukes, "Growing Pains," South Africa: The Good News, November 2, 2005, http://www.sagoodnews.co.za/arts_entertainment/growing_pains.html.

59. Gramsci's concept of cultural hegemony was formulated in his attempt to understand the failure of global capitalism and its European collapse under fascism in the 1930s. The term had originally been used in Marxist philosophical thought by Lenin to describe the power of the economic base. Gramsci extended it into the cultural realm to examine how capitalist ideology worked in cultural forms. His aim was diagnostic but also prescriptive. He hoped that his analysis would empower the spread of socialism throughout the world. See *An Antonio Gramsci Reader: Selected Writings, 1916–1935*, ed. David Forgacs (New York: Schocken Books, 1988).

60. Metro FM, http://www.metrofm.co.za/.

61. Fredric Jameson, *Postmodernism, or, The Cultural Logic of Late Capitalism* (London: Verso, 1991).

62. Ibid., 25.

63. Metro FM.

64. Eve Bertelsen, "Ads and Amnesia: Black Advertising in the New South Africa," in *Negotiating the Past: The Making of Memory in South Africa*, eds. Sarah Nuttall and Carli Coetzee (Cape Town: Oxford University Press, 1998), 228.

65. One can see the latest Castle Lager ad set in New York on You Tube at http://www.youtube.com/watch?v=4zmQBNnaAeQ.

66. The song is by Toto, a Los Angeles-based rock band, from their 1983 album, *Toto IV.*

67. Judith Williamson, *Decoding Advertisements* (London: Marion Boyars Publishers, 1978), 12.

68. Jean-Luc Comolli and Jean Narboni, "Cinema/Ideology/Criticism," *Screen* 12, no. 1 (1971): 27–36.

69. Roland Barthes, "From Work to Text," in *Modern Literary Theory*, ed. Philip Rice and Patricia Waugh (New York: Arnold, 1996).

70. Tom Masland, "Generation Born Free," *Newsweek*, April 2004.

71. Sarah Nuttall, "A Politics of the Emergent: Cultural Studies in South Africa," *Theory, Culture, Society* 23, no. 7–8 (2006): 263–278.

72. Sarah Nuttall, "Stylizing the Self: The Y Generation in Rosebank, Johannesburg," *Public Culture* 16, no. 3: 430–452.

73. Achille Mbembe, "The Banality of Power and the Aesthetics of Vulgarity in the Postcolony," *Public Culture* 4, no. 2 (Spring 1992).

2. State and Market Enter the Race

The epigraph is from the NFVF, *Consolidated and Final Summary.*

1. Gary Mersham, "Television: A Fascinating Window on an Unfolding World," in *The South African Handbook of Mass Communication*, ed. A. S. De Beer, (Pretoria: J. L. van Schaik Publishers, 1998), 211.

2. Ivan Bernier, "Local Content Requirements for Film, Radio, and Television as a Means of Protecting Cultural Diversity: Theory and Reality," Section 1, *Culture, Communications et Condition Féminine. Quebec*, http://www.diversite-culturelle .qc.ca/index.php?id+13386=1.

3. The IBA defines an independent producer as one who is not directly or indirectly employed by any broadcasting licensee and one who is not controlled or in control of a broadcasting licensee. Independent Broadcasting Authority Act, Review of Local Content Quotas: Discussion Paper, http://www.info.gov.za/view/ downloadfileaction?id=70333.

4. Nel, *Profile 2000.*

5. Independent Broadcasting Authority Act: Review of Local Content Quotas.

6. Richard Maxwell, *The Spectacle of Democracy: Spanish Television, Nationalism and Political Transition* (Minneapolis: Minnesota University Press, 1995), 33.

7. Joann Wilkie and Angelia Grant, "The importance of evidence for successful economic reform," http://www.treasury.gov.au/documents/1496/PDF/04_ Evidence_and_reform.pdf.

8. Estian Calitz, "Structural Economic Reform in South Africa: Some International Comparisons," *South African Journal of Economics* 70, no. 2: 103–122.

9. Ibid.

10. Ibid.

11. "A Report on the National Film and Video Indaba 2005, 18–19 August 2005—Midrand, Johannesburg," http://www.nfvf.co.za/documents.

12. Gauteng Film Commission, http://www.gautengfilm.org.za/live/content .php?item_ID=316.

13. Ibid.

14. See John Tomlinson's *Globalization and Culture* (Chicago: University of Chicago Press, 1999), 47, for an excellent discussion on how connectivity is at the heart of globalization, which Anthony Giddens defines as "the intensification of world wide relations which link distant localities in such a way that local happenings are shaped by events occurring many miles away and vice versa."

15. National Film Education and Training Strategy, Industry Discussion Document, October 2006, http://www.pmg.org.za/docs/2004/viewminute.php?id=4708.

16. He has also written and directed for television *Skooldae, n Lug Vol Helder Wolke, Familiedae, Brood Vir My Broer, Mattewis en Meraai*, and *Agter Elke Man.*

17. Elsaesser, *New German Cinema*, 113.

18. I discuss Dv8 projects later in the chapter under the subheading "Private Lessons."

19. Elsaesser, *New German Cinema*, 113.

20. In fact, it is more conservative when one considers M-Net's developmental film initiative, New Directions, aimed at encouraging and supporting the work of emerging African filmmakers, which I discuss later in this chapter. M-Net, or The Electronic Media Network, was founded in 1985 as an encrypted subscription channel. The channel broadcasts a mix of entertainment but is not allowed to carry news programming. In 1995, it expanded satellite transmission (DSTV) into sub-Saharan Africa. DSTV carries more than fifty channels, ranging from South African-produced content to international syndicated content, sports, and news. It has 1.23 million subscribers in forty-one African countries. There are also various "bouquets," or bundles of channels, available that cater to some of South Africa's expatriate communities.

21. See "Mickey Dube, A 'Disgusted' Filmmaker," http://www.africultrues.com/anglais/artices_anglais/40dube.htm.

22. LSM, developed by the South African Advertising Research Foundation (SAARF), stands for Life Style Measurement. It divides the population into eight LSM groups, with eight being the highest measurement and one the lowest. The measure offers a means of segmenting the South African market outside of demographics such as race, income, and education. SAARF developed the measure in the late 1980s with the intent of combining a variety of variables into a single ranking which would be stronger than any single variable and thus more useful for market segmentation. Thirteen variables were selected from a pool of seventy-one on the basis of their combined differentiating power. To test the validity of the measure, income and education were introduced to the index variables. Results showed that neither of these two variables contributed sufficiently to warrant inclusion. The index has changed over the years to reflect societal changes. There are now twenty-nine variables on the index. South African Advertising Research Foundation, SAARF Living Standards Measure, http://www.saarf.co.za.

23. Anton Harber, "Tread carefully on SABC funding," http://www.theharbinger.co.za/wordpress/2008/04/17/.

24. NFVF, *Value Charter*, 7.

25. Anant Singh, quoted in "The South African Film Industry," a documentary broadcast on the SABC 2 channel on June 5, 2000.

26. All figures quoted come from the week May 11–15, 2008. See http://www.tvsa.co.za/default.asp?blogname=tv_ratings&ArticleID=8206.

27. NFVF, Indaba 2001, *Distribution, Exhibition and Marketing Report* (Johannesburg: NFVF, 2001), 5.

28. Ibid.

29. The SA Film and Television Sector, *Cultural Industries Growth Strategy* (CIGS), Department of Arts, Culture, Science and Technology, Pretoria, November 1998.

30. Unlike the majority of surveys that link consumer satisfaction to movie content, this survey sought to identify the causal factors leading to declines in theater attendance. See PA Consulting Group, http://www.paconsulting.com/news.

31. Andrew Worsdale, "Screen Test for Local Film," *Mail and Guardian*, Za@Play, August 12, 1999.

32. Nu Metro Productions represents Warner Bros., New Line Cinema, 20th Century Fox, and Walt Disney Pictures (video). Ster-Kinekor Pictures represents Polygram Filmed Entertainment, Focus Features, Walt Disney Pictures (theatrical), Miramax Films, Universal Pictures (video), United International Pictures, Paramount Pictures, Universal Pictures, and Dreamworks SKG.

33. These are *Panic Mechanic* (David Lister, 1997), *Mr. Bones* (Gray Hofmeyr, 2001), and *Mama Jack* (Gray Hofmeyr, 2005).

34. Data taken from NFVF, South African Feature Film 2000–2007 document, p. 23, http://nfvf.co.za/sites/default/files/docs/Microsoft_Word_-_SA_feature_films_2000-2007.pdf.

35. Patrick Frater, "Dv8 Gets Ten-Picture State Backing," ScreenDaily.com, November 18, 2004, http://www.screendaily.com/dv8-gets-ten-picture-state-backing/4020996.article.

36. Ibid.

37. In its place came the production of documentaries, travelogues, and newsreels, which proved profitable enough on the global market to ensure their continuation for many years. A weekly newsreel, *African Mirror*, was produced from 1913 to 1984, making it the longest-running newsreel in the world. In addition to the newsreel, examples of documentaries and travelogues made include *The Dust that Kills* (a film on preventing miner's phthisis), *The Glorious Cape Peninsula*, and *Motorist's Paradise*.

38. John Botha and Eric Louw, "Film: The Captivating Power of Fleeting Images," in *Mass Media Toward the Millennium*, ed. A. S. de Beer (Pretoria: J. L. van Schaik Publishers, 1998), 189.

39. Mandla Langa, "Drag Film by Its Neck into New Millennium," *Sunday Independent*, November 9, 1997.

40. Ibid.

41. Ibid.

42. James Holsten and Arjun Appadurai, "Cities and Citizenship," *Public Culture* 8, no. 2 (Winter 1996): 190.

43. Neville Alexander, "Affirmative Action and the Perpetuation of Racial Identities," edited version of a lecture originally delivered at the University of Fort Hare, East London Campus, May 21, 2006, http://www.Workersliberty.org/node/6301.

44. Ibid.

45. NFVF, *A Report on the NFVF Film Indaba* (Johannesburg: NFVF, 2005), 14.

46. "Black" is a catchall term used by the government to include black Africans, "coloureds," and Indians.

47. Data taken from NFVF, South African Feature Film 2000–2007 document, 14.

48. NFVF, *A Report on the NFVF Film Indaba*.

49. Elsaesser, *New German Cinema*, notes these difficulties in the development of New German Cinema, which took the form of *autorenkino*, or a cinema of authors. *Autorenkino* did not, he argues, eliminate the contradictions so much as disguise them. It determined the political and administrative machinery put in place to fund films practically and it furnished the criteria that validated filmmaking as an "art." Once institutionalized, the ideology of self-expression became a surrogate economic category that worked in two different ways. As an auteur, the filmmaker was able to access and exercise a certain amount of financial clout within the subsidy

system. At the same time, the system used the auteur as a commodity for marketing German cinema abroad.

50. Adam Haupt, "Putting Words into Action," *Mail and Guardian*, April 9, 1998, 2.

51. See Jeremy Nathan, "The Business of Show Business," Mail and Guardian online, July 11, 2007, http://www.mg.co.za/articlePage.aspx?articleid=313647&area.

52. I discuss *Wa n Wina* in chapter 4.

53. See Thomas Elsaesser's *European Cinema: Face to Face with Hollywood* (Amsterdam: Amsterdam University Press, 2005): 57–82 for a brilliant discussion on international film festivals.

54. "SA Celebrates 11 Years at Cannes," SAinfo Reporter, May 16, 2008, http://www.southafrica.info/news/conferences/cannes11.htm.

55. "Drum Wins Top African Prize," March 5, 2005, http://www.bbc.co.uk/worldservice/specials/145_latestnews/page4.html.

56. Kinder, *Blood Cinema*, 6.

57. Philip Rosen, "Nation and Anti-Nation: Concepts of National Cinema in the New Media Era," *Diaspora* 5, no. 3 (Winter 1996): 375–402.

58. In "Nation and Anti-Nation," Philip Rosen offers an insightful discussion of the viability and utility of the trope of cinema vs. television and the kind of schema that it generates in terms of identities, the subject, culture, and the audience. Rosen argues that these oppositions, though widespread among film scholars and cultural theorists, do not hold. The concept itself has utility in film history as a way of stimulating and organizing research and pointing to the possibility of using cinema as a sphere of resistance to certain global practices.

59. "Dv8: Putting SA Films on the Map," SouthAfrica.info, Gateway to the Nation, October 20, 2003, http://www.southafrica.info/pls/procs/iac.page?p_t1=2780&p_t2=7380&p_t2.

60. Andrew Worsdale, "Tales of Township Life," *Mail and Guardian*, May 22–28, 1996, 3. Ramadan Suleman is the director of a recent South African film, *Fools* (1996), based on a short story by Njabulo Ndebele.

61. *ScreenAfrica* 15 (February 2003).

62. South Africa has a GDP of $239.510 billion (2005). It accounts for about 35% of the total GDP of sub-Saharan Africa. Although South Africa occupies only 3% of the continent's surface, it generates 40% of all industrial output, 25% of GDP, and 45% of mineral production.

63. This brief sketch can hardly do justice to the subject. I have included it as a background to the current situation, a situation in which South Africa is, for the first time, taking part. Anyone seeking a deep and full analysis and overview of the last thirty years of African cinema should consult Frank Ukadike's *Black African Cinema* (Los Angeles: University of California Press, 1994), Manthia Diawara's *African Cinema: Politics and Culture* (Bloomington: Indiana University Press, 1992), and Michael T. Martin, ed., *Cinemas of the Black Diaspora: Diversity, Dependence and Oppositionality* (Detroit: Wayne State University Press, 1995).

64. Isaac Julien and Kobena Mercer, "De Margin and De Center," in *Black British Cultural Studies: A Reader*, eds. Houston A. Baker, Jr., Manthia Diawara, and Ruth H. Lindeborg (Chicago: University of Chicago Press, 1996), 200–208.

65. John Matshikiza, "The World of African Film," *Mail and Guardian*, September 3–9, 1999.

66. Suleman directed *Fools* (1999), a co-production between France, Mozambique, Zimbabwe, SABC, and M-Net. It is based on a short story by South African writer Njabulo Ndebele.

67. Ukadike, *Black African Cinema*.

68. Matshikiza, "The World of African Film."

3. The Moment of Truth

The first epigraph is from Dullah Omar, former Minister of Justice (see http://www.doj.gov.za/trc/). The second epigraph is from Ingrid de Kok, "Cracked Heirloom: Memory on Exhibition," in Nuttall and Coetzee, eds., *Negotiating the Past*, 57–71.

1. The task of the Human Rights Violations Committee was to investigate human rights abuses that took place between 1960 and 1994, based on statements made to the TRC. The committee established the identity of the victims, their fate or present whereabouts, the nature and extent of the harm they had suffered, and whether the violations were the result of deliberate planning by the state or any other organization, group, or individual. Once victims of gross human rights violations were identified, they were referred to the Committee on Reparation and Rehabilitation. The enabling act empowered that committee to provide victim support to ensure that the TRC process restored victims' dignity and to formulate policy proposals and recommendations on the rehabilitation and healing of survivors, their families, and communities at large. The envisaged overall function of all recommendations was to ensure non-repetition, healing, and healthy coexistence. The President's Fund, funded by Parliament and private contributions, was established to pay urgent interim reparations to victims in terms of the regulations prescribed by the President.

The primary function of the Amnesty Committee was to ensure that applications for amnesty were done in accordance with the law. Applicants could apply for amnesty for any act, omission, or offense associated with a political objective and committed between March 1, 1960, and December 6, 1993. The cutoff date was later extended to May 11, 1994. The final date for the submission of applications was September 30, 1997. Being granted amnesty meant that the perpetrator was free from prosecution for that particular deed. (Information adapted from the TRC webpage, http://www.doj.gov.za/trc/.)

2. Alex Boraine, *A Country Unmasked: Inside South Africa's Truth and Reconciliation Commission* (New York: Oxford University Press, 2000), 89.

3. Catherine Cole, "Performance, Transitional Justice and the Law: South Africa's Truth and Reconciliation Commission," *Theatre Journal* 59, no. 2 (May 2007): 167–187.

4. Ibid.

5. Daniel Herwitz, "The Future of the Past in South Africa: The Legacy of the TRC," *South Africa: The Second Decade*, special issue, *Social Research* 72, no. 3 (Fall 2005): 540.

6. For a detailed description of the conditions for amnesty, see "Traces of Truth: Documents Relating to the South African Truth and Reconciliation Commission," TRC—Category 3—Amnesty, University of the Witwatersrand, http://truth.wwl.wits.ac.za/cat_descr.php?cat=3.

7. Truth and Reconciliation Commission of South Africa Report, Interim Report of the Amnesty Committee, vol. 5, chap. 3, http://www.info.gov.za/other-docs/2003.

8. Mahmood Mamdani, "Reconciliation without Justice," *South African Review* 10 (1997): 22.

9. Veena Das, *Critical Events* (Oxford: Oxford University Press, 1995): 37.

10. Pier Paolo Pasolini, "The Cinema of Poetry," trans. Marianne de Vettimo and Jacques Bontemps, in *Movies and Methods: An Anthology*, ed. Bill Nichols (Berkeley: University of California Press, 1976), 542–558.

11. Glauber Rocha, "An Aesthetic of Hunger," in *New Latin American Cinema: Theories, Practices and Transcontinental Articulations*, vol. 1, ed. Michael T. Martin (Detroit: Wayne State University Press, 1997), 59–61; Julio Garcia Espinosa, "For An Imperfect Cinema," in *New Latin American Cinema*, ed. Martin, 71–82.

12. Njabulo Ndebele, "Of Lions and Rabbits: Thoughts on Democracy and Reconciliation," in *After the TRC: Reflections on Truth and Reconciliation in South Africa*, eds. James Wilmot and Linda van de Vijver (Athens: Ohio University Press, 2001), 143.

13. See Antjie Krog, *Country of My Skull: Guilt, Sorrow and the Limits of Forgiveness in the New South Africa* (New York: Random House, 1998); Max du Preez, *Pale Native* (Johannesburg: Struik Publishers, 2004); Lyn S. Graybill, *Truth and Reconciliation in South Africa: Miracle or Model?* (Boulder, Colo.: Lynne Reiner Publishers, 2002); Neville Alexander, *An Ordinary Country: Issues in the Transition from Apartheid to Democracy in South Africa* (Oxford: Berghahn Books, 2003); Richard Wilson, *The Politics of Truth and Reconciliation in South Africa: Legitimizing the Post-Apartheid State* (Cambridge: Cambridge University Press, 2001).

14. Gideon Nieuwoudt died of lung cancer in prison in 1998 while waiting for the outcome of his amnesty application for the Motherwell bombing.

15. Andre Du Toit, "The Moral Foundations of the South African TRC: Truth as Acknowledgement and Justice as Recognition," in Robert I. Rotberg and Dennis Thompson, eds., *Truth v. Justice. The Morality of Truth Commissions* (Princeton, N.J.: Princeton University Press, 2000), 136.

16. Zenzele Khoisan, the lead investigator in the case, has written a memoir about his experiences. See *Time of the Jacaranda* (Cape Town: Garib Communications, 2001). The Gugulethu Seven story is also featured in the documentary *Long Night's Journey into Day* (Francis Reid and Deborah Hoffman, 2000).

17. Krog, *Country of My Skull*, 253–254.

18. *Red Dust*, Tom Hooper, 2004.

19. Claire Johnston, "Women's cinema as counter-cinema," in *Notes on Women's Cinema*, ed. Claire Johnston (London: SEFT, 1974), 29.

20. Laura Mulvey, "Visual Pleasure and Narrative Cinema," in *Visual and Other Pleasures*, ed. Laura Mulvey (London: Macmillan, 1975), 14–26.

21. E. Ann Kaplan, *Women and Film: Both Sides of the Camera* (New York: Methuen, 1983).

22. Stephen Neale, *Genre* (London: British Film Institute Publishing, 1980), 58.

23. Pam Cook and Mieke Bernink, eds., *The Cinema Book*, 2nd ed. (London: British Film Institute Publishing, 1999), 360.

24. Charles Derry, *The Suspense Thriller, Film in the Shadow of Alfred Hitchcock* (Jefferson, N.C.: MacFarland Press, 1988), 103.

25. Krog, *Country of My Skull.*

26. Ibid., 43.

27. Ibid., frontispiece.

28. Sarah Nuttall, "Telling 'Free' Stories? Memory and Democracy in South African Autobiography since 1994," in *Negotiating the Past,* eds. Nuttall and Coetzee, 75–88.

29. Nelson Mandela, *Long Walk to Freedom* (Randburg: Macdonald Purnell, 1994).

30. See Mamphela Ramphele, *A Life* (Cape Town: David Phillips, 1995). Ramphele qualified as a medical doctor in 1972 before going into exile as an anti-apartheid activist in 1977. In the post-apartheid years, she was appointed vice chancellor of the University of Cape Town (1996–2000). Subsequently, she was appointed as a director of the World Bank. She serves with a number of international foundations and plays a major role in black economic empowerment initiatives both globally and nationally. She does not hold a government office.

31. Nuttall, "Telling 'free' stories?," 75.

32. Noël Burch, *Theory of Film Practice* (London: Secker and Warburg, 1973).

33. Ella Shohat and Robert Stam, *Unthinking Eurocentrism: Multiculturalism and the Media* (New York: Routledge, 1994), 7.

34. *Ubuntu* is defined in various ways. The most well-known definition is based on the maxim, "a person is a person through other persons" (in Zulu, *umuntu ngumuntu ngabantu*). The ethic of ubuntu stresses community over isolation and the idea that one cannot develop humanity in isolation.

35. Langston Hughes, "Out of Love," in *The Collected Poems of Langston Hughes,* ed. Arnold Rampersad (New York: Vintage, 1995), 433.

36. Colin McCabe, "Realism and the Cinematic: Notes on Some Brechtian Theses," *Screen* 15, no. 2 (Summer 1974): 12.

37. Cook and Bernink, eds., *The Cinema Book.*

38. Interview with Ann Peacock, *In My Country,* DVD, Special Features.

39. Toby Miller, Nitin Govil, John McMurria, and Richard Maxwell, *Global Hollywood* (London: British Film Institute Publishing, 2001), 18.

40. Ibid., 2

41. Figures from the NFVF website, http://www.nfvf.co.za/documents.

4. Community and Pandemic

1. This discussion of Thabo Mbeki relies on work in Daniel Herwitz's book, *Race and Reconciliation: Essays from the New South Africa* (Minneapolis: University of Minnesota Press, 2003). It also relies on Herwitz's "Understanding AIDS in South Africa," *The Journal of the International Institute* 13, no. 2 (Winter 2006), and on Mark Gevisser's biography, *Thabo Mbeki: The Dream Deferred* (London: Jonathan Ball Publishers, 2007).

2. Malegapuru Makgoba, "Science, the Media and Politics: HIV/AIDS in South Africa," keynote address, 119th Nobel Symposium, Stockholm, 2001, p. 3.

3. "Letter by President Mbeki to Clinton, Blair, Schroeder, Kofi Annan and others," April 3, 2000, http://www.free-news.org/tmbeki.htm.

4. "Estimating the Lost Benefits of Antiretroviral Drug Use in South Africa," Pride Chigwedere, George R. Seage III, Sofia Gruskin, Tun Ho Lee, and M. Essex, *Perspectives, Epidemiology and Social Science* 49, no. 4 (December 1, 2008).

5. Joint United Nations Programme on HIV/AIDS, 2008 Report on the global AIDS epidemic, UNAIDS, http://www.unaids.org/en/KnowledgeCentre/HIVData/GlobalReport/2008/2008_Global_report.asp.

6. Simon Chislett with Laurence Dworkin, Alosha Ntsane, Theresa Armien, Susan Levine, Martin Cuff, and Don Edkin, "STEPS for the Future (Actually Life is a Beautiful Thing): An Introduction by the STEPS Project Staff," *Visual Anthropology Review* 19, no. 1–2 (Spring/Fall 2003): 10.

7. Ibid., 8–12.

8. All of this information on audience reception is taken from the STEPS Impact Study conducted by students of the University of Cape Town's Department of Social Anthropology, led by Dr. Susan Levine. Susan Levine, 2003 *Impact Study: STEPS for the Future: An Impact Study in South Africa, Lesotho and Mozambique of 36 Documentary Films about HIV/AIDS*. Study available at the STEPS for the Future website, http://www.steps.co.za.

9. Ibid., 37.

10. Ibid., 42.

11. Examples of these films are *Kukuli* (Luis Figueroa, 1961) and *Jarawu* (Eulogio Nishiyama and César Villanueva, 1966), made by the Cine Club Cuzco. Both combine fiction and documentary and are feature-length films.

12. See, among others, *Les Maîtres Fous (The Mad Masters)* (1955), *Moi, un Noir (Me, a Black)* (1959), *La Pyramide Humaine (The Human Pyramid)* (1959), *Chronique d'un Été (Chronicle of a Summer)* (1960), *La Punition (The Punishment)* (1962), *Le Mil (Millet)* (1963), *Rose et Landry* (1963), and *Année Zéro (Year Zero)* (1966).

13. Dennis McQuail, *Mass Communication Theory: An Introduction*, 3rd ed. (London: Sage, 1994). In chapter 5, McQuail describes six "types" of media theories outlining general principles of media performance, which he distinguishes from structure. The latter concerns itself with legal issues (freedom of the press) and material ones (regulation of channels, licensing, etc.). Performance refers to the ways in which the media carry out their chosen and assigned functions. His six "types" or "theories" (the term is used loosely) in historical order are as follows: authoritarian, Libertarian, Soviet, social responsibility, development, and democratic participant. Other theorists argue that there are only two basic types—authoritarian and Libertarian—with gradations in between. See J. Merrill, *The Imperatives of Freedom* (New York: Hastings House, 1974).

14. According to McQuail, the tenets of the social responsibility theory stem from the idea that "media ownership and operation are a form of public trust or stewardship, rather than an unlimited private franchise." They should therefore, as McQuail states, (1) provide a forum for ideas, (2) be free but self-regulated, (3) follow agreed codes of ethics and professional standards, (4) be truthful, accurate, fair, objective, and relevant. Further, society may need to intervene in the public interest. McQuail, *Mass Communication Theory*, 124.

15. Hans Magnus Enzenberger, "Constituents of a Theory of the Media," *Video Culture: A Critical Investigation*, ed. John G. Hanhardt (Rochester, N.Y.: Visual Studies Workshop Press, 1986), 96–123.

16. An example of participatory media, The Kayapo Indian Project (KIP) conducted by Tim Turner is animated by the idea that the liberatory and subversive capacities of video production are realized when the camera is placed in the hands of those who are usually the object of its gaze—in this case, the ethnographic gaze of

the anthropologist. As with Manet's great painting Olympiad, in which a prostitute stares boldly back at her "clients," thus reversing the ownership of the gaze, so the use of video by indigenous people reverses the conventions and hence the asymmetrical power relations inherent in ethnographic film use by non-indigenous people. In the process of learning how to produce their own videos and record the everyday lived events of their worlds, the participants go through a process of self-empowerment and transformation. In short, the argument is that societal development, which is usually a top-down process, begins from the very bottom with the psychology of the individual. Awareness begun at this level, in the act of doing or making representation and in the ownership of the product that emerges from such activity, is the real basis for a critical social transformation. See Tim Turner, "Defiant Images: The Kayapo Appropriation of Video," *Anthropology Today* 6, no. 6 (1992).

17. Main groups include such organizations as the Film and Allied Workers Organization (FAWO), the Campaign for Open Media (COM), and The National Information Technology Forum (NITF).

18. Since July 1, 2000, the IBA has been integrated into a new, larger regulatory body named the Independent Communications Authority of South Africa (ICASA).

19. This argument is made by Knut Lundby in Stewart Hoover and Knut Lundby, *Rethinking Media, Religion and Culture* (Thousand Oaks, Calif.: Sage, 1997).

20. Turner, "Defiant Images," 5–16.

21. *It's My Life* (Brian Tilley, 2001). The film is distributed in the United States by California Newsreel, P.O. Box 2284, South Burlington, VT 05407.

22. Béla Balázs, "The Visible Man, or the Culture of Film," *Screen* 48, no. 1 (Spring 2007): 91–105.

23. Hamid Naficy, *An Accented Cinema: Exilic and Diasporic Filmmaking* (Princeton, N.J.: Princeton University Press, 2001), 11.

5. Quo Vadis?

David James, *Allegories of Cinema: American Cinema in the Sixties* (Princeton, N.J.: Princeton University Press, 1989), 6; Karl Marx, *Capital: A Critique of Political Economy*, trans. David Fernbach, vol. 2 (New York: Vintage, 1978), 303.

1. Paul Willemen, "The Third Cinema Question: Notes and Reflections," in *Questions of Third Cinema*, eds. Jim Pines and Paul Willemen (London: British Film Institute Publishing, 1989).

2. Later, Teshome Gabriel's book, *"Third Cinema in a Third World—The Aesthetics of Liberation,"* reanimated and expanded the concept beyond the confines of person or place or even stylistics by emphasizing the ideology and consciousness of the producer.

3. Fernando Solanas and Octavio Getino, "Towards a Third Cinema: Notes and Experiences for the Development of a Cinema of Liberation in the Third World," in *Movies and Methods*, ed. Ben Nichols (Berkeley: University of California Press, 1976).

4. This practice often has rather risky results, as in Fredric Jameson's assertion that in third-world texts, the private individual's destiny is, "in the era of multinational capitalism," always a national allegory.

5. Ann McClintock, "Pitfalls of the Term 'Post-Colonialism,'" *Social Text* 31/32 (Spring 1992): 1–15.

6. Ibid.

7. Apparently, this is the way the term was first employed. As Russell Jacoby quoting Ajiz Ahmad notes, the term was first used in the 1970s in discussions about Pakistan and Bangladesh. Russell Jacoby, "Marginal Returns," *Lingua Franca* (October 1995): 30–37.

8. Cook and Bernink, eds., *The Cinema Book*, 115.

9. Stuart Hall, "Cultural Identity and Diaspora: Identity, Community, Culture and Difference," in *Colonial Discourse and Post-Colonial Theory: A Reader*, ed. P. Williams and Laura Chrisman (New York: Columbia University Press, 1994).

10. SA Constitution, chapter 2, section 16.

11. Peter Wollen, "Godard and Counter-Cinema: Vent d'Est," in *Narrative, Apparatus, Ideology: A Film Reader*, ed. Philip Rosen (New York: Columbia University Press, 1986), 120–129.

12. Naficy, *An Accented Cinema*.

13. Xoliswa Sithole, "The Mere Fact of Me is Political," in *Through African Eyes: Dialogues with the Directors, 10th African Film Festival*, ed. Mahen Bonetti and Perena Reddy (Yerevan: Printinfo JV LLC, 2003), 117–121.

14. Rob Nixon, *Homelands, Harlem and Hollywood* (New York: Routledge, 1994), 90.

15. Readers seeking more information on "pro-apartheid" cinema should consult Tomaselli's *The Cinema of Apartheid*. It is enough to say here that it was a cinema for whites only, aimed predominantly at the Afrikaans audience, and supported by state subsidy and Afrikaans capital. The white, Afrikaans-speaking audience was relatively large and stable. As a result, most Afrikaans films ran long enough to break even and qualify for the subsidy, which was rewarded on the basis of box-office returns. According to Pieter Fourie, the cinema of apartheid in the main generated a stream of non-critical, folksy tales characterized by what he calls an "idealistic conservatism." Fourie argues that most Afrikaans films communicated by means of obsolete symbols that had little intercultural value. They "painted a one-sided and stereotypical portrait of the Afrikaner" and ignored the social-political realities of the country. The Afrikaans film, with a few exceptions, stagnated during the past three decades and disappeared in the 1980s. An offshoot of the dominant internal cinema was the creation of a so-called "Bantu" film industry in the 1970s. This resulted in the making of a large number of films by whites for blacks in ethnic languages that validated rural life and demonized city experiences. Since government policy forbade black cinemas in the urban white areas (this would be seen as a concession to the idea of black urban citizenship), these films were screened in churches, schools, and community halls in the townships. The history of film distribution in South Africa has paralleled the history of the country in its racist and segregationist policies. Only in 1985 did the distributors manage to desegregate some cinemas, and for the first time, the cinema-going public was defined outside of racial boundaries. Silber, "Tax, Lies and Videotape."

16. See Martin Botha's "South African Short Film Making from 1980 to 1995: a Thematic Exploration" for details on the role of the IDAF in funding what he calls a "critical South African cinema," in *Communicatio: South African Journal for Communication Theory and Research* 22, no. 2 (1996): 51–56.

17. These were not the only motivating forces that signaled the beginning of the credibility crisis for apartheid. Job reservation was becoming increasingly dys-

functional in the capitalist economy of South Africa, which demanded a more efficient labor force, as was the legislation controlling the migration of blacks to the urban areas. The Durban workers' strikes in 1973 further underlined the lack of legal viability. The formation of the new black trade-union movement forced the government to adjust labor legislation in line with more international industrial trends. See Stanley B. Greenberg, *Legitimating the Illegitimate* (Los Angeles: University of California Press, 1987) and Stephen Friedman, *Building Tomorrow Today* (Johannesburg: Ravan Press, 1985) for excellent discussions on these topics.

18. Most of the films of this period are available through the Film Resource Unit (FRU), a non-governmental organization that operates as a film distribution and educational agency. FRU has an outreach program that screens South African and African films at alternative urban exhibition sites such as schools, libraries, universities, township bars (*shebeens*), and community halls. During apartheid, FRU operated underground, distributing banned film footage. It is committed to the idea of cinema as a tool in social development.

19. Deniz Kandiyoti, "Identity and Its Discontents," in *Colonial Discourse and Post-Colonial Theory*, ed. Williams and Chrisman, 376–391.

20. Sumita Chakravarty, "The Erotics of History: Gender and Transgression in the New Asian Cinemas," in *Rethinking Third Cinema*, eds. Anthony Guneratne and Wismal Dissanayake (London: Routledge, 2003), 79–99.

21. Lynn Steenveld, "South African Anti-Apartheid Documentaries, 1977–1987: Some Theoretical Excursions" (M.A. thesis, Grahamstown, Rhodes University). See also Keyan Tomaselli and Jeanne Prinsloo, "Third Cinema in South Africa," in *Movies, Moguls, Mavericks*, eds. Blignaut and Botha, 329–373.

22. Michael Chanan, "Introduction," in *Twenty-Five Years of the New Latin-American Cinema*, ed. Michael Chanan (London: BFI, 1982).

23. Kinder, *Blood Cinema*.

24. Manthia Diawara discusses in detail the differences between Anglophone and Francophone African cinemas in *African Cinema: Politics and Culture* (Bloomington: Indiana University Press, 1992).

25. Lewis Nkosi, "Fiction by Black South Africans: Richard Rive, Bloke Modisane, Ezekiel Mphalele, and Alex La Guma," in *Introduction to African Literature: An Anthology of Critical Writing*, ed. Ulli Beier (London: Longman, 1979), 222.

26. David Attwell, *South Africa and the Politics of Writing* (Cambridge: Cambridge University Press), 11.

27. According to Attwell, J. M. Coetzee has suffered attacks on his legitimacy as a South African writer with his attempts to escape realist constraints through the use of anonymously defined contexts and characters in his novels.

28. Caroline Christov-Bakargiev in conversation with William Kentridge. D. Cameron, C. Christov-Bakargiev, and J. M. Coetzee, *William Kentridge* (New York: Phaidon Press, 1999), 8.

29. Cameron, Christov-Bakargiev, and Coetzee, *William Kentridge*, 114.

30. Ibid.

31. Ibid.

32. Georges Méliès, "Cinematographic Views," in Richard Abel, *French Film Theory and Criticism: A History/Anthology, 1907–1939*, vol. 1 (Princeton, N.J.: Princeton University Press, 1988), 35–47.

33. Tom Gunning, "The Cinema of Attractions: Early Cinema, Its Spectator and the Avant-Garde," *Wide Angle* 8, no. 3–4 (1986): 63–70.

34. These are *Johannesburg, 2nd Greatest City After Paris* (1989), *Monument* (1990), *Mine* (1991), *Sobriety, Obesity and Growing Old* (1991), *Felix in Exile* (1994), *History of the Main Complaint* (1996), *Weighing and Wanting* (1997), *Stereoscope* (1999), and *Tide Table* (2003).

35. William Kentridge, *Thinking Aloud: Conversations with Angela Breidbach* (Walter Koenig: Cologne, 2006), 66.

36. "UK 'regrets' Mugabe gay protest," BBC Online Network, November 10, 1999, http://news.bbc.co.uk/1/hi/uk/514606.stm.

37. The "Simon" in Greyson's film is the same man in the STEPS film, *Simon and I*, discussed in chapter 4.

38. McCabe, "Realism and the Cinema," 10.

39. Nelson Mandela, "I Am Prepared to Die." Nelson Mandela's statement from the dock at the opening of the defense case in the Rivonia Treason Trial, April 20, 1964, Pretoria Supreme Court, http://www.anc.org.za/ancdocs/history/rivonia.html.

40. Information taken from "Carl Linnaeus," http://www.ucmp.berkeley.edu/history/linnaeus.html.

41. Michel Foucault, *The Archaeology of Knowledge*, trans. A. M. Sheridan Smith (London: Tavistock Publications, 1972), 7.

42. Carolus Linnaeus, Encyclopædia Britannica Online, June 26, 2008, http://www.britannica.com/eb/article-273183.

43. Andy Visockis, "*Proteus* (Canada, 2003)," Andy's Film World, February 29, 2008, http://andysfilmworld.blogspot.com/2008/02/proteus-canada-2003.html.

6. The Dialectic of Reconciliation in *De Voortrekkers* and *Come See the Bioscope*

The epigraph is from Duncan Petrie, ed., *Screening Europe: Image and Identity in Contemporary European Cinema* (London: BFI, 1992).

1. *De Voortrekkers* was directed by Harold Shaw, who was bought from England for the task, and written by Gustav Preller, a noted South African historian and champion of the Afrikaans-language movement. It was not the first feature film made by AFP: that was *The Kimberley Diamond Robbery*, made in 1910.

2. Thelma Gutsche, *The History and Social Significance of Motion Pictures in South Africa, 1895–1940*, 313.

3. The English title of the film is *Winning a Continent*. As Jacqueline Maingard notes, the English title signifies "much broader colonial aspirations" than does the Afrikaans one. Jacqueline Maingard, *South African National Cinema* (New York: Routledge, 2007), 16.

4. The Battle of Blood River was the name used by the Afrikaners. It is no longer politically astute to use that name. The currently accepted name is the Ncome River Battle.

5. At the time of its founding, the ANC was called the South African Native National Congress. It changed its name to the African National Congress in 1923.

6. Pallo Jordan, "From Colonialism to African Nationalism," Helen Suzman Foundation, http://www.hsfo.org.za/publications/focus-issues/issues-21-30/issue-28/from-colonialism-to-african-nationalism/.

7. Shohat and Stam, *Unthinking Eurocentrism*, 92–93.

8. See Ntongela Masilela's "The New African Movement and the Beginnings of Film Culture in South Africa," in *To Change Reels: Film and Film Culture in South Africa*, ed. Isabel Balseiro and Ntongela Masilela (Detroit: Wayne State University Press, 2003), 15–30.

9. Siegfried Kracauer, "The Mass Ornament," in *The Mass Ornament: Weimar Essays*, ed. Thomas Levin (Cambridge, Mass.: Harvard University Press, 1995), 75.

10. Miriam Hansen uses the phrase "referential realism" to describe *The Birth of a Nation* in comparison to what she calls the metarealism of *Intolerance*, which comments on competing modes of representation rather than on "reality." See chapter 7 in Miriam Hansen, *Babel and Babylon: Spectatorship in American Silent Film* (Cambridge, Mass.: Harvard University Press, 1991), 175.

11. Andre Bazin, "The Ontology of the Photographic Image," In *Film Theory and Criticism*, 6th ed., eds. Leo Braudy and Marshall Cohen (Los Angeles: Oxford University Press, 2004), 169.

12. For Ernest Gellner, nationalism is "primarily a political principle, which holds that the political and the national unit should be congruent." Ernest Gellner, *Nations and Nationalism* (Ithaca, N.Y.: Cornell University Press, 1983). Nationalism is an ideology which claims supreme loyalty from individuals for the nation and asserts the right of national self-determination. See also Walker Connor, *Ethnonationalism: The Quest for Understanding* (Princeton, N.J.: Princeton University Press, 1994) and Anthony D. Smith, *The Nation in History: Historiographical Debates about Ethnicity and Nationalism* (The Menahem Stern Jerusalem Lectures) (Hanover, N.H.: University Press of New England, 2000).

13. Judt, "The Old New Nationalisms." Both Eric Hobsbawm's and Trevor Ranger's essays in *The Invention of Tradition* (Cambridge: Cambridge University Press, 1983) and Gellner's *Nations and Nationalism* are examples of this approach. So too is Benedict Anderson's idea of the nation as an "imagined community," explained in *Imagined Communities*.

14. See Anderson's remarks on the role of time in the biography of nations, in which he draws an analogy between modern nations and modern individuals in terms of constructing their identities and subjecthood. According to Anderson, both people and nations are estranged from their pasts and use narratives of identity as the connective medium. Narratives of belonging backed up by "evidence" (family photos, relatives, and mementos) help the individual forge his or her identity to the forgotten past. They provide a biography that, like classical Hollywood cinema's narrative structures, has a beginning, a middle, and an end, a set of characters with which one can identify and a number of formal elements (*mise-en-scène, montage*) which permit such identification. However, there is a difference in the way the usage of narrative plays itself out on the national stage. While individuals have beginnings, as in the Old Testament's reiteration of who begot whom, and then proceed down through time from this point, nations come up in time. The biography of the nation cannot therefore be written in "evangelical terms" but must be fashioned in "up time." See Anderson, *Imagined Communities*.

I would argue that Anderson privileges the role of narrative in remembering the past but ignores its counter-role in forgetting it. Narratives, particularly those that attempt to narrate the self, can be used as distancing mechanisms, as ways of overcoming the past and moving into the present and the future. This use of narrative was, for example, evident in some of the autobiographies told at the Truth and Reconciliation Commission hearings. The impetus in some of these personal stories was not to connect the person to the past, but to "free" them from the memory of it, to get rid of its burdens and traumas.

15. Andre Bazin, "The Evolution of the Western," in *What is Cinema?*, vol. 2, trans. Hugh Gray (Berkeley: University of California Press, 1971): 149.

16. Isabel Hofmeyr, "Popularising History: The Case of Gustav Preller," in *Regions and Repertoires: Topics in South African Politics and Culture*, ed. Stephen Clingman (Johannesburg: Ravan Press, 1991), 61.

17. G. W. Eybers, *Select Constitutional Documents Illustrating South African History, 1795–1910* (London: George Routledge & Sons, 1918), 144–145.

18. Quoted in L. Thompson, *A History of South Africa* (Sandton, South Africa: Radix Press, 1990), 88.

19. Both Albie Sachs and Njabulo Ndebele have called for an abandonment of apartheid categories in search of a new social imaginary (Ndebele's phrase), or in Sachs' words, a new cultural imaginary. As Ndebele puts it in her essay "Redefining Relevance," what is needed is freedom from "the epistemological structures of oppression." Njabulo Ndebele, *Rediscovery of the Ordinary: Essays on South African Literature and Culture* (Johannesburg: COSAW, 1991), 58–73.

20. According to Thompson, drawing on various historical reports on the battle, each commando member had at least one gun and the expedition had two small cannons. The Zulu *impis* had no firepower at all. Thompson, *A History of South Africa*.

21. This primitive attempt at state-making failed when the British colonial authorities annexed the area in the early 1890s and the *trekkers* once again fled back across the Drakensberg Mountains and into the *Highveld*.

22. The event was also memorialized by the building of the Voortrekker Monument outside of Pretoria—a huge, squat, stone building shaped rather like a fat tea cozy and containing a symbolic sarcophagus for the martyred leader and friezes which depict the major events. The entire building is encircled by carved stone walls representing the *laager* or circle which the *trekkers* had formed by lashing together the wheels of their ox wagons, thus marking in stone the ideas of separateness, containment, and apartness. The monument does not open itself to casual viewing. Instead, a visitor has to enter the *laager* and then the tomb, and in so doing, just as when one enters a great cathedral such as St. Peters, become a temporary (if unwilling) convert.

23. It had, as Leonard Thompson points out, been tried and failed as early as 1870 and was central to Britain's imperialist philosophy and aspirations for southern Africa and beyond. See Thompson, *A History of South Africa*.

24. Ibid., 152–153.

25. Even the filming of some of the scenes from *De Voortrekkers* on the sabbath, a logistical necessity since the thousands of "Zulu" extras needed for the battle scenes were drawn from the mines and could only work on a Sunday, raised vehement complaints from the conservative Dutch Reform Church. Many in the Afrikaans community were hypersensitive to the smallest issue that might be interpreted as a sign of cultural contempt.

26. The practice of defining national identity in terms of an enemy or an "other" seems to be a well-used government strategy, particularly after periods of conflict. In Fassbinder's *Germany: History, Identity, Subject*, Thomas Elsaesser describes

how West Germany's new national identity was helped by the definition of a new enemy (really an old enemy), the Soviet Union, and by extension, East Germany. See Thomas Elsaesser, *Germany: History, Identity, Subject* (Amsterdam: Amsterdam University Press, 1996).

27. This view of South Africanism gradually broadened beyond the idea of a white race, although it took seventy-three years to do so. In 1983, the Tri-Cameral Parliament clearly indicated that coloureds and Indians were now included under the rubric of South African, but blacks were still excluded until the 1994 elections, which ended apartheid with a transcendent view of the nation based on democracy. Democracy is seen as the basis for generating a loyalty to the state, which can then form the basis for a nation.

28. David Bunn, "Whited Sepulchres: On the Reluctance of Monuments," in *Architecture, Apartheid and After*, ed. Hilton Judin and Ivan Vladislavic (Rotterdam: NAI Publishers, 1999). In terms of referencing accuracy, the book was printed as a companion to a traveling exhibition of the same name. The book's format is unusual in that it is arranged as a map with no page numbers.

29. Gustav Preller, *Piet Retief* (Melville: Scripta Africana, 1988).

30. Ibid., 54.

31. Ibid., 53.

32. In 1924, the National Party, under the leadership of Barry Herzog (the staunch supporter of Afrikaner independence), merged with the South African National Party to form a fusion government. Jan Smuts became deputy to Herzog. This joint government was rejected by certain members of the National Party who formed the Purified National Party and became known as the *Broederbond* or brotherhood.

33. Aletta Norval, *Deconstructing Apartheid Discourse* (London: Verso Press, 1996), 52.

34. Edwin Hees, "The *Voortrekkers* on Film: From Preller to Pornography." Unpublished paper presented at the South African Cultural History Conference, Two Centuries of British Influence in South Africa (1795–1995), Pretoria, June 29–30, 1995, http://www.und.ac.za/und/ccms/articles/voortrek.htm.

35. The film was funded by British capital since I. W. Schlesinger, the owner of AFP, had extensive financial interests in the British entertainment industry. This fact does not automatically translate into the film adopting a pro-English stance, nor, of course, does it account for the audience's reception of it, but it is yet another determinant in the film's production history.

36. See Ernesto Laclau and Chantal Mouffe, *Hegemony and Socialist Strategy: Towards a Radical Democratic Politics*, 2nd ed. (New York: Verso, 2001).

37. See Bhekizizwe Peterson's "The Politics of Leisure during the Early Days of South African Cinema;" Edwin Hees's "Contextualizing *De Voortrekkers*;" and Ntongela Masilela's "The New African Movement and the Beginnings of Film Culture in South Africa" for further discussion on *De Voortrekkers* and the dissemination of *The Birth of a Nation* in South Africa. All articles are in *To Change Reels*.

38. Slavoj Zizek, *The Sublime Object of Ideology* (London: Verso Press, 1989), 82.

39. The exclusion of "foreign elements" became a major trend in white politics in the thirties and forties, as evidenced by the introduction in 1930 of a Quota Bill by D. F. Malan, the leader of the newly formed National Party (then called the Purified National Party). The bill limited immigration from "scheduled" countries, which included Greece, Latvia, Lithuania, Poland, Russia, and Palestine, but did not place

limitations on immigrants from "non-scheduled" countries, which included Germany. A loophole opened for German Jews fleeing Hitler's Third Reich. In response to the growing numbers of the South African Jewish community, a second Aliens Bill was passed. Although specifically avoiding direct reference to Jews, the bill prohibited the immigration of all those not in command of a "European" language. Under the bill, Yiddish did not qualify, thus permitting the exclusion of Jews from the Eastern European countries. In a virulently anti-Semitic speech, Malan singled out the South African Jews as scapegoats, not only for the poverty of the Afrikaners due to their control of commerce, but also for the divided and fragmented condition of the society in which they operated as a "state within a state." See Milton Shain's book, *The Roots of Antisemitism in South Africa* (Charlottesville: University Press of Virginia, 1994). Like the Portuguese traders in *De Voortrekkers*, in a speech delivered in Stellenbosch in April 1937, Malan accused the Jews of doing "everything in their power to keep the Afrikaners from uniting, as they feared that South Africans would rise from their lowly and insignificant position to save South Africa for the South Africans." Cited in Norval, *Deconstructing Apartheid Discourse*, 46.

40. An example of such a project is the mammoth docudrama, *Die Bou van 'n Nasie (They Built a Nation)*, which is a self-conscious act of taking back that which *De Voortrekkers* had offered and rewriting it so that Afrikaners would truly receive the self-representation they had historically "earned" for themselves. Made by AFP in 1938 but funded by the Publicity and Travel Division of South African Railways and Harbors at the height of Afrikaner dissatisfaction with the Fusion government, *Die Bou van 'n Nasie* was intended for publicity purposes abroad to encourage trade. Locally it was shown at the Voortrekker Centenary celebrations. The film's intent was exactly that of *De Voortrekkers*; namely, to project an image of national unity in the country. Once again, the myth of the Great Trek was placed in the service of that projection. The film begins historically with Bartholomew Diaz's voyage in 1486 around the coast of South Africa and then moves rapidly to paradisiacal scenes of Van Riebeeck and his men establishing his "garden" at the Cape, as was his mandate from the Dutch East India Company in 1652. Happy aboriginals—the so-called Hottentots or San people—who cooperate with him in his cultivation of the Cape scamper around him on the rocks looking for crayfish. There is much to say about the overtly racist discourse in the film which positions the natives as savages and the whites as civilizers. But the important point for my argument is how quickly the conflict between Dingane and Retief becomes the film's focal point. Once again the nation, through this reenactment of the master narrative of the Great Trek, is able to reproduce itself as white and male. Except that is not quite true. *Die Bou* foregrounds the contribution of the Afrikaner in the construction of the national culture and history. The contribution of the English, not to mention that of the blacks and all others, is elided. The film is an aggressive projection of Afrikaans nationalist politics.

41. Mangosuthu Gatsha Buthelezi, "Speech Delivered by the Minister of Home Affairs (Chairman of the House of Traditional Leaders) at the Inauguration of the Ncome/Blood River Monument - 16 December 1998," South African Government Information, http://www.search.gov/za/...previewdocument.jsp?.

42. Ibid.

43. Solomon T. Plaatje, *Native Life in South Africa* (London: P. S. King, 1916).

44. Solomon T. Plaatje, *Mhudi* (Kimberley, South Africa: Lovedale Press, 1930).

45. Tom Lodge, *Black Politics in South Africa since 1945* (Johannesburg: Ravan Press, 1983), 1.

46. It is easy to read these political enactments in objective terms, that is, as reactions to particular material conditions of the moment: the pressing problem of Afrikaans "poor whitism" which threatened the ideal of white unity; the desire to bridge the economic gap between the English and Afrikaners by the Fusion government of Louis Botha and Jan Smuts, and the looming "threat" of a dispossessed, disappointed, increasingly nationalistic urban black (native) population.

Such a reading fails to take into account the larger discourse of segregationism that preceded the Acts and justified them as natural expressions of white supremacy.

47. Charles Taylor, "Two Theories of Modernity," *Public Culture* 11, no. 1 (Winter 1999).

48. Dilip Gaonkar, "On Alternative Modernities," *Public Culture* 11, no. 1 (Winter 1999).

49. For thirty years, the African National Congress worked in alliance with white liberals as an "extra-parliamentary loyal opposition" in the hope of changing South Africa into a non-racial democracy. Only in the 1960s did African nationalists come to the conclusion that apartheid could not be reformed through acts of Parliament, but would have to be radically destroyed.

50. Leo Charney and Vanessa Schwartz, "Introduction," in *Cinema and the Invention of Modern Life,* ed. Leo Charney and Vanessa Schwartz (Los Angeles: University of California Press, 1995), 3.

51. Gutsche, *Motion Pictures in South Africa,* 386.

52. Peterson, "The Politics of Leisure."

53. Phillips Newsletter, November 3, 1925; Bantu Men's Social Center 1927 Annual Report.

54. Brian Willan, *Sol Plaatje: A Biography* (Johannesburg: Ravan Press, 1984), 304.

Filmography

7 Fragments for Georges Méliès (William Kentridge, 2003, South Africa)
A Luta Continua/The Struggle Continues (Jack Lewis, 2001, South Africa/Finland)
Any Child is My Child (Barry Feinberg, 1989, South Africa)
Between Joyce and Remembrance (Mark Kaplan, 2004, South Africa)
Bicycle Thieves (Vittorio de Sica, 1948, Italy)
Birth of a Nation, The (D. W. Griffith, 1915, United States)
Blink Stefaans (Jans Rautenbach, 1981, South Africa)
Blood Diamond (Edward Zwick, 2006, United States)
Boesman and Lena (Ross Devenish, 1974, South Africa)
Boy Called Twist (Tim Greene, 2004, South Africa)
Broer Matie (Jans Rautenbach, 1983, South Africa)
Bunny Chow (John Barker, 2006, South Africa)
Cape of Good Hope (Mark Bamford, 2004, South Africa)
Catch a Fire (Philip Noyce, 2006, France/United Kingdom/South Africa/United
    States)
Chicken Biznis—The Whole Story (Ntshaveni Wa Luruli, 2000, South Africa)
Chip of Glass Ruby, A (Ross Devenish, 1963, United Kingdom)
Christmas with Granny (Dumisane Phakathi, 1998, South Africa)
Cinderella of the Cape Flats (Jane Kennedy, 2004, South Africa)
City of Blood (Darrell Roodt, 1983, South Africa)
City of God (Fernando Mireilles, 2002, Brazil)
Come Back Africa (Lionel Rogosin, 1959, United States/South Africa)
Come See the Bioscope (Lance Gewer, 1997, South Africa)
Constant Gardner, The (Fernando Meirelles, 2005, United Kingdom/Germany)
Conversations on a Sunday Afternoon (Khalo Matabane, 2005, South Africa)
Cry Freedom (Richard Attenborough, 1987, United States/United Kingdom)
Cry, the Beloved Country (Zoltan Korda, 1951, United Kingdom)
Cry, the Beloved Country (Darrell Roodt, 1995, South Africa)
De Voortrekkers (Harold Shaw, 1916, South Africa)
Die Groen Faktor (Koos Roets, 1984, South Africa)
Die Kandidaat (Jans Rautenbach, 1968, South Africa)
Disgrace (Steve Jacobs, 2009, Australia/South Africa)
Don't F*** with Me, I Have 51 Brothers and Sisters (Dumisane Phakathi, 2004, South
    Africa)

Drum (Zola Maseko, 2004, South Africa)

Eendag op n Reendag (Jans Rautenbach, 1975, South Africa)

Felix in Exile (William Kentridge, 1994, South Africa)

Fiela se Kind (Katinka Heyns, 1988, South Africa)

Fools (Ramadan Suleman, 1997, South Africa)

Foreigner, The (Zola Maseko, 1997, South Africa)

Forgiveness (Ian Gabriel, 2004, South Africa)

Freedom Square and Back of the Moon (Angus Gibson and William Kentridge, 1988, South Africa)

God is African (Akin Omotoso, 2001, South Africa)

Goodbye Bafana (also released as *The Color of Freedom*) (Billie August, 2007, South Africa/United Kingdom/Germany)

Good Fascist, The (Helen Noguiera, 1991, South Africa)

Guest, The (Ross Devenish, 1977, South Africa)

Gugulethu Seven, The (Lindy Wilson, 2001, South Africa)

Ho Ea Rona (We Are Going Forward) (Dumisane Phakathi, 2002, Lesotho)

Hijack Stories (Oliver Schmitz, 2000, Germany/France/United Kingdom)

History of the Main Complaint (William Kentridge, 1996, South Africa)

Hotel Rwanda (Terry George, 2004, South Africa/United Kingdom/Italy/United States)

How Long (Must We Suffer . . .)? (Gibson Kente, 1976, South Africa)

In Darkest Hollywood: Cinema and Apartheid (Peter Davis and Daniel Riesenfeld, 1993, United States/Canada)

In Desert and Wilderness (Gavin Hood, 2001, South Africa)

Ingrid Jonker: Her Lives and Time (Helen Noguiera, 2007, South Africa)

In My Country (John Boorman, 2004, United Kingdom/Ireland/South Africa)

It's my Life/Ma Vie en Plus (Brian Tilley, 2001, South Africa/Finland)

Jannie Totsiens (Jans Rautenbach, 1970, South Africa)

Jim Comes to Jo'burg/African Jim (Donald Swanson, 1949, South Africa)

Jobman (Darrell Roodt, 1988, South Africa)

Joburg Stories (Oliver Schmitz and Brian Tilley, 1997, South Africa)

Jock of the Bushveld, (Gray Hofmeyr, 1986, South Africa)

Johannesburg, 2nd Greatest City After Paris (William Kentridge, 1989, South Africa)

Jump the Gun (Les Blair, 1997, South Africa/United Kingdom)

Katrina (Jans Rautenbach, 1969, South Africa)

King Hendrik (Jans Rautenbach, 1965, South Africa)

Kini and Adams (Idrissa Ouedraogo, 1997, Burkina Faso/France)

Las Hurdes. Terra sin pan /Land Without Bread (Luis Buñuel, 1933, Spain)

Last King of Scotland (Kevin Macdonald, 2006, United Kingdom)

Last Supper at Horstley Street (Lindy Wilson, 1985, South Africa)

Letter to My Cousin in China, (Henion Han, 1999, South Africa)

Long Night's Journey into Day (Frances Reid and Deborah Hoffman, 2000, United States)

Mama Jack (Gray Hofmeyr, 2005, South Africa)

Mamza (Johan Blignaut, 1985, South Africa)

Mapantsula (Oliver Schmitz, 1988, South Africa/Australia/United Kingdom)

Marigolds in August (Ross Devenish, 1978, South Africa)

Max and Mona (Teddy Mattera, 2004, South Africa)

Mine (William Kentridge, 1991, South Africa)

Miner's Tale, A (Nic Hofmeyr and Gabriel Mondlane, 2001, South Africa/Finland)
Moffie Called Simon, A (John Greyson, 1986, Canada)
Monument (William Kentridge, 1990, South Africa)
Mother to Child (Jane Thandi Lipman, 2001, South Africa/Finland)
Mr. Bones (Gray Hofmeyr, 2001, South Africa)
My African Mother (Cathy Winter, 1999, South Africa)
My Country, My Hat (David Bensusan, 1981, South Africa)
Native Who Caused All the Trouble, The (Marnie van Rensburg, 1989, South Africa)
Night Stop (Licinio Azevedo, 2002, South Africa/Finland)
Oh Shucks—I'm Gatvol (Gray Hofmeyr, 2004, South Africa)
Old Wives' Tale, An (Dumisane Phakathi, 1998, South Africa)
On the Wire (Elaine Proctor, 1990, United Kingdom)
Pappa Lap (Jans Rautenbach, 1971, South Africa)
Place of Weeping (Darrell Roodt, 1986, South Africa)
Promised Land, The (Jason Xenopolous, 2002, South Africa)
Proteus (John Greyson, 2003, South Africa/Canada)
Quest for Love (Helen Noguiera, 1988, South Africa)
Reasonable Man, A (Gavin Hood, 1999, France/South Africa)
Red Dust (Tom Hooper, 2004, South Africa/United Kingdom)
Sarafina (Darrell Roodt, 1992, South Africa/France/United Kingdom/United States)
Sarie Marais (Joseph Albrecht, 1931, South Africa)
Saturday Night at the Palace (Robert Davies, 1987, South Africa)
Schoolmaster, The (Jean Delbeke, 1991, South Africa)
Schweitzer (also known as *Lambarene/Light in the Jungle: The Story of Dr. Albert Schweitzer* (Gray Hofmeyr, 1990, United States)
Sexy Girls, The (Russell Thompson, 1998, South Africa)
Simon and I (Beverley Palese Ditsie and Nicky Newman, 2002, South Africa/Finland)
Sobriety, Obesity and Growing Old (William Kentridge, 1991, South Africa)
Sometimes in April (Raoul Peck, 2005, France/United States/Rwanda)
Song of Africa (Emil Nofal, 1951, South Africa)
Son of Man (Mark Dornford-May, 2006, South Africa)
Stereoscope (William Kentridge, 1999, South Africa)
Stick, The (Darrell Roodt, 1987, South Africa)
Storekeeper, The (Gavin Hood, 1998, South Africa)
Story of a Beautiful Country (Khalo Matabane, 2004, South Africa/Canada)
Story of an African Farm (David Lister, 2004, South Africa)
There's a Zulu on My Stoep (Gray Hofmeyr, 1993, South Africa)
Tide Table (William Kentridge, 2003, South Africa)
Triomf (Michael Raeburn, 2008, South Africa/France/United Kingdom)
Tsotsi (Gavin Hood, 2005, South Africa/United Kingdom)
Ubuntu's Wounds (Sechaba Morojele, 2001, United States/South Africa)
U-Carmen e-Khayelitsha (Mark Dornford-May, 2005, South Africa)
U-Deliwe/Orphan (Simon Sabela, 1975, South Africa)
Ukamau (Jorge Sanjines, 1966, Bolivia)
Wa n Wina (Dumisani Phakathi, 2001, South Africa/Finland)
Wah Wah (Richard Grant, 2005, United Kingdom/France/South Africa)
Waiting for Valdez (Dumisane Phakathi, 2002, South Africa)
Walk in the Night, A (Mickey Madoda-Dube, 1998, South Africa)

Weighing and Wanting (William Kentridge, 1997, South Africa)
Windprints (David Wicht, 1989, South Africa)
Wooden Camera, The (Ntshaveni Wa Luruli, 2003, South Africa)
World Apart, A (Chris Menges, 1988, United Kingdom/Zimbabwe)
World Unseen, The (Shamim Sarif, 2007, United Kingdom)
Yawar Malku (also known as *Blood of the Condor*) (Jorge Sanjines, 1969, Bolivia)
Yesterday (Darrell Roodt, 2004, South Africa)
Zonk! (Hyman Kirsten, 1950, South Africa)
Zulu (Cy Endfield, 1964, South Africa/United Kingdom)
Zulu Love Letter (Ramadan Suleman, 2004, South Africa/France/Germany)
index, Saks, *Cinema in a Democratic South Africa*

Index

Lucia Saks is Assistant Professor in the Department of Screen Arts and Cultures, University of Michigan, Ann Arbor. She holds a Ph.D. in critical studies from the University of Southern California's School of Cinematic Arts. From 1997 to 2002, she was director of the Media and Communication Program at the University of KwaZulu-Natal. Currently she teaches at the University of Cape Town in the Centre for Film and Media Studies.

Printed and bound by CPI Group (UK) Ltd, Croydon, CR0 4YY

13/04/2025

14656545-0005